658.82

NO-NONSENSE
MARKETING

16 SEP 1998

080447

BRN 50099

NO-NONSENSE
MARKETING

101 Practical Ways to
Win and Keep Customers

VICTOR H. PRUSHAN

JOHN WILEY & SONS, INC.

New York · Chichester · Weinheim · Brisbane · Singapore · Toronto

This text is printed on acid-free paper.

Copyright © 1997 by Victor H. Prushan.
Published by John Wiley & Sons, Inc.

All rights reserved. Published simultaneously in Canada.

Reproduction or translation of any part of this work beyond that
permitted by Section 107 or 108 of the 1976 United States
Copyright Act without the permission of the copyright owner is
unlawful. Requests for permission or further information should
be addressed to the Permissions Department, John Wiley &
Sons, Inc.

This publication is designed to provide accurate and authoritative
information in regard to the subject matter covered. It is sold with
the understanding that the publisher is not engaged in rendering
legal, accounting, or other professional services. If legal advice or
other expert assistance is required, the services of a competent
professional person should be sought.

Library of Congress Cataloging-in-Publication Data

Prushan, Victor H., 1936–
    No-nonsense marketing : 101 practical ways to win and keep
customers / Victor H. Prushan.
        p.   cm.
    Includes index.
    ISBN 0-471-15707-4 (paper : alk. paper)
    1. Marketing—Management. 2. Strategic planning. 3. Competition.
4. Customer services. I. Title.
HF5415.13.P78   1997
658.8—DC20   96-42473

Printed in the United States of America

10 9 8 7 6 5 4 3 2 1

To Florence,
my wife and best friend

Acknowledgments

I first started thinking about this project after I had attended an authorship workshop at the National Speakers Association headquarters in Tempe, Arizona, in September 1994. It was what I learned there from representatives of the publishing world, and from many fellow speakers who had become authors, that got the juices flowing and gave me the motivation to finally sit down in front of a blank computer screen and get to work.

Writing is supposed to be a lonely occupation. During the course of preparing this book, however, I spoke with and received encouragement from so many people that loneliness would be the last word I'd use to characterize the experience. The truth is, it was a lot of fun. Now that this book has become a reality, I must pause to thank those many people who contributed their time and knowledge so willingly to help me get through this.

A major thanks goes to my good friend Marsha Lewin, who read some of my early scribbles and thought enough of them to pass them on to her editor at John Wiley & Sons. Fortunately for me, that editor was Ruth Mills. Throughout, Ruth encouraged me to say what I wanted to say the way I wanted to say it, but she never hesitated to tell me when I missed the mark and suggest a *better* way. What more could you ask for?

Special thanks are in order to my fellow management consultants and good friends who contributed the gifts of their expertise. Specific help for this book came from Dick Pinsker, who provided his thoughts on hiring sales and marketing people; from Jim Carey and his take on compensating the sales force; from Bill Birnbaum with his insights into planning and the planning

Acknowledgments

process; and Shell Alpert, who taught me so much about direct marketing.

I want to express my sincere appreciation to H. L. Singer at Powers Process Controls; Merrill Skeist at Spellman High Voltage; Ron Madison at EG&G Flow Technology; Don Skinner at Eltron International; Brian Heimbigner of RCC; Philip Alford of Tekelec; Jerry Hudspeth of Parrish Financial Servicing Company; "Dabo" Dabasinskas of Howell Electric Motors; Randy Hoffman, Rick Sill, and Peter Williams of Magellan Systems; and Joe Atchison of Poly-Optical Products. Thank you all for your feedback on what it takes for a company to compete successfully. Thanks, too, to my friend Steve Sereboff who suggested the approach to the final chapter. Giving more than expected is one of the most important messages of this book.

Thank you to all my clients, past and present. I hope you've learned from me; I know I've learned from you.

Supportive families make it all possible. It's even better when family members have business experience and skills that I can call on when I need it. Thanks to Marc Prushan for his input on personal selling, Paul Prushan and Robert Prushan for their thoughts on management, and my wife, Florence, not only for her management expertise but also for her assistance and constructive comments throughout, and for her own special version of Marketing's 4 Ps—*pushing, prodding, patience,* and *putting up with* me. Without her it could never have happened.

Finally, I wish I could personally thank Murray, Thelma, and Bernard. I think they would have been proud.

V.H.P.

Contents

Contents

Contents

Contents

Contents

Contents

Introduction:

So You're Marketing-Oriented, So What?

This is a book about marketing, from a marketer's point of view. I've been involved in marketing for my entire career. I started out as a field sales engineer for a division of a Fortune 500 company, then worked my way up the sales and marketing ladder with companies large and small. I've carried a sample bag and a catalog case, and I've spent a lot of time on red-eye flights. There was a time I thought jet lag was the way you were *supposed* to feel. I've worked with overseas agents and manufacturers' representatives and distributors and my own field salespeople. As a product manager I chased my customers' orders through manufacturing and did more than my share of arm-twisting and cajoling to get products out the door. I've seen and been a part of the good, the bad, and the ugly. In other words, I've been around.

I have observed hundreds of companies in my marketing consulting practice and in my public seminars and private workshops. Like most of us, I've read about the successful ones, the likes of Hewlett-Packard, Motorola, Federal Express, Nordstrom, the ones that consistently make the "excellence" lists.

But I also see the ones who muddle along, barely keeping their heads above water. Like the CEO of a manufacturing company I ran into a while back who had been in business for 15 years and was beside himself with joy that annual sales volume would finally reach a million dollars. Or the companies that hit the five or ten million dollar level and linger there for years without any growth, then slip backward. Or the start-up company that never gets going. Or the major multinational sitting on its obsolete technology, helplessly watching as the upstarts find—and successfully bring to market—new ways to do the same things, only cheaper, faster, and better.

Joy and Reality

Among the joys—and frustrations—of marketing as a discipline is that there is little or no discipline. There are few hard and fast rules to follow. The ones that do exist are pretty much innocuous. Produce quality products. Price them right. Provide good distribution. Promote effectively. Focus on customer needs. Build satisfied customers.

Let's face it, did a manager or corporate executive ever tell you that he or she didn't care about customers? Didn't care about what was going on in the marketplace? Did you ever hear an executive confide that profits weren't important? Of course not. *Everyone* cares about customers. *Everyone* wants to do a great job for them. *Everyone* wants to make money and be successful. So when you tell me how marketing-oriented you are, or how focused you are on customer needs, please forgive me if I have trouble stifling my yawn.

A quality product and a focus on customer needs doesn't ensure marketplace success. Those things are important, but they aren't about winning. They are more about losing. If you don't have a quality product or if you don't focus on your customer, you lose. But if that's all you have and do, you still lose.

Why? Because first, last, and always, it's a competitive world. Unless you are fortunate enough to be first on the market with a hot new product or service, you are probably locked up in a competitive struggle. If you and your competitor do all the same things, how does a customer distinguish one from the other? If you are not looking for a way to set yourself apart (*differentiate* is the marketing buzzword), I'll put up some money that says your competitor is. And signing up more customers. And racking up more sales.

Marketing Basics Isn't Basic Marketing

One of the great challenges of international travel is to communicate with other people in their own language. When I first visited France after years of high school and college French behind me, I noticed that no one there spoke basic or intermediate French. Everyone spoke just French. If I was going to get along, I had to learn to speak the way they spoke, idioms and all. In the real world, I learned, there is no such thing as basic French.

This book is about getting back to basics, but it isn't about basic marketing. It is about getting back to good marketing. In the real world, there is no such thing as basic marketing, or intermediate or advanced marketing, for that matter. There is only good marketing or bad marketing. Bad marketing may as well be no marketing. You either do it or you don't.

Successful marketing is usually identified *after* the fact. Succeed and your marketing effort was superb. Come up short and your marketing obviously failed. If you do it right, you have a winning product or service that makes a lot of money. If you don't do it right, you are out of the game.

Pattern of the Book

This book is a list of items to help any company or any organization put together a successful marketing program. I have tried to make it more a "do" list than a "don't" list. "Don't" lists pose a dilemma. If you *don't* do something, what do you *do* in its place? I have always believed that marketing is a proactive discipline. Success comes to those who seize the opportunities, to those who act instead of wait. With a few exceptions, I have concentrated on the positive rather than the negative.

Is the list definitive? Obviously not. With enough time and thought, 101 ways might grow to 1,001.

Are some of the items controversial? I expect so. I have argued most of these points with clients and associates. Controversial or not, they reflect more than 30 years of experience and observation.

Will any of this help? If you have an open mind and are willing to shatter a myth or two, I am sure of it.

Victor H. Prushan
Thousand Oaks, California
January 1997

1

THE VIEW FROM THE TOP

The truth is, marketing isn't about the marketing department. It's about the whole organization. And top management is responsible for the whole organization. Management sets the tone. The skill (or lack of it) that management shows in conducting the day-to-day business of the company has its effect.

I work with a lot of companies in technology-based businesses. In many cases, the President and CEO is the guy who started the business in his garage. It's his baby. He's an engineer with a dream come true. He runs his own company. He's making good money. He's doing what he wants, when he wants, how he wants.

Company presidents are usually the best salespeople of all. I think the best thing that can happen to a salesperson on a difficult call is to have the company president along. He knows the technology cold. After all, he invented it. He can make decisions on the spot. He doesn't have to call anyone for permission to cut price or promise an early delivery or whatever else a customer needs. Buyers are impressed and flattered. What the boss may lack in formal sales training he makes up for with sincerity and knowledge.

But selling isn't marketing; it's only a part of marketing. It's in the marketing issues that management can either make or break the company. Providing the leadership and the marketing decisions that advance the company's ability to compete—today and tomorrow—is something only *management* can do.

That is what this chapter is about.

1 BEWARE OF THE MODEL OF THE MONTH

We are obsessed with tools to improve our businesses. Give us a model or a set of forms to fill in or a set of meeting agendas and we will make our companies successful. If they don't work, not to worry. There's another model with another set of forms and another set of meeting agendas following right behind that might just do the trick. And another and another.

Alphabet Soup

Run to the business section of your nearest bookstore for a selection of the latest and greatest management tools, programs, and models, each one guaranteed to take your company (and your career) to new heights. To succeed, today's manager goes through an alphabet soup of programs and practices, a list as long as, well, the alphabet.

How can you face your shareholders if you don't adopt TQM; pressure your vendors or indulge your customers with JIT; get registered to ISO (9000 or otherwise); build a house of quality with QFD; increase margins and improve delivery times with DFM, MRP, and CIM; improve on TTM; spread the word over an EDI?

Joining the old standbys—like portfolio analysis, product/market expansion grids, PIMS, and the experience curve—are the new buzzwords and techniques of the day—business process reengineering and downsizing and rightsizing and competitive benchmarking and conversion and strategic outsourcing and, my latest favorite, mass customization, the oxymoron to end all oxymorons.

These are the subjects of conventions, conferences, seminars, magazine articles, books (both nonfiction *and* fiction), staff meetings, lunch conversations, and, no doubt, pillow talk.

This is not to say that all these tools are just quick-fix solutions without substance. Who in his right mind would advise against quality improvement? Improving the manufacturability of the product or shortening the time it takes to get new products to market are noble objectives. And if you have to conform to a customer's Just-in-Time (JIT) requirements, you do it. No ifs, ands, or buts.

There is a downside, unfortunately. Change—major change— is expensive and may not produce the results you are looking for. Several years ago, one of my clients engaged the services of a major consulting firm to help the company implement a Total Quality Management (TQM) program. After two years of meetings, conferences, forms, and checklists, not to mention more than one million dollars in fees, the client shut down the program. Senior managers were frustrated that they couldn't see any revenue or bottom-line benefits. Everything soon got back to "normal." No more meetings on TQM, no more forms, no more checklists. And about the same market position they held before they started.

We are all familiar with how the American automobile industry lost a significant share of its market to Japanese manufacturers. Starting in the late 1960s, Japanese automobile manufacturers gradually increased their market penetration and eventually captured the "quality" position. For years American car owners had complained about the quality of the home-built product. Given an alternative, buyers jumped for the Japanese cars.

Faced with embarrassment, declining revenue, and lost profits caused by losing share to a foreign competitor, Detroit fought back. Huge investments in quality programs have paid off. Quality has improved greatly. Bleeding from losing market share has stabilized, or at least slowed. Things have been looking up.

But where does it go from here? Suppose that Magnanimous Motors' new Fireball 8000 is rated by the automotive press and *Consumer Reports* as a great new car, just as good as its nearest Japanese competitor. It's priced about the same. Comes with similar features and option packages. It's quiet and tight. Economical and reliable. Stylish. Just about everything you'd want in a family car. Just about everything competition has had for years. So who needs it?

It isn't that these models and techniques aren't useful or even critically important. The problem with the herd instinct in bringing TQM and similar improvement techniques to the firm is not in the concept but in the *expectations*. If you and your competitors are furiously working to improve quality and performance, it stands to reason that TQM only levels the playing field. When quality is a given, competitive pressure intensifies.

Models for success are really models for keeping up. Do whatever it takes to improve your performance, but don't expect any of this to give you a competitive edge. If you think otherwise, you are fooling yourself, your staff, and your shareholders. But not the marketplace.

The real bright spots for the American automobile business are new products such as minivans and sport utility vehicles, products that foreign competitors have not exploited so well. Let's see how that works: quality new products filling unserved needs, priced right, promoted well. I do believe that's called *marketing!*

2 THROW AWAY YOUR MISSION STATEMENT

Most business plans, strategic plans, or marketing plans start with a mission statement. This is usually an opening sentence or paragraph or two describing corporate philosophy or vision or how management sees the company and its place in the world. Usually pretty heady stuff. Heady stuff but often a waste of time. I never really understood why companies bother.

Some years ago I was doing a marketing planning seminar for an industrial products company. The company had been in business many years and was, by most standards of measurement, successful. In the room were about 30 of the company's sales and marketing people and some senior managers, including the CEO. When we got to the subject of mission statements, I asked if they would tell me theirs. After a brief moment of silence, every head in the room turned to the CEO, who sheepishly admitted that he knew it but couldn't repeat it verbatim.

Excusing himself, he went back to his office to find his company's mission statement. Returning about a half hour later, he stood before the group and read from a large notebook, which I assumed to be Copy #1 of the corporate plan. The mission statement filled almost two pages and, when he was through, I still wasn't sure what kind of business the company thought it was in.

I have rarely heard of an employee who knew the company mission statement. Moreover, I've never heard of managers actually paying attention to it, even when they should. Which may be why a lot of companies get themselves involved in new ventures or acquisitions they have no business getting into. Mission statements are often sprinkled with ideals like making the company a great place to work, protecting the environment, satisfying customers, and, of course, making a profit for the shareholders, who will live happily ever after. What's different about that?

Mission statements simply aren't realistic. They rarely reflect what companies do on a day-to-day basis to grow or even survive. The desire to make a profit is a fundamental part of doing business. It shouldn't require restating. The fact that you have satisfied employees is reflected in your ability to produce and deliver products and services that make money. Other than that, nobody cares. Especially customers. Your concern for the environment shows your good citizenship but it doesn't do much to set you apart from competitors who feel the same way you do. Even polluters say they are environmentalists.

Throw away the mission statement. Chances are no one will know it's gone.

3 DEFINE YOUR BUSINESS WITH A POSITION STATEMENT

Rather than spending the time to create flowery-sounding mission statements, think through what you are and what you do and, even more important, how you are seen in the marketplace. I tell my clients (those who are willing to see my way regarding mission statements) to write a different kind of statement, a "position" statement, if you will. Some call it an elevator speech, a statement describing your company that you can present to a key prospect in the short time it takes for an elevator to go from the lobby to the executive suite.

A position statement describes you in three dimensions, all external to the company. *External* is the key. What happens inside is irrelevant to the marketplace. Your customers couldn't care less about what you do inside your company walls, as long as you satisfy their needs.

First, you want to name the type of customer you serve. Airframe manufacturers. Research laboratories. Working women. Whatever fits you. Second, tell what you do for those customers, or what you provide. Hermetically sealed switches. Fresh bread. Power supplies. Rental cars. And, third, tell how you do it, or what technology you use. Silicon. Gallium arsenide. Liquid crystal displays. All-natural ingredients.

Of course, the three dimensions, or parameters, can be in any order. Just be sure the statement is clear and logical. Look at these examples:

ABC Instrument Company serves the defense and aerospace industries with high reliability temperature measurement and control devices for space applications, using nonmechanical, solid-state materials.

With a statement like that, you wouldn't expect ABC to provide back patio outdoor thermometers. But if the company finally decided it had better get back into commercial markets, it might well change its statement to:

ABC Instrument Company manufactures and markets digital instruments for high accuracy temperature measurement and control in the food processing industry, using proprietary solid-state materials.

Or try this one:

DEF Plating Company provides the automotive industry with specialized plating services for decorative components on vehicles subject to severe environmental conditions.

This tells the world that DEF does what a lot of other platers don't. And it positions DEF to get more money for its service.

Here's the one for my firm:

VHP Associates *provides marketing consulting services for business-to-business manufacturing and service firms, applying back-to-basics techniques to planning, strategy, business development, and related marketing-mix issues.*

I will let that one speak for itself.

4 MAKE SURE YOUR COMPANY POLICIES ARE IN SYNC WITH YOUR STRATEGIES

Some years ago my wife and I went into a department store to buy a washing machine. I can't tell you the name of the store, but a very tall building in Chicago is named after it. The price was right for the machine we selected and the features were what we wanted. We were sold. Someone had to be home to accept delivery, so we asked whether the store could set up its schedule for a specific time. That way, we would spend the least amount of time away from our jobs. Not possible, the salesperson said. It was not their policy to set up time of delivery any more specifically than the day of the week. They would call us the day before and tell us whether it would be in the morning or the afternoon.

It was *their policy,* not *our needs,* that mattered most. The delivery trucks were loaded for the most efficient routing, regardless of customer needs or wishes. And if that wasn't satisfactory, there was nothing the salesperson could do about it. The burden was on us.

Since we couldn't come to an agreement, we went across the road to an appliance specialty store. They had an acceptable machine for an acceptable price. When we asked when they could deliver the washer, the response was, "How soon can you get home?" They got our business. Two hours after the store visit, the washer was installed and working.

The department store's marketing strategies were well executed and successful. They advertised heavily. They stocked their locations with a wide range of products that could satisfy virtually every appliance need, and priced them fairly. Whatever it took to get customers in the store they did and did well. But the customer walked out without buying because the store policy set up an impossible burden on the customer. Go figure.

A Fly in the Ointment

In 1993 Intel, the dominant force in microprocessors for personal computers, introduced its state-of-the-art Pentium chip. As luck would have it, someone, somewhere uncovered a "bug" in the Pentium that produced calculation errors in certain obscure uses. To err is human, to forgive divine, to stonewall is perilous. Intel announced its "policy" to replace the chip only if the owner could show that he or she used the computer in those specific applications where the error would show up. All others please step aside and let the most worthy pass. The furor this policy created caught Intel's management by surprise.

I assume that Intel's goal for the Pentium was to sell as many as possible to as many computer makers as possible in as short a time as possible. The Motorola/IBM/Apple consortium had just introduced the PowerPC chip and Intel had a huge market share to protect against possible inroads. Its strategy for the Pentium would have to include terrific prices, and the ability to meet high-volume demand with a reliable, well-made, well-designed product. Somewhere in Intel's business philosophy, I'm sure, it addresses total customer satisfaction, responsiveness, and so on, and so on. Did its hard-nosed replacement policy serve its marketing goals and strategies? Gimme a break!

Eventually Intel changed its policy, agreed to replace chips for anyone who asked. The hubbub died down, Intel continued its market leadership. Pentium-based PCs resumed their role as the standard and the industry went on about its way. But the price was high. Intel is no longer a "can do no wrong" kind of company. It is human, after all.

Competing in the Open Skies

It wasn't so long ago that TWA was my international airline of choice. That was the time when TWA and Pan Am were the two

U.S. carriers on the North Atlantic route. Whenever I had a choice, it was TWA for me. How things have changed. Today TWA struggles. Its international presence has shrunk to miniscule proportions as it has sold off key routes to generate enough cash to keep it going. Strapped for cash, it probably operates the oldest fleet of planes of any major carrier in the country.

I always had the impression that TWA was a reluctant participant in the frequent flyer craze that now is so much a part of airline marketing programs. It's just an impression, mind you, but I can't think of anything innovative it ever brought to its frequent flyer program. To me, it seemed like the airline offered the program because everyone else did. My real hangup about TWA was that, to me, it seemed to go out of the way to make it difficult to be a participant, or at least to cash in on some of the rewards that are so important. Let me tell you about an experience where policy and strategy were at odds.

I hadn't flown much on TWA for a while. I found it went to fewer and fewer places I want to go. Still, I had accumulated a number of points that I didn't want to lose. I didn't have enough points for a free first-class trip and vacation to Europe, but there was enough points for at least a domestic free ticket. Because I am a good son-in-law (I really am), I suggested to my wife that I could get a ticket for her mother to come spend some time with us.

If it only had been that easy. It was TWA's policy, I learned, that frequent flyers may only obtain free tickets for themselves or their family members *with the same surname*. That meant that I could get a ticket for *my* mother but not for *my wife's* mother. Unless she had the same name as me. Now that would be highly unusual. Not impossible, of course, but the genetic implications of most of the possibilities are too bizarre to dwell on.

There was an out. The TWA telephone sales representative stated that, if she didn't have the same surname, then I must show *written proof* that this woman was truly my wife's mother. Pause for a moment and reflect that I was only applying for a free airline ticket, not citizenship. In any case, I protested that I could hardly know where to find such a document. How many of us posses written proof that ties us to our in-laws? For some of us that could even be very undesirable, something we might not even want other people to know. (I assure you that this wasn't the case with me.) Regardless, the phone agent pointed out quite forcefully that that was the rule. No proof. No ticket.

You may be surprised to know that deep in our records was a document that listed my mother-in-law and my wife, indicating that they were truly mother and daughter. The day was saved. The ticket was issued. My grateful mother-in-law enjoyed her vacation and we enjoyed having her with us. What might have happened if she had a name different from my wife's maiden name? Suppose she had remarried—she is a widow—and had a different name altogether? Who knows? I might still be struggling.

I am dead certain that there is nothing in TWA's marketing plan, if it has one, that calls for frustrating and angering customers. On the contrary, the company advertises vigorously to win and keep customers. Its strategy is undoubtedly one that calls for doing everything humanly possible to put people in seats and fly them to wherever they want to go. But its policy did just the opposite. It was originally instituted to prevent frequent flyers from selling their points to third parties, "cheating" the airline out of its rightful fare revenue. Although this policy no doubt was effective in preventing some of these unauthorized sales, it also assumed TWA's customers were guilty until proved innocent. That isn't the kind of policy that endears a customer to a supplier. As I said earlier, I don't fly TWA all that often anymore.

If your corporate policies conflict with your ability to service your customers properly, the policies have to go. Otherwise your customers will.

5 KNOW WHAT IT TAKES TO WIN IN YOUR BUSINESS

6 KNOW WHAT IT TAKES TO FAIL

What does it take to win in a specific business? What does it take to lose? I've put these two together because to know one is to know the other. What are the critical factors that have to be in place for a company to succeed? In planning jargon these are called Critical Success Factors (CSF), Key Success Factors (KSF), or sometimes, believe it or not, Key Factors for Success (KFS). The reader will no doubt recognize a similarity among these three terms. Whatever we call them, I strongly recommend that you know what they are for your business. When it comes to building strategies, those are the things you concentrate on.

I was fortunate, recently, to have some clients in the electronic power supplies business. In simple terms, a power supply is the component within an electronic system, such as a computer, that converts line voltage, for example, 120 volts AC, into the kind of electrical power the system can use. At last look there were more than 1,000 different makers of power supplies around the world. A 1% market share would make you a dominant force in that business. You get the idea that the competition is intense.

Beyond normal good business practices, to succeed in a business like power supplies you've got to do the things—and do them right—that customers look for when selecting a supplier. Most customers use power supplies in the equipment they build and sell. So one critical factor is the ability to meet customer delivery requirements *all* the time. Slow down or shut down a production line and customers will dump you as fast as they can qualify another source. Sometimes faster.

Power supplies are usually selected after system designers figure out all the other things they need. Often at the last moment. By then the customer's engineers are in a god-awful rush to get their hands on a prototype so they can see if their design is going to work. The second critical factor, therefore, is the ability to deliver prototypes on short notice for customer evaluation. That takes a special kind of engineering organization to handle those requirements without interfering with other activities like developing new products or maintaining the existing product line.

Finally, a power supply may be a stepchild in a system designer's priorities, but it doesn't mean you can palm off yesterday's technology on tomorrow's products. Customers demand the latest and greatest, and if you don't give it to them someone else will. So the third critical success factor is the ability to respond with improved technology and performance to meet the changing needs of the customer.

Perhaps an individual manufacturer, serving a particular market segment, would have a different set of key factors for its own specific circumstances. Regardless, by understanding what it takes to win—or fail—in the business, you now can focus on developing strategies and programs that address what is truly important.

In the airline business, empty seats mean revenue lost forever. In hotels, when a night goes by with a room unsold, that revenue is lost, never to be recovered. You can't make up for it tomorrow or next week because your capacity in the short run is fixed. These industries use parameters like passenger-seat miles, load factors, or occupancy rates as the measure of good or bad performance. The idea in businesses like these is to concentrate on filling seats or filling beds. *Nothing else really counts.* To get passengers or guests you need sophisticated reservation systems, convenient schedules or locations, smiling and helpful employees, a heavy promotion budget. With them you can compete. You may even succeed. Without them you will surely fail.

There are issues unique to each business, including yours, that you must address. Know them and win. Ignore them and fail.

7 DON'T SACRIFICE LONG-TERM SUCCESS FOR SHORT-TERM GAIN

Here is a fable for our times.

Alice Ambitious has just been appointed Vice President of Sales and Marketing for the International Widget Corporation. Alice is highly qualified for her new job. She has an MBA from a well-known and highly respected B-school. She has had more than ten years with the company in various positions in customer service, field sales, and product management. She is very familiar with the widget market. Alice is good at her job. She is a marketing pro.

Alice is dedicated to maintaining her company's market leadership. She knows that today's widget enjoys a good market position, but she sees trouble ahead. Customers are beginning to shop price. The last major buy from a top OEM customer produced an uncomfortable round of price concessions to hold on to the business. Not only is there rumor that IWC's number one competitor is testing a newer, smaller, cheaper version, but there is even some talk about a university research lab that is working on a technology that will turn the market upside down, possibly making widgets obsolete.

At the CEO's staff meeting for department heads and senior managers, Alice raises the issue of investing in some engineering development that will keep the existing widget line current and, at the same time, getting approval to start looking for the next generation of products.

The discussion is heated. The Vice President for Engineering argues that his staff is fully extended maintaining the existing line. He could use some more money to hire a couple of new engineers and a technician or two to work on some new designs he's been tinkering with that he hopes will keep the company ahead of the competition. As for R&D, he still thinks that the widget serves such a basic and essential purpose, there is little or no chance that customers could or would redesign their products using another technology.

The Chief Financial Officer argues against Alice's proposal, saying he doesn't know where the money would come from. The company just paid its shareholders a generous dividend for the eighth consecutive year. Cutting back the dividend would worry Wall Street and the share price would drop. Besides, revenue and profits are up. Why rock the boat?

The VP for Operations says he would rather invest the money in building a factory in Mexico. The lower costs would improve profits. The Sales Manager, who was bitterly disappointed when the VP job went to Alice instead of him, argues for lowering widget prices so the company can be more competitive. "The future is now," he shouts.

The meeting deteriorates into an argument over whether or how much they should cut price and what are the minimum margins acceptable. Somehow, the idea of putting some money into new product development is no longer on the table.

In the end, the CEO thanks Alice for her ideas but chooses not to accept any of them. He decides that the company needs to hold on to market share and be as "aggressively competitive as possible." He read a book somewhere that said the best approach for a market leader facing an aggressive competitor was to lower prices before the competitor's new product hit the market. The idea was to lower the customer's incentive to switch. The meeting is over.

The Sales Manager is triumphant. The VP for Engineering mutters all the way back to his office, something about too much work, too little help. The VP for Operations puts the meeting completely out of his mind, races back to his office to get ready for the next meeting with the shop stewards on plant safety. The CFO leaves the plant for his lunch appointment with his bank's loan officer. The CEO spends the rest of the day preparing for next week's board meeting. The thought of bringing up long-term investment when cash flow is so tight is not an option. First things first, he thinks.

Alice goes back to her office, closes the door, and pulls up her resume on her computer screen. Six months later, Alice finds a new job in a new industry. At the same time International Widget Corporation has successfully beaten back the competitive challenge. Although everyone is sorry to see Alice go, they are all too busy making big money to miss her for long.

The scene shifts forward five years. The only widget business around is for replacement parts on old equipment. Doodads are now the technology of choice. The widget market is over. IWC has nothing to take its place. Layoffs leave the company a shell of its former self. Eventually the company is acquired and merged into another organization. Its identity disappears. End of story. Cue the funeral dirge. Roll credits.

An Apple a Day Isn't Enough

Look no further than Cupertino, California, for a well-known, real-world illustration. It wasn't long after Apple Computer introduced the Macintosh in 1984 that it became the darling of personal computer users. It was revolutionary. It was easy to use. It was reliable. It was lovable. Its competition, the IBM-compatible computer, with its DOS operating system, couldn't do things nearly as well and was a headache to set up and install; hooking up peripherals like printers, scanners, modems, video cards, and the rest could be a nightmare. You would think the business world would have leaped at the opportunity to buy something obviously so much better. Wrong.

First, there were problems with the design. The Mac didn't look like a serious computer. It had a small, black-and-white screen. Business wanted larger screens in color. OK, Apple said. We can do that. And they did.

The Mac didn't have all the software that business needed. OK, Apple said. We can fix that. Software developers flocked to put out Mac applications, until everything you could do on a DOS machine you could do on a Mac. Better.

You need more memory? You got it. You need internal hard drives? You got it. You want lower prices? Uh, oh. Sorry. Get lost!

The price premium for buying a Mac was higher than most corporate buyers were willing to pay. Can you blame them? If you were planning to buy a desktop computer for everyone in your company, maybe ten, maybe a hundred, maybe thousands, would you be concerned about cost? Yes. If most of your people use their computers for word processing and spreadsheets, and maybe sneak in a game of solitaire when the supervisor isn't looking, would you pay more money for terrific graphics? No. You would probably buy a couple of Macs to keep your graphic arts department happy. Everyone else would get IBM-compatibles, preferably no-name clones, if the price was right. And that's what happened.

From Apple's point of view, high prices meant high margins and high profits. The stock price soared. The Mac was a better computer and worth more money, so management thought. Besides, what was the point of lowering prices if they could sell everything they could build?

What is the point, indeed. The point, of course, is that the high price discouraged volume purchases. Corporate buyers looked at the Mac as a high-priced toy. Without volume purchases, the company could never gain market share. And still can't. Probably never will.

This example isn't about pricing strategy. That comes in a later chapter. It's about ignoring the future and concentrating on *short-term gains*. In spite of its troubles, Apple remains a viable company with great products and a remarkably loyal customer base. For the moment. The sad part is thinking about what *might* have been, or what may yet come to be.

8 DON'T SACRIFICE SHORT-TERM GAIN FOR LONG-TERM SUCCESS

What good is the future if you can't get through *today?* Let's look at what happens to Alice Ambitious when she moves on to her next job. Alice took the position of Vice President, Marketing for Consolidated Skyhook because she was impressed with the company's plans for the future. A heavy R&D budget would guarantee a steady stream of new products, avoiding the situation that caused her so much frustration at IWC. But Consolidated Skyhook wasn't paradise, Alice was quick to find out.

The President and Chief Executive Officer started the company by coming up with a hot new approach that made skyhooks the technology of choice. In addition to the role of CEO, the founder had given himself the collateral title of Chief Scientist. In that role, he spent almost all of his time working with his engineering and research groups on a family of new products that would help preserve Consolidated's technology leadership. After 20 years, the company was well ahead of its competitors in sales and market share. Even so, growth had slowed in recent years, and sales levels had been static for the two preceding years.

Alice's warm feelings about Consolidated's new product development program, the reason she joined the company in the first place, were starting to ebb. True, the new products were exciting. The little market research the company did indicated that customers would appreciate all the new features and benefits. But it was taking altogether too much time to get them out. The CEO was a perfectionist, and he wasn't going to let the new product line go until he was absolutely sure it did all the things he wanted it to do. "I won't risk getting caught with big warranty charges just because I rushed this product to market before it was ready," he would say when pushed by his marketing department.

In the meantime, Alice had an existing product line she had to move to keep the company in business. Trouble was, cash flow was getting tight. All the money the company could spare was going into development. There were several things Alice wanted to do to keep the current skyhook line viable. The industry trade show was a must to keep the company's name in front of the market. The sales force was starting to complain about the company product literature and brochures. There hadn't been a new data sheet printed in two years. The advertising budget was way down. Advertising in the trade journals had been the company's best source of sales leads. Worst of all, two of five customer service representatives had left to take new jobs and the company wasn't going to replace them. That meant the other three clerks were overloaded with phone inquiries, order expediting, and an occasional quality complaint.

Speaking of quality, Alice was beginning to hear some grumbling that product quality was beginning to suffer. The purchasing department had just instituted a major effort to lower the cost of components. Some longtime vendors with known reliability had been replaced with suppliers offering lower prices. But was the company seeing the bitter fruits of that policy? Customer returns were increasing, an almost unheard of circumstance in the 20-year company history.

At the weekly staff meeting, Alice reported that sales were holding at an even level, but competition was getting tougher and tougher. If Consolidated didn't take steps immediately to correct some of the problems she was seeing, sales were going to start dropping off, never mind grow. After all these years, she commented, there is no conceivable reason for product quality to fall off. Especially after all the money and time put into TQM programs!

The Manager for Procurement expressed his resentment that anyone would think purchasing policies would impact on product quality and sales. On the contrary, smart purchasing cut the cost of material by almost 5%. "And that goes right to the bottom line," he beamed. "Of course, we *have* had some vendor problems, I'll admit, and we're looking into it."

"But don't forget, every change we made had Lou's approval," he said in his best defensive manner.

Lou, the Director of Engineering, pulled the bloody knife from between his shoulder blades without comment, then mumbled something under his breath (but loud enough for everyone to hear) about high sales commissions and making millionaires out of mediocre salespeople. Lou wasn't willing to give up a dime of his budget to help Marketing. After all, the future of the company rested with his ability to get those new products out, no matter how long it took. That took people and money.

The Chief Financial Officer sympathized with Alice but concluded there was no money available for additional marketing expenses. On the other hand, lower revenues projected for the next quarter are going to make the Board very unhappy. *Very* unhappy. She suggested that perhaps Alice should consider cutting back in other areas. Perhaps Lou was right, she offered. Sales commissions *were* getting too high.

Alice did not respond, but if looks could kill . . .

The CEO cleared his throat. Staff meetings were a bore for him. Let's get this over with, he thought, I've got more important things to do. If I knew this Ambitious woman was such a complainer, I probably would never have hired her.

"Look, folks, I don't have to tell you how important this new line that Lou and I are working on will be to the company. When this gets to market we'll blow the competition away. I don't think we should spend a lot of money on promoting the old products. In six months we'll want to put all our resources into promoting the new.

"Alice, take a look at your budget and see where you can find some economies. Cut out a trade show, cut down on travel, whatever it takes. Let's hang tough, everyone."

Then he turned to his Chief Engineer. "Lou, let's go. We've got to get back to that life test data. Can't understand why it failed so early. . . ."

Six months later, the company experienced its first downturn in almost 15 years. Two of the company's five leading customers had allowed International Skyhook, Consolidated's main competitor, to bid on some new applications. International's lower price and impressive reliability data carved away a third of Consolidated's business with these customers in almost no time at all.

When Alice and the Sales Manager visited the two companies in hopes of recovering the lost business, one of the buyers commented that he hadn't seen anyone from Consolidated in months. "I thought you folks had lost interest in our business," he said, "or did you cut out your travel budget?"

Once again, Alice saw the handwriting on the wall. It's time to move on, she thought. Maybe I'll become a consultant. That sounds like a fun way to make a living.

And she did. And it was. And she lived happily ever after.

As for Consolidated Skyhook, it was a case of lost market share, lost revenue, and late to market, so late that the product was probably obsolete before it got out the door.

End of fable. Back to reality.

New products are the drivers that take the company into the future, but it is your existing business that helps you meet payroll, pay the bills, keep the company's name in front of prospects and customers. Nobody deliberately sets out to kill the goose that laid the golden egg. But by cutting down on expenditures for marketing and product improvement, by "value engineering" to the point where product performance is affected, your product line becomes less attractive. You don't want it to happen and you don't expect it to happen, but business falls off and almost never comes back. And if you are not ready to replace the line with the next latest and greatest, you are a gone goose.

9 FOCUS ON REVENUE, NOT COST CUTTING

Help me out if I'm wrong, but it was always my understanding that positive cash flow means more money coming in than going out. It means you have two things to worry about—bringing in the business and, at the same time, keeping your costs down. Bringing in the business means get the order, deliver the product, invoice, receive check, deposit check. Simple. The things sales and marketing are designed to do. What we call revenue.

Of course, no good manager need be told to control costs. If you haven't learned that by now, turn in your company car and your cellular phone and consider writing poetry as a second career. On the contrary, most managers are *obsessed* with cost. When times are tough, the first thing the manager is likely to do is review the cost structure. Cut staff, cut budgets, delay payments, whatever it takes.

A great mystery to me is why companies going through difficult times do exactly the opposite of what it takes to turn them around. If cost cutting is the surefire way back to success, then how come it's so hard to come back from the bad times? Is there a single "everyone's-heard-of-them" company that has ever cost-cut its way back to true market leadership after a major downturn? Not one that I know of. Not IBM, not General Motors, not Pan Am, Digital Equipment, McDonnell Douglas, Macy's, or the Pittsburgh Pirates.

Sure, some return to profitability. After all, that's the whole idea behind cost cutting. McDonnell Douglas's commercial jet operation has been struggling for years to maintain a presence in the air transport business. After round upon round of cost cutting, the company regained some measure of profitability at a compatible sales volume and cost structure.

But as far as market leadership goes, forget it. Boeing and Airbus are so far ahead that McDonnell Douglas has been relegated to niche player. On the bright side, they have one or two products that appeal to some of the airlines, so they continue to hang on, even put together a few years of good times, even grow a little. But suppose sales volume again declines. What then? Another round of layoffs and cost cutting, and maybe, just maybe, a lower break-even point. How long can that go on?

As an occasional dieter, I have been known to claim that I am too short for my weight. If I spent enough time on a medieval torture rack, perhaps I could eke out a few more centimeters. But a much easier, less painful, more rewarding solution is to try to lose a few pounds. The real issue for the company that experiences a sales downturn is not that costs are too high; it's that the company must get its revenue back. But instead of focusing on building up sales—and revenue—the company starts slashing costs.

I live in Southern California, the center of the universe for the defense and aerospace industry. Some of the biggest companies and employers here are the giants that sell airplanes, electronics, and all manner of military hardware to fight hot and cold wars. Like any major industry, defense and aerospace has spawned a countless number of smaller manufacturing and service companies that fill places in the industry's food chain, from raw materials to finished product.

In recent years the industry has had a tough time. The Soviet Union no longer exists. What has taken its place is struggling with capitalism, free elections, and McDonald's. The need for defense products still exists but not on the scale required for the past 50 years. Government procurement has been cut back drastically.

Only a fool would go along with "business as usual" under those conditions, and there are few fools in defense and aerospace. The industry's response, however, has been predictable. Closed plants, mergers, acquisitions, and mass layoffs of production workers, engineers, and white-collar staff. At a time when all industries are adopting a "lean and mean" look, defense and aerospace has become positively anorexic.

And where has all that downsizing got them? More closed plants, mergers, acquisitions, and mass layoffs of production workers, engineers, and white-collar staff. And throw in a few bankruptcies for good measure.

Cutting costs can be painful. *Very painful.* Typically, the company will try to be fair to all departments and cut costs across the board. That means the sales and marketing departments have to bear their share of the burden. Sales staff? Cut. Customer service staff? Cut. Advertising? Cut. Trade shows? Cut. Sales commissions? Cut. Travel budgets? Cut. New products? Cut or delay.

The effect of all this cost cutting is to *compound* the revenue problem. If marketing people can't visit customers and prospects, and can't promote products and services, how can you expect to get sales going again? And if you don't turn around the sales decline, where is the revenue?

Controlling costs makes sense in the short term. No one suggests ignoring costs when you don't know how you are going to make payroll next week. But beyond the short term, *cost cutting only prolongs the inevitable.* It can only slow down, possibly stop, the bleeding. Healing and *recovery only* come from *increased sales.*

In industries such as defense and aerospace that are going through fundamental changes, cutting costs and waiting for the market to turn around won't work. That market is not coming back for a long, long time. For most participants, the only solution is to take existing capabilities and skills and focus them on getting into new products and markets. "Conversion," as they call it these days, isn't *easy.* For much of weapons-oriented technology, there probably is no commercial outlet. But there is no viable alternative. Eventually it becomes increase sales or die. That's what good marketing is designed to do.

In this chapter I've talked about a few things I think are almost exclusively within the decision-making prerogatives of senior management. If top management doesn't make the decisions in these cases, or if they don't concern themselves with these issues, chances are nobody else will. If management makes the wrong decisions, it has no one to blame but itself.

There are other subjects, of course, that are more precisely marketing issues, and we'll get to look at those in the remaining chapters. Nevertheless, many of those topics are still of vital interest to the boss. I never saw a CEO who wasn't deeply involved in pricing decisions, for example. The smaller the company, the more likely the CEO is right there in most, if not all, of the marketing decisions. Once again, *marketing isn't only a job for the marketing department.* It's the job of the entire organization, including top management. Read on.

2

DEALING WITH A COMPETITIVE WORLD

If you have any kind of business success, you have plenty of customers and more than your share of competition. Viable businesses attract competitors like lightbulbs attracts moths. If you don't have competition, you are either fortunate or, more likely, you don't have much of a business. In fact, competitors can be a *blessing* instead of the curse we so often think of them as. Let's talk about a few things that deal with the way we approach competition and a competitive market.

10 FORGET ABOUT MARKET SHARE

An electronics manufacturer contacted me recently for help in understanding his market. He wanted to know the exact size of the served market, his company's share of the market, and the shares of each of the major competitors. The company's sales had been flat for a long time, and management was trying to develop a strategy to get moving again. Should they invest heavily to increase share, or would they be better off investing in new business opportunities?

To push for a bigger share of a small mature market would likely bring a price war that none of the participants wanted or could afford. On the other hand, if the market was bigger than originally thought, maybe it would be worth the cost of a major sales and marketing effort. Deeper penetration of an existing market would be much less risky than investing in a new venture.

Let's look at this logic. First, after so many years of operating in this market, why would management now think there was a great untapped block of business just waiting for some savvy marketer? Not likely, and I think they knew this in their hearts. Second, how much is it worth to know exactly how big the market is? Once you know, what will you do with the information? Will it make any difference in your strategy, assuming you had one? For big players in, say, soft drinks or consumer packaged goods, small increments of share could mean millions of dollars in revenue. An accurate assessment of market share has a big impact on how much money to spend on advertising or sales promotion. In smaller business-to-business markets this is rarely the case.

Realistically, a company that's been in the same business for 10 or 15 years should have a very good idea of what's what in the core market. It may not have the exact numbers, but that shouldn't stop it from making the right decisions.

Back in the seventies and eighties all the great gurus from the business schools and major consulting firms preached that market share and profitability were not just related; they were "cause and effect." Gain market share and greater profits would follow as naturally as the sun comes up in the morning. We were enamored—

obsessed—with experience curves and growth-share matrices. Electronics giants like Texas Instruments and Raytheon introduced new products with surprisingly low prices in hopes of building up market share. With increased business, that is, experience, their costs would go down and their profits would go up. It didn't always work out that way, but the legacy remains. Market share has always been very important to most companies, if for nothing other than as a measure of how well they are doing against competition. But other than bragging rights, what does a heavy concern with market share do for you?

In some cases, market share measurement isn't even *possible*. For example, can you define your market precisely in dollars or units? And, more important, do your competitors define it the same way? If the answer is no to either of these questions, what is the point of the exercise? If your industry is typical of most, competitors' products and markets overlap rather than coincide exactly. It isn't uncommon for two strong companies to claim 60% shares of what each considers the same market. Few companies serve exactly the same market segments or define their markets in exactly the same way.

It is true that some industry trade associations collect sales statistics from their members. From those gross numbers, the individual member can "easily" compute market share. If there were 5,000,000 widgets sold last year and we sold 500,000, voilà, we have a 10% share, assuming that all the players reported, and all the players reported accurately. An interesting pair of assumptions. Even then, *so what?* Would it make any difference in our strategy if our actual share were 15% instead of 20%? What if it were only 12%?

If market share is so important, perhaps you should redefine your market. Every company could probably define its actual market so precisely it could claim a 100% share. That kind of exercise will make you and your board of directors feel good, but what practical purpose would it serve? For most players, market share is a "nice to know" rather than a meaningful statistic. There are enough profitable companies with small shares of large markets to make the whole idea of linking share and profitability merely academic.

What is the point of keeping score when most of you aren't even playing the same game, never mind on the same field? Stop worrying about market share and go after all the business that is out there.

11 COMPETITION CAN BE A LIFESAVER, NO KIDDING

You may not like it, but deep inside you know that competition is a necessary evil in a market economy. Here's an example. For a time I was national sales manager for a small New England electronics company. The company, which no longer exists, was funded with venture capital to produce and market a marine collision avoidance system for oceangoing commercial ships. A collision avoidance system, for all the landlubbers out there, is an electronic navigation aid that computes the course and speed of other vessels in the area and advises the ship's watch officer of their "closest point of approach," or CPA. The system even makes recommendations for evasive action. The smallest CPA, of course, is zero, which means your ship and the target are sharing the same space (an unhappy situation for a mariner that would no doubt ruin his whole day).

Prior to the invention of this product, watch officers would do all their plotting manually on the face of radar screens or on special plotting paper. Manual plotting is OK when the ship traffic is light, but in certain parts of the world, the English Channel, for instance, the traffic is so heavy, the plotting load becomes a real burden. The collision avoidance system was able to automate the process and track many targets simultaneously, a real breakthrough in marine safety.

At the time, there were no rules governing or requiring the use of this new technology, so the early going was tough. Depending on market conditions, shipowners can make lots of money, but most of them are reluctant to share much of it with suppliers, particularly if they don't have to. We had to comb the world looking for shipping companies that were willing to put money into safety equipment that mariners got along without for thousands of years.

With each system at about $75,000 a pop, this was a tough sell, but slowly, ever so slowly, the business grew. Then came what we thought would be our undoing. A major U.S. company with greater resources, a broader product line, and a more-experienced sales force entered the market with a competitive product. We would never be able to keep up, we thought. Although we knew we had a better approach to the problem solution, we feared that the competitor would bury us.

But wait! Sales actually picked up. Our competitor was selling systems and building up its share of the market, true, but we were managing to keep our sales up, in fact grow substantially. How to explain it?

When we were alone acting as missionaries to get new prospects to see the light, potential customers would decide whether or not to buy. More often than not, they would say no. That's the way it is when you are promoting a new concept. But with two of us getting around the industry extolling the virtues of these systems, the decision process was shifting, no longer *whether* to buy, but *whose system* to buy. A not so subtle distinction.

The increased competition actually worked in our favor. As we both signed up new customers, we were both building up an impressive reference list that lent credibility to our claims. Their salespeople were calling on customers we couldn't get to. Once these customers were convinced to buy, we were usually given a chance to pitch our product, too. And we were successful in enough of those instances to maintain our market leadership.

In his book *The Marketing Imagination* (Free Press, rev. ed., 1986), Theodore Levitt proposed that "the more producers there are of a new product, the more effort goes into developing a market for it. The net result is very likely to be more rapid and steeper growth of the total market." When IBM made its personal computer design open for all to copy, the PC business boomed. Certainly IBM lost considerable market share but still it sold huge quantities of computers. It would be hard to see how IBM would have been better off if it had had no competition all these years. Any troubles it's had have had more to do with management decisions than competitive pressures. Competition forced down prices and expanded the market so that even IBM benefited from it.

Don't get me wrong. I am not saying that competition is all sweetness and light, nor am I suggesting you take your competitors to lunch and thank them for making you work hard. What I am saying is that they will be there, whether you like it or not. And even if they *are,* there is no reason to panic. Competition, especially for new products, is probably more of a plus than a minus. Take advantage of it.

12 DON'T UNDERESTIMATE THE COMPETITION

Confidence and self-assurance are the main elements of a winning attitude that makes for marketplace winners. Most successful marketers I've known are understandably proud of their products and their companies. Most of them genuinely believe their products are better than the competition. They have no trouble making that point to customers and prospects.

That's fine as far as it goes. Trouble is, it usually isn't enough. The customer has to feel the same way or you are just fooling yourself. The first guiding principle for dealing with competition is that you should not *underestimate* the competition. Competitors are probably as good as you are. Competitive products are probably as good as yours. In some cases they could even be better.

Don't pump yourself up so high that you lose sight of reality. You leave yourself wide open for a competitive surprise. Business history is full of cases where market leaders underestimated the potential of competitors and let them get a foothold in the industry. The American auto industry underestimated the potential of Japanese imports. Goodyear underestimated Michelin. Remington Rand underestimated the potential of IBM. IBM underestimated the strength and appeal of Compaq. Compaq underestimated the marketing skills of Dell and Packard Bell. Apple underestimated the entire PC industry. And so it goes.

It is much safer to assume that your major competitors are just as good as you. And why wouldn't they be? Their executives get degrees and MBAs from the same schools. Their staff attends the same seminars. They read the same books. They call on the same customers. They have access to the same market information. If investment is an issue, they have access to the same capital markets. As far as most customers are concerned, your competitors' products and their customer service are probably just as good as yours. If you believe otherwise, you lose.

When you minimize the capabilities of the competition, you leave yourself vulnerable to making poor choices, such as keeping your price too high, too long. Here is where hubris takes over from sound business judgment. Management says its product is better; therefore, it is worth more. Customers don't always see it that way, however, and the sales force can't get that message across. Or management says something like "We don't want to get into a price war. We're keeping our prices where we think they should be." Trouble is, they are wrong. Competitors leap in with lower prices and the whole business is in the tank.

Some people take their existing customers for granted. Here's that hubris word again. If you want to lose customers, just assume you can never lose them. If you assume that your position with a key customer is solid, you could be right. Or *wrong*. Are you willing to take that risk? You can't always count on customer loyalty, first because customers are always going to act in *their* own best interests, not *yours*. Second, competitors are pursuing your customers actively. Eventually they will break through.

13 DON'T OVERESTIMATE THE COMPETITION

Sometimes we act like our competitors have super powers, especially when they are market leaders or rank close to the top. Market leaders set the standards, and the rest of the pack follows along or makes do with what's left over. Those who make computer printers probably see Hewlett-Packard in their dreams. HP can do no wrong. And what retailer doesn't envy Wal-Mart for what it has done and what it has built? Or Nordstrom, a company that has become a metaphor for excellence in customer service? If you are an Airbus executive, how does it feel every time Boeing announces another big sale of the 777? Ask Apple and Motorola how they feel about 90% of the world's PCs shipping with Microsoft operating systems and Intel microprocessors. These are all formidable companies with strong market positions, and I sympathize with anyone who has to go to work every day worrying about what to do about competing with them.

Nevertheless, let me share something with you about your competition. They are probably worried as much about *you* as you are about *them*. Even market leaders get spooked when new challengers look like they are making all the right decisions. Every one of them is vulnerable to a smart, clever, innovative competitor. Every one of them makes a mistake once in a while that gives the other players some hope. Wal-Mart got plenty of negative publicity for its alleged practice of setting up in small towns and devastating the local retail trade. Nordstrom's expansion nationally caused the usual growing pains and strain on profits. Hewlett-Packard has been in and out of and back in the personal computer business. And, of course, who could forget Intel's famous Pentium fiasco, which I referred to in Chapter 1? Like my dad used to say, they still put their pants on one leg at a time.

Most people would rather be safe than sorry. Whether that means taking an umbrella with you in case it rains, or backing up your computer files on a regular basis, we are encouraged and indeed usually do take the safe route. After all, losing your computer files because you didn't back up your hard disk can destroy your business. So why is it those who play it safe so often end up being sorry? Because when you *overestimate* the competition's abilities and success potential, you make questionable decisions. Here are a few possibilities:

- You set your prices too low because you fear your competition will undercut your usual price. No one likes to "leave money on the table," but that's what happens. Your assumption is based on the idea that competitors can always lower their prices to match or even undercut you. Thus you price yourself low enough to hope it won't happen. Maybe.

Maybe not. What you've done, though, is make a customer very happy. Which isn't a bad thing, of course, except you'd like to make a little *profit* out of the exercise. But you don't.

- You concede business that could have been yours. You do this with rationalizations like "our competitor has the inside track with this customer," or "we're probably priced too high for this application," or "if we go after this business, we won't be able to serve our existing customers." Whatever the stated reason, you let the business get away because you don't think you can beat the competition.
- You make promises you will have a hard time keeping. You think the only way to get the business is to promise something you know (or think you know) the competition can't do. Like unreasonably short delivery schedules or no additional charges for tailoring the product to a specific customer request.

You will recall from the previous section something similar to the following: Competitors are probably no smarter than you. Their executives attend the same seminars, read the same books, go to the same business schools as you and your people do. You have access to the same market information and intelligence they do. Competitive products are probably not better than yours. Customers don't see all the differences between you and your competition. Unless you *are* inferior, there is no point acting that way.

14 RESPOND TO OPPORTUNITIES AND THREATS IMMEDIATELY

Action delayed is opportunity lost. Consider this scenario.

Your main competitor has always enjoyed the lion's share of the market. You have struggled to keep up, trying to maintain a respectable number two position. One day your sales representative gets you on the phone to pass on a piece of marketing intelligence he's come across in his travels. You learn that the "enemy" is experiencing severe problems with the labor force at its plant in Malaysia. The pickets are up, the factory is shut down, and the local government is on the side of the workers. An early settlement or resolution isn't likely. "There but for the grace of God go I," say you.

"I wonder how they are taking care of their customers," you pose to your associates. With a little discretion and a lot of digging you find that the answer is "not very well." One particular account of theirs that you've been eager to crack is about to shut down its production line because of the impending parts shortage. It turns out that you can deliver a similar part, fully qualified, competitively priced, and, best of all, *available*. Your people go in, make their presentation, and a grateful buyer places a major order with you. The frog has turned into a handsome prince, and you all live happily ever after, the wicked competitor never recovering its lost market share.

That is what is known as responding quickly to an opportunity. Second example. You are the market leader. You have good relations with your customers. Your products, while hardly state-of-the-art, are reliable and competitively priced. One day a sales representative gets you on the phone (coincidentally, the same guy who told you about the Malaysian labor dispute; if only he could sell as well as he could hear) and tells you about a competitor's new product that looks like a killer. The results that have come back from the beta site testings were very positive. A major marketing effort is about to begin. "We gotta do something."

You meet with your staff to decide a strategy. The first thing you decide is to lower your price. That takes away some of the incentive for any of your customers to try the new product. In conjunction with the price decrease, you announce the upcoming availability of your next generation product. It won't be available for another year, but getting the word out now lets the market consider the option of doing nothing until your product gets there. Which is exactly what you want them to do. IBM was notorious for this in the heady days of the mainframe business. Usually, a new product announcement by IBM would "freeze" the market. Customers considering a competitor's computer would defer their final purchase decision until they had a chance to compare their current candidate with IBM, everyone's favorite in that market. With that kind of business practice, is it any wonder why IBM dominated the computer world?

A press release or two announcing some corporate personnel changes or some particularly good quarterly results or perhaps a third-party testimonial by one of your satisfied customers gets some needed ink. By the time your competitor is ready for market, the whole industry is buzzing about *you*, not them. Their new product announcement is lost in the noise.

That is what is known as responding *quickly* to a threat.

Labor disputes aren't the only things to capitalize on, of course. Competitors have problems for any number of reasons. I remember a company in the semiconductor business that ran into production problems. Seems like they lost the manufacturing touch for a while and production yield went from 80%, normal for that product category, to less than 10%, a disaster by anyone's standards. By the time their process got back under control, competition had walked off with a huge portion of market share. Sales volume dropped off to almost zero. It took years, literally years, to get back into the good graces of major customers and recapture some of that lost business.

But whatever the opportunity or threat, there is no way you can turn it to your advantage unless (1) you have an intelligence system that gives you *enough advance warning,* and (2) you act *quickly.*

15 DO ONLY WHAT YOU DO WELL WHERE YOU DO IT WELL

Tom Peters and Bob Waterman, coauthors of *In Search of Excellence,* advise you to "stick to your knitting." Your "knitting" is what marketing academics call your core competencies. Core competencies are what you do best, things you do so well that they are the main reason you can stay in business. Successful strategies are based mainly on your strengths, the things you do better than your competitors.

Exxon knows how to find oil, refine it, transport it, and sell it. When it thought that diversification was a great idea, it funded start-up companies in the office equipment business. What did Exxon know about office equipment? Once you got past the fact that it used a lot of photocopiers and typewriters, not very much. Most of these ventures failed.

IBM was always noted more for its sales organization and marketing skills than for its technical expertise. It's taking nothing away from its engineers, but the company got to be the dominant force in the computer industry because it marketed and sold its products better than most.

Dell Computer is successful because it has a unique method of selling its products. While others fight for retail shelf space, Dell merrily rolls along selling through telephone and mail order.

The U.S. aviation industry is loaded with examples of companies stepping outside their core competencies, mostly in changing their services.

United Airlines derives its main strength from carrying passengers long distances in big planes. It is the leading carrier across the Pacific and remains a major factor in U.S.-Europe and U.S.-South America travel. When it competes head-to-head with American Airlines or Delta, it holds its own. But when Southwest Airlines threatened to take over the lucrative California market, United had to reorganize itself completely to remain competitive in a state where it had been the leader since the beginning of the air transport industry. Shuttle by United is its new "airline within an airline," put together with a different cost structure from the parent and a different way of operating. Less time at the gate. Fewer passenger amenities. Concentrating exclusively on the short-hand market. Even so, Southwest has pulled ahead. United claims the Shuttle is here for the long run. Maybe so, but the struggle has no end in sight. And profits are nowhere to be seen.

Southwest, on the other hand, is an expert at short runs. That is its strength, and it is almost unbeatable at it. When it started out in Texas, it quickly dominated that market and made lots of money doing it. It has one of the lowest costs per passenger mile of any airline in the world. The airline has cleverly put together a route structure one leg at a time. With each new route, it either takes over the leadership position or it threatens the existing leader. Now Southwest is talking about extending some of its routes to the U.S. Northeast. Be careful.

America West Airlines started out in the same mode as Southwest. Short runs. High profits. Then the company got overambitious, adding long-range routes, bigger planes, and more overhead, so much additional cost that it almost flew itself out of business.

U.S. Air is a major carrier in the eastern United States. It controls most of the traffic at its main hub in Pittsburgh. Some years ago, however, it got caught up in the acquisition craze and bought PSA, a regional carrier with a very good reputation and loyal customer base, particularly in California. U.S. Air itself is a regional carrier and now it was entering a region it had no experience with. By the time the debacle ended, U.S. Air was gone from California, older and perhaps wiser, but certainly poorer.

All the companies I mention here do something so well that they do or can dominate their markets. On the other hand, when they step out of their primary strength, they can, and most do, get into trouble.

What are you good at? You must be good at *something*, otherwise how do you stay in business? Whether it is marketing, engineering, volume manufacturing, unique distribution, or anything in between, recognize what it is, exploit it, and be *very cautious* about deviating from it.

16 EXPLOIT COMPETITIVE WEAKNESSES (HIT THEM WHERE IT HURTS)

In June of 1996 Oscar de la Hoya won professional boxing's super-lightweight division World Boxing Council championship in a fourth-round technical knockout over reigning champion Julio Cesar Chavez. The immediate cause of Chavez's defeat, aside from de la Hoya's youth and exceptional boxing skills, was a major cut over the eye, a cut that de la Hoya went after relentlessly, hitting it repeatedly until it was bleeding so badly the referee had to stop the fight.

In baseball, runners steal second base because the pitcher's motion is slow enough to allow the runner to start for second base before the pitch is thrown. By the time the catcher gets the ball, it's too late to throw out the runner. The best base runners learn all there is to know about pitchers and their weaknesses, then exploit them in every possible situation. In a game I saw recently, Eric Young of the Colorado Rockies stole *six* bases off Los Angeles Dodger pitching. The runs he set up by his baserunning were enough to provide the Rockies with their margin of victory.

The successful pro football quarterback knows where to send his receivers to take advantage of any weakness on the part of the defensive backfield.

Lest we take the sports metaphor too far, my point is that there are always weaknesses on the part of your competitors. Once you know them you have to do something about it, or it wasn't worth the trouble to discover them. If you actually *know* that a competitor has a problem that can be exploited, and you don't take advantage of it, you pretty much deserve what you get.

In the next chapter, on planning, I mention the specific areas to look for in evaluating your own firm's strengths and weaknesses. The same characteristics will apply when cataloging competitive weaknesses, except that you will have more trouble uncovering the details.

The first place I look for weaknesses is on the front lines, with the sales force. They may be weak in certain territories with inexperienced or indifferent or invisible salespeople, or all of the above. You exploit that by sending in your best and most professional salespeople. Buyers don't like to deal with incompetents. Their mistakes can just as often hurt the customer as help. Concentrating on customers that have been neglected by competitors is bound to be a winner.

Look for gaps in your competitors' product lines. If you can offer a more complete package, you have an advantage (*their* weakness) to exploit. I have worked for a few small companies and one of my major frustrations was seeing a competitor talk about the broad scope of their line compared with the shallowness of ours. Their advantage lay in their ability to supply a more complete package and "bundle" the whole offering together with a single price. Many customers find this an attractive proposition. (Caution: See Number 44 for another slant on this point.)

Look for inefficiencies in operations. Do their warranty policies stack up well against yours? If not, it could indicate a lower level of quality or reliability. This is a great talking point with a customer when you are comparing competing proposals.

Is your competition a smaller company living from day to day? There is always the risk of cutting corners, or worse. Are they short on cash? Now is the time to let customers know how strong and dependable you are. Warning: *Avoid arrogance.* In our society we still root for the underdog. Don't let this point come back and bite you.

Is there a technological difference? Point out how important it is to go with the added benefits of your advanced technology, not the technology itself but the benefits of that technology.

Business isn't war and isn't sports. But it *is* about winning. Exploiting competitive weaknesses is an important path to the winner's circle.

17 KNOW WHAT YOUR COMPETITION IS GOING TO DO NEXT

Knowledge is power, and nothing gives you more power in a competitive world than a good insight into your competition. Wouldn't it be nice to know what your competitors' next moves were? I am not suggesting that we install a spy in their midst. That is, at best, unethical. More than likely, it is illegal. I am suggesting that we pay attention to all the information available about our competition that is available through perfectly legal and aboveboard methods.

How Much Do You Know about Your Competitors?

When clients ask me what is a practical amount of competitive information they should be trying to collect, I tell them I would like to know as much about my competition as I know about my own company. In effect, there is no limit. The more you know, the better off you are. Even if it doesn't seem useful at the time, related data can show a pattern or a trend that would indicate some action or activity you would not otherwise have known. In this case, any news is good news. No news is bad news. These are some of things I would make a particular effort to find out about competitors:

- Who are their major customers? If your sales force can't help you on this, you probably need a new sales force. They should be calling on these people on a regular basis trying to get a piece—or a bigger piece—of their business. If you find out there's a customer you didn't know about, you might want to ask yourself why. And as long as you are chasing after their customers, you definitely want to know how their customers feel about them.

- Are they profitable? I like to know this because it gives me a clue to the way they operate in a competitive situation. If they need the business real bad, will they lowball their prices? Is there a clue here to quality and reliability? Staying power? The ability to support their customers over time?

- What are their plans and strategies? What moves are they likely to make during the next five years? How would you like it if your competitor knew your plans and strategies? That's why you should be making an effort to anticipate what they intend to do, both short and long term. Think of the joy in beating them to the market with a new product you are both working on, or dropping your price before they do, or lining up some exclusive distributorships before they get a chance to. That happiness comes from knowing what they are going to do next or knowing so much about them that you can guess with a high degree of probability in being correct.

- What are their major strengths and weaknesses? How do their strengths and weaknesses compare with your own? This gets right to the heart of my comment above about knowing all you can possibly know about a competitor.

Compare them with your own organization with respect to financial strength, organization, research and development expenditures, physical resources, plant capacity, sales and marketing skills, distribution, market position, and so forth.

Where Do You Go?

The sources of competitive intelligence data are so wide-ranging, it is beyond the scope of this book to list them all. The more common sources, and the ones you are most likely to have available to you, include:

- Trade shows and conferences, particularly product displays and conference papers.
- Advertising copy and product literature are good sources of competitors' product features and benefits and offer insight into how they position themselves.
- Competitors' home pages on the Internet's World Wide Web. The more sophisticated the company, the more detailed its web page seems to get. A good source.
- In-house publications can clue you in on inside information about managers, plans, facilities, new product development, and so on. You name it and it was, is, and will be there.
- Other suppliers sometimes willingly share information about a mutual competitor, especially when the competitor in question is the industry leader everyone wants to knock down a rung or two.
- Your own sales force is out there in the big wide world talking to buyers and technical people, sitting in reception rooms chatting with other salespeople, coming away with *priceless* information about competitive price, products, and so forth. They should be feeding that information back to the home office as quickly as they can get to a phone.
- Customers may or may not have ulterior motives, but many seem well disposed to sharing a competitive price or letting loose a piece of useful information. It depends a lot, of course, on the sort of relationship your salesperson has with the customer.

- Financial disclosures and reports are always available for public companies. I've known people to buy a single share of a competitor's stock just so they could receive company information regularly. For private companies, you probably can get at least a Dun & Bradstreet report. In this age of the Internet, all these company data are available on-line.
- Trade associations sometimes publish information about their membership, including market share data. Even if there is nothing in print, there is no telling what a judicious phone call to the association's executive director might yield.
- When companies issue press releases, they are deliberately putting out information about themselves. Every once in a while you can link information in the press release with an item learned from another source and . . . well, you get the concept.
- Direct inquiry. Never underestimate the benefit of asking for information directly. Pick up the phone and give your competitor a call. Sometimes they will hang up on you. Sometimes you can get someone on the line who'll pour out his or her soul, and the company's private information. You'd be amazed at what you can learn just by asking. Be warned, however, that there are laws against collusion. Don't get yourself in a discussion that can be construed as such. And of course you should avoid one-on-one meetings with no one else around.

One of my favorite places to gather information is at a competitor's booth at a trade show. Here is a technique I use with reasonable success. I usually pick the late part of the afternoon, when the booth staff is getting leg weary. Without any deception on my part or any attempts to disguise who I am, I just start looking around their display to get a feel for the line, how busy the booth is with serious lookers, and so forth. By judging the quality of the overall display you get a take on their promotion expenditures and how they are trying to position themselves.

Sooner or later I am approached by one of their salespeople who, at this hour of the day, would rather be off his feet with a tall cold beer than answering inane questions from a lot of people whose sole interest is collecting catalogs, or so it seems. His reaction at this point, should he put two and two together and see that I am a competitor, is rarely negative or defensive. Usually, it's something in the nature of comradeship, a we're-both-in-the-same-boat kind of greeting, maybe even some bravado like, "I've got something you don't have." When I ask my simple questions such as "What's new?" or "How's it going?" chances are he's going to tell me a lot more than his management would like.

From such chance encounters I've learned of design delays, management changes, quality problems, new product and market intentions, even things about ongoing customer negotiations. Some of the more useful tidbits you can pick up this way deal with *other* competitors, the common enemy. As long as I haven't misrepresented myself or hidden the fact that I work for or represent a competitor, I see nothing unethical about standing by as someone dumps tons of useful information on me. There are times when I wish I had a tape recorder in my pocket. Of course, *that* would be unethical.

3

GOOD PLANNING
IS GOOD MARKETING

Marketing and planning are interlocked. Like Siamese twins, one can't do without the other. Any plan that doesn't have a strong focus on marketing isn't much of a plan. Any marketing program that doesn't try to follow some predetermined plan isn't much of a marketing program.

From time to time I will have a discussion with a prospective client and we'll talk about the company's marketing plan. In a depressingly frequent number of cases, my contact will show me what he calls a marketing plan, but what I see is just a forecast and a budget. Other times he'll say that his company doesn't have a written plan but he knows pretty much what the company has to do to compete successfully. I even had one CEO tell me with a straight face that in his industry, planning was ineffective. He was not in the kind of business where he could ever put together a plan and stick to it. I think he was wrong. I will always think that.

By now you will probably have concluded that I am a bit of an iconoclast, even something of a curmudgeon. I confess I don't mind poking some fun at pretension, especially new business "theories" that restate the obvious and repackage what management should be doing all along. When it comes to planning, however, I am a rigid, humorless fundamentalist. I believe in the truth of the good book, especially any book that tells you how to write and implement a marketing plan. Actually, you don't really need a book about planning. You just need a little common sense.

18 PUT TOGETHER A WRITTEN MARKETING PLAN

If it isn't written down, it isn't a plan, it's a dream. Dreaming is fine, but for most mortals, reality is what pays the bills. When it comes to business, converting dreams to reality involves setting goals and putting into gear the actions that will get you to those goals. Getting those goals and actions down in writing so you can share them with the rest of your management team will go a long way toward converting your dreams to reality. The whole process is called planning, and the written marketing plan is the end product of that process.

The Planning Model

Planning doesn't have to be complicated. The simplest outline I know is the three-question model that sums up for me what planning is all about. These questions are:

- Where are we now?
- Where do we want to be?
- How will we get there?

The first question calls for an understanding of who you are, what you do, the competitive environment, the economy, and all those other factors that influence your ability to compete successfully. Planners call it the Situation Analysis (more about this in Number 19). Once you know all that, and you have a firm grip on your capabilities and limitations, your place in the marketplace, so to speak, you can come up with a realistic target to shoot for. In planning jargon, it's called setting objectives. You can express objectives any way you want. You can even call it anything you want. Some people use the term "goals" instead of "objectives" and some even draw a distinction between the two. The differences are too subtle to worry about; consider the terms interchangeable. Marketing objectives are usually stated in terms of sales volume, but I've also seen them in terms of margin, profit before taxes, and very often market share (but by now you know how *I* feel about market share—and if you've forgotten, review Number 10!).

Whatever objective you decide on, and the only opinions that count are those of you and the rest of the management team, I strongly recommend that your objective be expressed in some numerical form. "Increase sales to $10,000,000" is a lot more forceful than merely, "increase sales." The most important reason to express your objective numerically is so that you have some way of measuring how well you are doing or have done. Without quantifying the goal (or objective), any increase, even a single dollar, would satisfy the terms of the objective.

Now you know where you are and where you want to be. The hard part comes next. Getting there requires actions—strategies and tactics. If you want to grow the business by 20% next year (your objective), how do you expect to do it? A good way to look at strategies and ensure you've covered all the bases is to think of them in terms of the marketing mix. Product strategy. Pricing strategy. Promotion strategy. Distribution strategy. Add on one or two that don't fit neatly into these categories, like selection of target market and positioning, and you've got it all covered. Ask and answer questions like "What do I do with my product line (or pricing structure, promotion mix, distribution channels and so forth) to get to my objective?" "What markets should we serve?" "How should we position ourselves?"

But strategies, if you want to use that word, are too general to do much good. You have to break down each strategy into more basic elements. These, no surprise, are called tactics. Tactics are the details. The specifics. Who does what, starting and ending dates, expected results, what it will cost. Good marketing plans spell out these details clearly and precisely. Everyone knows that planning implementation is critical. *Implementation* is getting down to the details.

If you want to expand on the three-question model, you may find it more to your liking to go with a more-detailed marketing plan outline. There are probably as many recommended outlines for marketing plans as there are marketing plans. Figure 3.1 is a reasonable, generic plan outline you can follow that will cover the basics. Tailor it to your specific needs. You are the one who has to live with it.

Figure 3.1

MARKETING PLAN OUTLINE

I. EXECUTIVE SUMMARY

II. DEFINING THE ORGANIZATION AND ITS GOALS

III. SITUATION ANALYSIS (Where are we?)
    Economic and Industry Forecasts
    Business Unit Forecast
    Description of Markets Served
    Competitive Environment
    Present Marketing Mix
    Key Factors for Success
    Strengths, Weaknesses, Opportunities, Threats (SWOT)

IV. MARKETING OBJECTIVES (Where do we want to be?)
    Net Sales, Profit, Gross Margin, Market Share, etc.

V. MARKETING STRATEGIES (How will we get there?)
    Market
    Product
    Price
    Promotion
        Advertising
        Sales
        Sales Promotion
        Publicity
    Distribution

VI. TACTICS (Action Programs)
    Specific actions related to each of the above strategies
        What will be done?
        How will it be done?
        When will the action begin? Completed?
        Who is responsible for seeing that it gets done?
        How much will it cost?

VII. PROCEDURES FOR MONITORING, EVALUATION, AND CONTROL

VIII. CONTINGENCY PLANS

IX. PRO FORMA FINANCIAL STATEMENTS, BUDGETS

Keep the process *simple.* Planning isn't an end in itself, it's a *means* to an end. If it gets too complicated or the process is too lengthy, people are likely to lose interest and you will come up with a plan that no one buys into. Worse, it will never be implemented.

And one last thing. Probably the most important prerequisite for a successful marketing plan is for the CEO to be 100% supportive. This is one of those cases where leadership really counts.

19 SWOT IS NOT FOR FLIES

The first step in the marketing planning process is a realistic company self-assessment, that is, the Situation Analysis phase of the process. The operative word here is *realistic*. This is not the time for flowery phrases and utopian statements. If your plan is going to have a fighting chance of successfully guiding your company into the future, you've got to be truthful and honest about your company's situation. This is the time to get it all out on the table, to hold nothing back. SWOT (Strengths, Weaknesses, Opportunities, Threats) analysis is the heart and soul of the Situation Analysis. The SWOT exercise gets us to put things in perspective. Here are a couple of checklists I use when I work with clients on the planning process. These are some of the things you should be looking at. Your own situation may suggest some others.

To identify internal strengths and weaknesses, you should look at:

- Internal organization
- Technical expertise
- Research and development
- Customer service
- Reputation
- Labor agreements
- Manufacturing capabilities
- Financial health
- Promotion effectiveness
- Management skills
- Information systems
- Sales force
- Scope of the product line
- Market position
- Quality
- Distribution network
- Pricing policies
- Plant and facilities

To identify external opportunities and threats, look at:

- State of the economy
- Competition
- Demographic trends
- New technologies
- Pending legislation
- Social changes

- Market growth or contraction
- Changes in the labor supply
- Political issues
- Critical materials and supplies

The purpose of the SWOT exercise is straightforward. The idea is to develop strategies and action programs that will exploit your strengths and outside opportunities, minimize or counteract your weaknesses or outside threats. Simple.

Why is this so important? Here's a brief example. Once I was given the assignment to facilitate a small company's planning process. The management team had a pretty good idea of what it wanted to do and where it wanted to go, but it had never gone as far as putting together a written marketing plan.

Based on what it had done in the past, what the sales staff had reported as "sure thing" orders, and some additional business with a high probability of successful closing, the group had set what looked like a realistic sales goal for the following year. The next step was to agree on the strategies to get them there.

The key strategy for realizing the sales target was early introduction and delivery of two new products that were in the development stage at the time. The CEO, the Marketing Vice President, the Chief Financial Officer, and assorted other team members all agreed on the strategy. The Chief Engineer dissented.

"We are limited in our engineering personnel," he advised. "I have enough people to get out one of these products but not both. Pick which one you want." In fairness, he sounded a little bit more managerial and professional than that, but the message was clear. Engineering was a finite resource. Use it any way you want, but you can get only so much out of it. Sure enough, when we had gone through our SWOT analysis, we identified the shortage of engineering talent as a definite "weakness."

In theory, of course, the process should have noted the discontinuity between product strategy and available engineering resources before we got to that point. Nevertheless, the process worked as it should have. Analyze the situation. Set realistic objectives. Develop strategies to meet the objectives. Once the disparity was identified, the team turned to possible solutions. Fortunately, the objective did not have to be changed. There was still plenty of time to acquire additional engineering talent by hiring new people and filling in gaps with outside contractors. The CEO immediately authorized the engineering department to move ahead. New employees were on board far enough in advance to ensure that both products, critical to the company in meeting its goals, were completed and delivered on time.

When it comes to setting objectives and developing strategies and detailed actions, it all starts with SWOT and the Situation Analysis. Skip this step and you are almost guaranteed a marketing plan that is *useless*.

20 SET REALISTIC OBJECTIVES—WITH A STRETCH

My wife and I have a little joke we play on each other from time to time. Whenever one of us expresses a desire for something luxurious or outrageously pricey, the other will comment, "Well, if you are not going to have something, you might as well not have something very expensive." It's a silly play on words, but it helps us put things in better perspective. When it comes to setting business objectives, it is one thing to reach for the stars and altogether another to have a realistic chance of getting there.

The marketing plan is no place for unachievable, unrealistic goals. I once read a business plan for a start-up company assuring potential investors that, "with aggressive sales and marketing effort" (whatever that was supposed to mean), projected sales from start-up through the second year of operations should reach $200,000,000 (emphasis mine). Going from start-up to $200 million in only two years for this particular company was patently absurd. It had a nice little product, but its market was limited and the product's benefits weren't terribly significant. Prospective investors recognized these issues immediately and avoided this company like the plague. Of course, the company never got off the ground and went out of business very soon. Fortunately, it didn't take anyone else's money with it.

Of History and Hockey Sticks

In the planning process, historic patterns will tell you, at least at first look, whether you've come up with reasonable short-term objectives. If it looks unrealistic on the face of it, your justification problem is all that more serious. This is what I call a hockey stick projection. Lay a hockey stick on the ground and adjust it so the blade points upward. If your growth from year to year is flat or essentially linear, and your projected growth turns upward sharply so that the plot looks like that hockey stick, you've got some explaining to do. Say your typical growth rate is about 5% a year. You *may* be able to double your business the next year, but those who have a vested interest in your business have a right to be skeptical, at least until you've proved otherwise. Unless you're going for the Stanley Cup, hockey stick projections have no place in your business.

But if planning were only about meeting goals set by linear projections, the process would be essentially a waste of time. Good marketing planning and good goal setting should present some level of "stretch." Meeting a forecast isn't a big deal. You know where all that business is coming from anyway. That's just maintaining the status quo.

The way I like to look at planning and goal setting is to think something like this:

I know we can achieve sales of $XXX next year. I will not be satisfied with achieving that level. I am really looking for $XXX + 20%. When I went through the Situation Analysis and SWOT exercise, I came away convinced that there were sufficient opportunities to achieve that level, and our own strengths include the resources to get us there. Therefore, we must think through and develop the correct strategies and detailed programs that will get us to $XXX + 20%. I will expect nothing less.

Compaq Computer has grown from revenue of $4.1 billion in 1991 to $14.8 billion by the end of 1995. Eckhard Pfeiffer, the CEO, keeps his company on a plan to grow between 20 and 25%

each year. There is *no way* you can get a company to grow that fast by maintaining the status quo. Compaq is on an aggressive track of acquisition, strategic partnering, aggressive pricing, and investment in new opportunities, both internal and external. Pfeiffer follows the model. He sets the objective first, then implements the strategies that will get them there. Judging from the company's record, those objectives are realistic. And a big stretch.

21 EXPAND THE PLANNING TEAM

What's wrong with this scene? A busy marketing manager running an understaffed department in a tough competitive environment answers the phone late one afternoon to hear the company president's latest request. "We have a board meeting coming up in two weeks. Please put together a marketing plan that I can look at and approve by next Thursday. That way I'll be in good shape to present the plan to the board when we go over next year's budget."

At least he said "Please."

The marketing manager closes her office door and starts working on the "plan." A week later she emerges with two copies of an impressively bound document in hand and carries them to the boss's office where the two executives start going through the plan quickly. After about ten minutes, the meeting ends with a phone call from the manufacturing manager reporting the latest crisis on the production floor.

The president makes his pitch to the board of directors. Each director nods approval. Life goes on. The good news is the plan is looked at daily. The bad news is that the only one who sees it is the night cleaner dusting the bookshelf it sits on.

Planning Is a Team Effort

The marketing plan is not just the marketing manager's plan, or the plan for the marketing department only. It is the plan for the *whole company*. Those responsible for implementation should be involved in the process. Anyone whose input or performance is critical to the success of the plan should be on the planning team. Marketing plans require commitments to performance and completion dates. Those who can commit their departments to milestones must be on the team. In my experience a typical planning team looks something like this:

- *Chief Executive Officer*—Provides the leadership and direction that goes with the job.
- *Marketing Vice President*—By definition is responsible for the successful development and implementation of the plan.
- *Chief Financial Officer*—If we're talking about money—and we are—the CFO has to be involved.
- *Chief Engineer or Senior Product Designer*—Makes the commitment to product development schedules and assignments.
- *Operations Manager or Head of Manufacturing*—If you can't make it, you can't deliver it. If you can't deliver, you can't invoice. If you don't invoice, well, you get the idea.
- *Human Resources Manager*—Takes care of the staffing requirements.
- *National Sales Manager; Product Managers/Application Engineers; other marketing service people responsible for market research, advertising and promotion, customer service, etc.*—If it has to do with sales and marketing, these are the people who will see that it happens.

It sounds like a long list and it is supposed to be. Practically speaking, not everyone is involved from start to finish, but every one of these people has an input and must commit time and resources and accept responsibility for some part of the plan. Without assigning and accepting responsibility it is less a plan than an exercise in essay writing.

22 MEASURE PROGRESS AND RESULTS AGAINST PLAN

You've finished the plan, all the responsible parties have signed their agreement and acceptance in blood, everyone breathes a sigh of relief and charges through the door to win this one for the home team. You now have two choices. You can look on the planning process as an interesting exercise and a learning experience but, oh, what a relief it is to get back to the real world, or you can see the process as the first step to achieving all that you can. Is there much of a choice? The only choice is to get on with the implementation as soon as possible. With the first step out of the way, the implementation process begins. Putting all those strategies and action programs to work to get you moving and competing and winning is what implementation is all about.

If you are really serious about successful planning and implementation, then you probably want to know how well you are doing toward reaching your goals. Some kind of periodic review should be in place so you can answer the "how are we doing?" question. Consultants in the planning process (me included) will tell you that the written completed plan begins to lose its validity upon completion and approval of the finished document. The world changes, and the assumptions made in the planning process become less correct as time goes by. Competitors don't stand still, the economy goes up or down, customers change requirements. New technology comes out of the lab and captures the market's imagination. All these factors, and dozens more, impact on your ability to keep up with your strategies and goals. Some of it may be beyond your control. Some of it may be your fault. Variances are inevitable.

Track Variances

Variances, an elegant word for the differences between what you did and what you thought you would do, can come from any number of causes. Set aside those variances where you actually did better than you had hoped. Although that may not always be such a good thing, they are obviously the more desirable alternatives. Suppose your plan calls for hitting an annual sales volume of $10 million, evenly spread out over the year at $2.5 million a quarter. At the end of the first quarter you look at the numbers and you actually did $2 million, $500,000 short. You missed your objective by 20%. What does it mean? Maybe nothing, maybe plenty. Sometimes the cause of a small variance can be relatively unimportant, like a customer releasing an order later than you had hoped. Those are the things that even out over the year. The ultimate result is what you had hoped for anyway.

But you missed your goal by 20% and that, by any standard, is a big number. The problem is more serious, perhaps dangerously so. Did you overestimate demand? Was it because competition got their product out before you did? The variance may point to a flaw in the strategy. Reviewing progress against the plan sometimes indicates that strategies that seemed like good ideas at the time are in need of change. If you let it slip, the situation can only get worse.

Schedule Periodic Reviews

How often should you review your plan progress? Even the most-experienced planners shouldn't let more than a quarter slip by without checking up. Those new to the process, or those in volatile, fast-moving industries should never let more than a month go by without a check. If you do, you run a big risk in missing a key indicator that you are moving off plan. More important, you risk missing your goals.

23 PLAN FOR CONTINGENCIES

I believe in Murphy's Law. I believe that bad things can happen when you least expect them to happen. A company I once knew had a nice little business selling a system to public utilities that burned oil for power generation. The company supplied a black box with sensors that monitored the exhaust gas going up the stack to determine the completeness of the combustion process. When the price of fuel oil had reached superhigh levels, the product was in demand to help the utilities improve their fuel efficiency. Business was good in the heady days of high oil prices.

But then a strange thing happened. The price of fuel oil began to drop. And drop. And drop. Before you could say OPEC, the price had dropped so low that the utilities were less and less interested in spending money on instrumentation to save them less money than the instrumentation was worth. The company's business went down like a rock dropped from, well, a power plant smokestack.

The company scrambled around for more business. It was able to identify one or two applications for its technology outside the utilities arena. Niche markets in niche markets. Not enough to sustain them. Eventually the company died.

Bad things do happen to good people. Something happened in the marketplace to diminish demand for the product. It was beyond management's control. Kismet. Fate. The luck of the draw.

But was it? Think of it this way. Customers buy your product because the price of oil is very high, higher than historical levels. Is it reasonable to assume that the price of oil will always stay high?

What happens if it goes down? Will it *ever* go down? Is there something that you can do to prevent it from happening? Not likely, unless your brother-in-law is a Saudi sheik. Is it something you can plan for? You bet! Of course, it isn't always possible to anticipate an event in the outside world. If you could, you wouldn't be doing what you are doing now. You would be taking advantage of your prescience to become a billionaire at the expense of the rest of us. But if something is out there that could happen to hurt your business and you can anticipate it, even if you can't predict it, you should be doing *something* to prevent your business from going in the tank.

When was the last time you asked yourself why customers use your product? Not only why they use you instead of your competition, but why they use a product like yours at all? In the example I've cited, customers used the product because it helped them to save on overall fuel costs. If fuel costs weren't a problem, which eventually turned out to be the case, there was little or no reason to use it. End of business. If that was a contingency that had any likelihood of occurring, management should have anticipated it and gone out looking for additional markets or coming up with new products to spread out the risk. Easier said than done, certainly, but what choice do you have?

Lest you think this is a unique situation, how many American companies that concentrated on the defense business were ready to shift to commercial markets when the cold war came to a screeching stop? Could it have been anticipated? Maybe not in terms of precise date and time, but any company relying on a single customer in a single market ought to ask a few "what if" questions.

Look Ahead—The Fun Is in the Anticipation

Savvy marketers take nothing for granted. They are always questioning, always asking questions, forever skeptical. They ask themselves those traditional "what if . . ." questions that are so easy to ask on spreadsheets but so difficult to ask when your business actually depends on it. What if interest rates drop? What if interest rates rise? What if my competition gets to the market before I do? What if we have an exceptionally hot summer? Cold winter? If there is some outside event or condition that will seriously impact your business—good or bad—you had better be thinking about it. Even if you can't think of an immediate solution or response, you have at least *identified* the issue and can begin the response process.

24 DON'T LET PLANNING INTERFERE WITH DOING

Every moment you spend around a conference table or at a so-called planning retreat (why we would use the word *retreat* to describe a session preoccupied with going forward is a source of some amusement) working on the future is time you no longer have available to getting you there. In accounting terms, it is an opportunity cost, the cost of giving up revenue-generating activity while you contemplate your corporate navel. I say this at great risk of being misunderstood. This chapter should have convinced you that I am a believer in planning and the planning process. But I also believe there is great risk from an *obsession* with planning.

My most important criticism of planning is that it can waste a lot of time for a lot of very valuable people in the organization if the process isn't organized properly. A growing practice these days is to use someone, usually from outside the organization, to act as a facilitator. This can be very helpful during the actual group planning sessions. A facilitator can move the process along, function as an arbiter in case of disputes, ensure that all members of the planning team get a chance to talk and make a contribution, and help tie it all together into a coherent document used to guide the company for the next time period.

Without a facilitator, planning sessions either muddle along or, more likely, the CEO dominates the discussion and ramrods through his or her own ideas. While obviously undesirable, the possible plus side of this condition is that the process might move along much faster.

Too Much Planning, Not Enough Time

Planning may be hit or miss with some companies, but others are so deep into the process, it borders on obsession. In an earlier incarnation, I was marketing manager for a group within a major defense and aerospace company. It was routine in this company to make quarterly presentations to senior management on how we were doing with respect to our plans and forecasts. Planning really shouldn't be used in this context. Tracking progress against forecast was about as far as we went.

Unfortunately, we started getting ready for these presentations four to six weeks in advance. If you do the math, you will see that we spent almost *half* our time preparing for presentations. Not much time left for implementation. Typically, we focused on our *presentations,* rather than *content.* Armed with stacks of overhead transparencies, pointers, marking pens, and a healthy share of guts, we would march up to the projector and do our thing. The division manager or group vice president would sit back and absorb it all, commenting once or twice about a particular number or issue. Once the review sessions were over, it seemed only a few days would go by and we'd have to start all over again. In this company, planning seemed to be much more important than implementation. Planning is not—or should not be—all consuming. It's still more important to leave time for getting the work done.

Corporate Planners

A word about the corporate planning department. For some companies, caught up in the need to map out their future, planning is so highly regarded that they establish planning as a corporate staff function. The concept of the corporate planner misses the point. The implementers have to be part of the process. If line managers don't take the major share of the process, the plan doesn't have a prayer of working. Line managers will always have the final responsibility for implementing strategies and meeting planning objectives. Farming out all but the clerical parts of the planning process dilutes the influence and incentive of the line manager.

4

LOOKING FOR MARKETS
AND CUSTOMERS

Marketing is about customers—finding them, satisfying them, keeping them. Without customers you have no business. Here is a fundamental truth: Until your prospects become customers in sufficient quantity to sustain your business, you haven't done an adequate marketing job. Remember your products or services are intended to satisfy the needs of a *customer.* Your efforts to define the market are always in terms of *customers.* Your promotional message is intended to attract and influence a *customer.* The price you show on your invoice will be paid by a *customer.*

All your inside efforts, even those you think are unrelated to marketing, should be focused on customers. Unless you are so big that you can afford to devote huge sums of money to basic scientific research, your development effort should be centered on products that serve your present or intended customer base. What other reason could you have for doing what you do? Unless you concentrate on identifying and signing up customers, you are wasting precious time.

Have I made my point? End of sermon. Let's get on with it.

25 FOCUS: ON MARKET SEGMENTS, TARGETS, AND NICHES

In the movie *The Graduate,* Dustin Hoffman as Jonathan is approached by a family friend at a graduation and homecoming party in his honor. The friend feels the urge to offer career advice to the recent college graduate and sums it up in one word, "plastics." Jonathan listens respectfully, then moves to his other guests. You may do the same after you read this, but I can't help offering a word to reflect the role of the marketing manager.

Focus. Focus on segments, target markets, niches.

Let's go back to the basics. And I mean the *basics.* There is not a product or service in the world that can be used by everyone. None. Every market contains a finite number of customers at some level below that of the total human race. I wish that message were more universally understood and accepted. Since you can't sell to everyone, the question arises of who *can* you sell to.

We normally think of customers clustered in markets, that is, sets of customers with a common need. Good marketing includes identifying those markets in which you have the best chance for success in matching your skills with those needs. If you define the market *too narrowly,* you risk underestimating the potential for your product or service. Define it *too broadly* and you end up with "prospects" who couldn't possibly have a common need. Including them in your program wastes time and money. This is all called segmentation.

For example, what is the computer market? Is the bank that needs a huge mainframe part of the same market as a small businessperson working from home? Compaq and Cray Research both sell computers, but they obviously don't serve the same sets of customers. Mercedes Benz and Hyundai both serve the automobile market, but beyond that you can't say they have many customers in common. If you are considering the purchase of a Hyundai, chances are you won't be comparing it with the Mercedes down the street. Picking out the right segments to go after is called target marketing.

I recall the case of a power supply company that I was working with to put together a business plan. Sales had been down for an uncomfortably long time, so the sales manager had his people out combing the landscape for new opportunities. The company's main business was selling into large computer systems and big-ticket medical electronics. But as far as the sales manager was concerned, if the company was going to be in that business (the way he defined it), it had better look at all sorts of power supplies. Typical prices for the company's products ran from a few hundred dollars to a thousand and up. Most of company's line represented the state-of-the-art technology demanded by their customers. The sales force was encouraged to bring in applications that demanded prices in the five- to ten-dollar range, the kind of power supplies that plug into the wall and drive your telephone answering machine or a cassette recorder, usually made in the Third World for next to nothing. No way the company could compete against them. It wasn't for lack of ability, either. Their engineers could design a product like that on the back of a cocktail napkin. But why?

Fortunately, the CEO recognized that these applications were diluting the company's resources without adding to the revenue stream. It wasn't the technology that eluded them. It was the ability to build something *cheaply enough* to compete in the high-volume low-price end of the market. He did the right thing by shutting down the effort. Wrong product, wrong market for the company.

"Find Me a New Market"

Once in a while prospective clients will admit that their business is a little flat and that they don't see many growth opportunities in their current market. So they ask me if I can help find new markets for their product line. Of course, some conditions are attached to such requests, the main one usually being that they aren't interested in any extensive redesigns or development projects. "But I just know there are new markets we ought to be hitting" is the typical comment.

Who are they kidding? For industrial marketers especially, something I learned a long time ago is that the product defines the market and, conversely, the market defines the product. Which means that the company has designed its product to meet the specific needs of a specific customer base. To identify another untapped market for an existing product begs the question, "Why weren't you selling to them all along?" Even if there was a similarity in usage, other markets will by this time have developed other solutions. Those solutions will have met unique technical and pricing needs dictated by the unique nature of these markets.

To illustrate, when you open the lid of your clothes washing machine during the spin cycle, the machine shuts down immediately. The "door interlock" switch that handles this job must possess some very specific characteristics. First, it has to be robust enough to meet the appliance's voltage and current requirements. Second, it has to survive for a long time in an unfavorable environment brought about by hot water, soap, and bleach. Third, it has to be cheap. It's a home appliance, after all, not the space shuttle.

That's the point. Every switch manufacturer in the world can design a device that meets the first requirement, electrical. Every switch manufacturer in the world can design a device that meets the second requirement, environmental. But a very small number can do both and still meet the price requirement, or even want to.

Summary: Find a market you can serve *well* and target it. Offer a product that meets the *special needs* of this target market. Don't expect to sell that product *anywhere else* without investing in major design changes. In other words, *focus.*

26 NEW CUSTOMERS—THAT'S WHAT IT'S ALL ABOUT

Finding new customers is more expensive than holding on to the ones you have. There is enough empirical evidence for us to agree on that. Besides, intellectually, it sounds correct. Still, whether you are a retail store in a strip mall or a major multinational, you lose customers from time to time. *Attrition is normal,* even for the best of us. You will lose some customers to competition, some because they go out of business, some because their needs have changed, and perhaps a few, hopefully very few, because they don't want to do business with you any more.

For whatever the reasons, you can't keep all your customers all the time. You have to replace the ones who leave at the same time you are looking for more customers to sustain your growth. Growth means new customers, of course, but even standing still means new customers. Take the following examples.

Cadillac has always been the top luxury car built in America. For most of my life it was a metaphor for quality and luxury. We compared other top of the line products to the Cadillac. The Cadillac of ballpoint pens. The Cadillac of lawn mowers. When you finally arrived at the top of your profession, it was a Cadillac in your driveway that let everyone know. Those glory days are behind us now. European and Japanese luxury cars have preempted the quality cachet. New cars. New metaphors. "Built like a Mercedes," "As quiet as a Lexus."

Unfortunately for this division of General Motors, its remarkably loyal customer base is getting older and, well, dying out. The so-called baby boomers and yuppies who could afford luxury don't want living rooms on wheels. They buy European and Japanese cars. Somewhere along the way Cadillac lost these people. It will be engaged in a struggle for the foreseeable future to get them back. The only way to do that will be with new products that appeal to a younger buyer. Somehow or other Cadillac will have to convert the car buyer who says, "for the same $40,000, I can have a BMW," to one who says, "for the same $40,000, I can have a Cadillac." Good luck.

Even when Apple Computer's fortunes took a dip in 1995, the company could count on a large and loyal customer base to stick with it. For the most part it has. Unfortunately for Apple, the market has been expanding rapidly and Apple isn't getting its share of the growth. That means that with normal attrition, Apple hasn't been bringing in enough new customers to keep up with the market. In the long run, if there is a long run for Apple, it will have to get back to its heritage of cutting-edge technology to strengthen its faded image. That's the only way it will turn around its shrinking customer base.

A loyal customer base only works for you so far. It establishes a business base. It is nice to know you have them, but it really is a case of the market saying, "fine, but what have you done for me lately." In other words, it's irrelevant. That's why airlines run ticket sales. They already have their so-called loyal customers locked up in frequent flyer programs. But it isn't *enough*. It's the rest of us they want to capture. The added increments of discretionary travelers can be the difference between profit and loss for the accounting period.

I will admit that sometimes an obsession with new customers can get you in trouble with your existing base. Consider this. Did you ever dine in a fine restaurant and when it came time to pay the check, you were told that the establishment didn't accept your particular credit card? American Express has done an admirable job of seeing that most good restaurants in the country, perhaps the world, accept Amex cards from their patrons. Restaurant owners are assured by American Express that its card members spend more on food and merchandise than holders of any other card (actually, I'd prefer to be known as a customer. "Member" implies that I might have something to say about how the company is run, like I belonged to a private club).

For a credit card issuer the real customer is the merchant who accepts the card. Profit on the individual cardholders, particularly those who pay off their bills in full each month, is comparatively small. The fees they charge merchants on each sale is where all the money is, and American Express has been known to charge its merchants higher fees than any other credit card issuer. So much so, by comparison, that merchants have been grumbling for years.

One day the revolution began. A group of Boston restaurants openly defied Amex, told them they would accept the card no longer. This could have been the start of something big. Remember that if it weren't for the Boston Tea Party and later events, American Express today might be known as British Express. (Doesn't have the same ring, does it?)

Cooler heads eventually prevailed. American Express promised to lower its fees and the Boston eateries went back to honoring the card. Further, Amex made the remarkable admission that its salespeople had been compensated too much on the basis of new customers to the neglect of its existing base. From now on, Amex vowed, future sales compensation would be weighted heavily toward customer (meaning merchants) satisfaction and customer retention. End of story.

Summary: You can't exist on your loyal customers. Like an addiction, you need more. Without stepping on the toes of your regular customers, you've got to get out and hustle for new ones. *Do it.*

27 GET TO THE DECISION MAKER

As a salesman and as a management consultant, I learned the hard way that almost anyone in an organization, including the lobby receptionist, can say no to your offering or proposal. In fact, I've had a telephone operator abruptly tell me that her company didn't hire management consultants, then hang up on me. Didn't do my ego much good, but it did spell out the problems I was going to have getting into that company. Depending on the money value, very few, perhaps only one person in the prospect's organization, can say yes. As they used to say on "Mission Impossible," your job, if you choose to accept it, is to find that person.

Different proposals call for different decision makers. As a rule of thumb you can always expect that the higher the dollar value of the project, the higher in the organization the final decision maker will be. Office supplies don't have the financial impact of, say, a new mainframe computer. What can be left to a commodities buyer for one purchase goes all the way to the CEO for another, even majority consent of the board of directors for another.

I don't want to make it sound any easier than it is. Getting to decision makers can be tough. Even if you know who they are, you have "gatekeepers" to protect them and lower echelon employees to run interference for them. Besides, you have human nature working against you on at least two planes. One, people do not want to admit that they can't make the decision at their level. Therefore you will experience delay after delay. Not only will non-decision makers not make the decision, they won't pass the information on or introduce you to the decision maker who can. Second, salespeople feel a sense of obligation to their good friends, the buyers. They don't want to step on buyers' toes, go around them, confront them with the tacit accusation that they're useless when they really need them.

Many salespeople are guilty of overreliance on the relationship they have established with a particular contact in the customer or prospect organization. In a typical exchange, the salesperson makes a new product presentation to his longtime contact, lunch pal, golfing buddy. The contact assures the salesperson that he is very interested in this product, his company not only *could* but *will* buy thousands of dollars worth over the next year. He assures the salesperson he will take it up with his boss at the first opportunity. The salesperson goes away from the call giddy with anticipation, announces his success to his boss, ups his forecast by several percentage points, then moves on to the next opportunity. Deep down in his heart, though, he knows that his buddy isn't the real decision maker. But what can he do? Going around him risks embarrassment and hard feelings. He'd probably lose the order and never get another chance at this customer. Better to let the contact sell for him on the inside.

Fast-forward to the next visit to this customer. So far no order has been received, no meetings scheduled for design clarification. Our hero asks his good contact for an update on the status of the new product and when they can start talking about purchase orders. The contact assures him that everything is OK, but he hasn't had the time yet to talk with his boss and pin him down on an evaluation program for the new product. "Right now, he's on an overseas business trip. But I'll try to catch him as soon as he gets back next month." And on it goes. More meetings. More messages conveyed to the boss. Still no order.

It is always a delicate issue as to whether going directly to the boss is an insult to your main contact. Many salespeople are reluctant to do that. Of course, the salesperson should have sought out the boss early in the program. The longer it took, the more it would look like he was going around his contact's back. The chances of this situation turning around and actually getting the order are virtually nil. It may even be—this actually happens more often that we would like to think—that the decision maker is out negotiating with his favorite vendor, and the order could get placed without you even knowing about it. Sad.

In my business I have to start at the top. In most companies the CEO or division manager or maybe a senior vice president makes the final decision on engaging a consultant. Inevitably, I am passed down the line to other managers who will define their problems for me and, should I be successful, will work with me during the course of the assignment. But having started at the top, it will be easier to get back there, if necessary, to close the deal.

Summary: If your offering is of true value, sooner or later someone will say yes. Find that someone *sooner* rather than later, and save yourself a lot of worry and lost sleep.

28 TAKE YOUR SHOW ON THE (OVERSEAS) ROAD

When you evaluate which target markets to focus on, geography should be one of your main considerations. All things being equal, it is unquestionably easier to work with customers next door than customers halfway around the world. I would have to say that for some businesses, it doesn't make any sense whatsoever to incur the expense and the risks associated with international markets. The main criterion would be whether you could be competitive after incurring all the additional costs unique to international sales. For some products, shipping costs are so high and competition so well established in foreign markets you would best forget about it and stay close to home.

At the other end of the spectrum, the nature of certain industries *requires* you to maintain an international presence. Industries like transportation, telecommunications, information technologies, petrochemicals, and the like are international in scope. Companies serving these markets are expected to have an international presence. That's where all the customers are.

It's the vast majority of manufacturing and service companies in between that have go/no-go decisions to make. Check it out. You may be surprised at the opportunities open to you.

It's a Big Beautiful World Market Out There

Here is a typical response to a question I often put to prospective clients, "Do you export?"

"Sometimes."

Possible translations:

1. Not if we can help it.
2. Only if the order falls on my head.
3. Huh?

Many companies take a pragmatic approach to international sales. For most of them, the United States is a huge market, with plenty of opportunities. Why bother with export licenses; culture, language, and currency differences; and the expenses of getting to the customer? The risks and problems associated with international business just aren't worth the hassle of trying to do business in that environment. Especially considering the size of the home market. Of course, if something should come in over the transom, so to speak, well, they wouldn't turn it down. But actively engaged in international marketing? No way. Not an unusual attitude, nor is it incorrect on the face of it. But maybe, just maybe, they are giving up some terrific opportunities.

And those opportunities could go right to your bottom line. In 1996 Coopers & Lybrand, the big-six public accounting and consulting firm, reported on a study it ran on companies choosing or choosing not to go after export markets. As reported in *The Wall Street Journal,* exporters in the C&L sample grow at a faster rate than nonexporters, 31.3% versus 24.9%. Lest you think it's only a manufacturing thing, more than half the companies in the study were in the service sector. If you want to question the methodology, the validity of the results, or how they selected their sample, take it up with Coopers & Lybrand. For me, there's enough empirical evidence here to point you toward international markets on the basis of growth alone. This is something American companies, with their huge home markets have always been slow to discover, even though European and Asian companies view international markets as *fundamental* to their business health.

So What's in It for You?

In spite of the potential problems with exporting, look at some of the benefits:

- You may find you get *better margins* on your international sales, even with the added costs unique to exporting.
- There could be *less competition*. The fact that you are able to penetrate those markets may indicate you are filling a need that was unserved by weak local competition.
- Immediately upon taking the step overseas, you will serve a *much bigger market* than the one you were used to. And, of course, bigger markets mean more customers and revenue.

Take the case of the California wine industry. Between 1986 and 1995, U.S. wine exports grew seven times, with the California segment accounting for 90% of that growth. In 1995 California wine producers shipped more than $200 million worth of wine to overseas markets, from Asia to Europe. The exporters aren't only the major producers like Gallo and Robert Mondavi, but small boutique wineries as well.

Wine making is a difficult business. Some years, because of weather, disease, or both, there is a shortage of good grapes and good wine. Then the industry can barely serve its domestic market. But most years, production is high, too high for the domestic market to absorb. So it's on a plane to far off places to sell, sell, sell. Based on the figures above, wineries have been very successful at it. Even in an occasional bad year, some international markets have grown so important that the industry can't cut back its exports. Last, growing overseas has the added effect of increasing the industry's prestige. The more widespread the industry's prestige, the greater the overseas growth. Cheers.

Or take the case of Lisle, Illinois-based Molex, Inc. You may never have heard of it, but it is a *$1 billion company* whose products are in virtually every sort of electronic equipment imaginable. In the worldwide market of electronic connectors, it ranks *second* with 5% of an estimated $20 billion market, behind giant AMP, Inc., another company you may never have heard of. (Such is the fate of the components manufacturer.)

From its founding in 1938 until 1970 the company stayed close to home. Then, looking to get a piece of the Japanese television business, it opened its first overseas plant in Japan. Today, to cover its international markets, it has 45 plants in 21 countries around the world. It no longer has to export. Local needs are served by local plants. A full 70% of its business comes from international sales. Seventy percent and growing. Although it took them 57 years to get to a billion dollars, management says they will be at $2 billion by 2000. Not bad results from a realization made a long time ago that they were in a *global* business.

Summary: Keep your passport current and expand your business into international markets. You can't afford not to.

29 GO FOR NICHES YOU CAN OWN

General Electric management has a policy that they will not stay in any market in which they can't rank at least number two as a supplier. And if they have to be number two, they want to be an *important* number two. That policy seems to hold true in any market they are in, whether it is major appliances, aircraft engines, medical imaging systems, or lightbulbs. GE puts into practice the essence of good marketing and good market segmentation, that is, focus on markets to which you can bring the necessary skills and resources to give yourself a competitive advantage.

Then *dominate* those markets. Not a bad lesson from one of the best marketing companies in the world.

But GE is an industrial giant, far removed in size and revenue from most other manufacturing or service companies. What about the rest of us?

Big fish in little ponds eat what they want. Little fish in big ponds get eaten. Where would you rather spend your time? For a smaller company to be successful in today's marketplace, it has to concentrate its activities on smaller target markets in which it can be a dominant player. Mix it up with the big kids on their turf and you'll come away with a bloody nose. At best.

The essence of niche marketing is that you focus on small market segments that larger companies aren't interested in. Without the competition from companies with virtually unlimited resources, you can concentrate on your customers.

Vive la Différence

Good niche marketing doesn't just mean ignoring bigger markets. If that's all it were about, bigger competitors would swoop in and take the business in a minute. They would consider it just another incremental piece of business, no different from the mainstream. All it would take would be more selling costs, not a major factor for them.

To avoid that, you *differentiate* to accommodate the specific needs of the niche. It could be a special technological twist. Competition may consider that the segment is too small to guarantee a sufficient return on investment. In the early PC days, IBM stayed with the mainstream corporate accounts it felt comfortable with and let Apple tailor special products for the education and desktop publishing markets.

It could be a product offered at a price and margin too low to be of interest to others. The Japanese car industry got a foothold in the United States by bringing in small, inexpensive cars for an economy-minded segment. Detroit didn't think it was profitable enough to compete. As it turned out, the Japanese concept of high quality along with low price served a bigger niche than anyone expected. Detroit has been scrambling to catch up ever since.

It might be that the niche can only be reached through unusual distribution channels. Tupperware sells to consumers at home gatherings rather than in retail stores. Avon sold cosmetics door-to-door, at least until the two-income family became the norm and no one was home when the Avon lady called. Dell and Gateway 2000 sell computers via telephone and mail order to a niche that knows what it wants and doesn't need a retailer to explain it and back it up with service.

Niche marketers all of them.

Avtech Corporation in Seattle sells electronic and electrical equipment to aircraft manufacturers. Some of what it sells, like cabin lighting or windshield heaters, is hardly the stuff of breakthrough technology. Yet the designs must be tailored to a unique environment and the customer can be very demanding. Competition for this business is spread out among companies of similar size and anonymity all over the world. The biggies just don't see the profit in going after it.

When they do, they can get into trouble. In Chapter 2 I mentioned working for a manufacturer of marine collision avoidance systems. One day we woke up and found IBM looking longingly at our market. In those days there was a famous saying, "No one ever got fired for buying IBM," so we were concerned. Very.

We shouldn't have been. I can only figure that IBM saw our market as another outlet for its minicomputers. It was already doing business with the major shipping and oil companies of the world with its big computers, so I guess the company thought it would be able to leverage on its contacts with top management. Good reasoning, but not good enough.

One of the world's foremost marketing companies forgot that you still have to give customers a reason to buy from you besides your logo. IBM gave us trouble for a while but it was eventually blown out of the water (pun intended), competing for and losing business at the major oil companies it thought it owned. Management at the major oil companies, who wouldn't dream of using any mainframe computers but IBM, couldn't see the connection between mainframes and operational equipment.

Summary: Tailor products to the specific needs of a narrow market and enjoy more profit with fewer competitors.

30 SPREAD OUT YOUR RISK

I am nervous about single-product and single-customer companies. It's too easy for something to go wrong. A glitch in a product process. Declining demand. Predatory pricing from a competitor. A new technology. What might be a minor—even a major—inconvenience for a company with a diverse line spells gloom and doom for the narrowly focused. Successful companies spread out the risk.

The long-term prospects for single-product companies are generally not very good. Few will remember Computer Memories, a California-based company that produced hard disk drives for the personal computer industry. The company developed a relationship with IBM and became a major supplier of drives for the IBM PC line. Over time IBM became Computer Memories' biggest customer, accounting for more than half its total sales volume; I've heard as high as 80%.

Unfortunately for Computer Memories, its product quality was a continuing problem. IBM became less and less tolerant of the poor quality and eventually put the company on notice that it was about to discontinue the purchase agreement. Try as it might, Computer Memories couldn't get its act together. IBM finally cut the company off. Even with six months notice, losing more than half your business is a trauma few of us can recover from. Computer Memories is now a memory.

If you've been using personal computers for a while, you probably remember Ashton-Tate, the company that pioneered database management systems software (dbms) for the personal computer. The program, called dBase, was the standard by which all other database management programs were compared. I wouldn't be surprised if the word *database* was an Ashton-Tate invention, that's how closely identified they were with the generic category of database management.

Although the company grew and prospered, all was not sweetness and light. Ashton-Tate was essentially a one-product company. dBase remained the bread-and-butter product, no matter how much the company tried to diversify the business and get into other computer applications. And try it did. It brought out word processors and graphics programs, but nothing made much impact. Its version of dBase for the Macintosh flopped.

But dBase itself rolled on, maintaining its position as the industry standard. The market depended so much on dBase that any program bugs caused immediate furor. Should A-T be late with an upgrade, the negative reactions were intense. Which became the norm. Upgraded versions were delayed and delayed and delayed. When they finally came out, they were, as they say about software, "buggy." The market was very disappointed. Competitive products made deep inroads in dBase and there wasn't anything else to take up the slack. When business declined, A-T got itself into financial problems. Eventually it merged with its major competitor and disappeared.

Then there are the "one-market" companies. Whenever there is a prolonged labor strike at General Motors, Ford, or Chrysler, suppliers get hurt, sometimes bad enough to go out of business. During recessions, when air travel passenger loads drop off, airlines cut back on purchases and usually defer deliveries of new aircraft. The aircraft manufacturers in turn buy less. At the end of the chain is the small one-product, one-customer, one-market company. When the cold war ended, countless companies in the defense and aerospace business scrambled around for business. What can a think tank think about *now* if all they've thought about for 40 years was defense strategy? Conversion, defense to commercial, was the only way to long-term survival. The big companies purged and merged. Most of the little companies weren't attractive merger and acquisition candidates. Unless they too could convert, it would be an ugly time. For some, it has been.

Summary: Total reliance on any single aspect of your business could be bad for your health. Murphy's Law has not yet been repealed.

31 USE MARKET RESEARCH TO FILL IN THE BLANKS

Mention market research to executives in small- to medium-sized companies and they will admit its importance. It's getting them to *practice* it that is so difficult. Perhaps it's their fear of how much it would cost. Perhaps they've been burned in the past by spending money and not getting much value in return. Perhaps they are so busy living from day to day they can't imagine taking the time to think of their future. And maybe they think they know all there is to know. There are probably dozens of other excuses.

Market research doesn't have to be expensive. Market research *can* fill information voids. Market research isn't just for the giants.

Chances are that many of you have at one time or another bought an industry study that discusses general trends and provides some overall statistics and facts about the state of the market. You can buy these reports from a number of different companies. Some specialize in various industries; some offer catalogs of reports as varied as chicken farming and satellite communications. The benefits are that they are relatively inexpensive and give a quick overview of market trends. The downside is that most of the time they are *too general* to do you much immediate good. Frankly, I never found any of these reports particularly useful beyond providing an overview for the appropriate section of the company's business plan.

The next step up the chain is the multiclient study. Multiclient studies are conducted by industry specialists under contract to several clients who share the costs of the project. They usually retain exclusive rights to the information for a period of time following completion. It is a wonderful way to get your hands on a study that you would have paid $100,000 or more for if you contracted for it yourself, for a small fraction, depending on the number of clients supporting the project. The upside is you get detailed, useful information. You may even have a say in the content and the overall approach to the study. In the multiclient studies that I have produced, I made sure the issues of specific interest to the clients were covered. The downside is that by the very nature of the vehicle, you will probably see considerable information that has no relevance to your specific needs. And of course multiclient studies will cost you more money than the widely available overviews. All in all, though, not a bad choice if you want to see more about an industry than you can get from your day-to-day activities.

Then there is the market research that is designed solely to answer *specific* questions. These are the answers you can use *immediately* to develop or implement your marketing strategy. You commission it and you pay for it. It can be expensive, but you generally get what you pay for. The utility of the information depends on the professionalism of the researcher, naturally, but it also depends on how well thought out are the questions you pose, and what you want to do with the answers. Questions that I have been called on to answer for clients in the past include:

- What is the *best price* to set for a new product?
- What is the *size of the market* for a new product?
- What is the *competition* doing about a particular issue?
- What are the *performance requirements* for this new product?
- How do we *compare with our competition* in a particular area?
- What are the *best distribution channels* to get us into this new market?
- What are the *price/performance characteristics* for a new product?

And so forth. These are not necessarily questions that can be answered with enough detail in a general industry overview. *All this costs money.* Most of the market research you should be doing can be done by your own staff. Collecting marketing intelligence data should be an ongoing process anyway. There isn't much point in farming that out. A product performance specification shouldn't be beyond the capability of any product manager. The same goes for pricing and distribution issues.

There are times, however, when circumstance dictates that you buy the services of outside researchers. It may be for confidentiality. You don't want to tip off the competition that you are looking in a certain direction. It may be because you don't have the available personnel. Lack of talent is one issue, but there is an opportunity cost associated with taking a manager away from one important job and into another. And third is objectivity. I have seen managers get so wrapped up in a project that they can't or won't accept any outside information that differs from a preconceived opinion.

Summary: Market research is *good*. Not doing it is *bad*. Do it.

32 GET MORE BUSINESS FROM EXISTING CUSTOMERS

Part and parcel to holding on to your existing customers is to get more business from them. The more business you get from each customer, the more products or services you provide, the more likely they will remain with you. Essentially you want to get all their new business and get a bigger split of their existing applications.

The Name of the Game Is Account Penetration

For many years the prevailing purchasing strategy was to qualify several vendors for a particular product or service. Multiple suppliers was a safe "don't put all your eggs in one basket" policy. In case one supplier got into trouble, the buyer still had backup alternatives. Buyers also were not averse to playing one vendor against another, ensuring the most favorable terms, best possible price, and so forth. The more vendors, the more intense the competition for the business, the more likely the buyer could come out of it with the best possible deal.

As part of the reengineering mania, it has become a growing act of faith that multiple vendors are no longer a good deal for the buyer. I suppose it relates to documentation requirements, parts lists, and standardization issues. For whatever reason, it is now fashionable to sponsor a winner-take-all shoot-out among the several competitors. Even without this extreme action, buyers are still narrowing down their supplier lists. Not only is there a growing opportunity to get more business from certain customers, it may be the only way you can survive.

When customers are intent on splitting orders among several vendors, you have to see that you get a bigger share, not necessarily the biggest (although that would be the most desirable outcome) but bigger than you normally have a right to expect. Certainly you are not even in the race unless you have a history of superior performance, so you can't count on that for getting a bigger share. Superior performance is expected. If yours is significantly better than your competitor's, you are home free.

But the competition's performance can be pretty good, too, as I suggested in Chapter 2. If that's the case, the way to a bigger share of a customer's business is through better marketing and better salesmanship. You have to give the customer a *better* deal: price, terms and conditions, warranty, special packaging, hand-holding, whatever it takes.

Take the case of Universal Widget. Universal is a marketer of industrial products sold mainly to OEMs (Original Equipment Manufacturers), that is, to companies that incorporate Universal's widgets in their end products. A few years ago Widget finally broke through with a major prospect by getting specified on a new model. This is a high-end model and counts for only about 10% of the customer's volume, so Universal has about 10% of the customer's total widget business. It's a good start, but not good enough for Universal's management. For Universal to further penetrate this account, it has to ensure it gets specified on *every new model* that comes out. Further, Universal has to convince the buyer to be *at least a second source* for all the other ongoing widget business. If a competitor is ever going to trip over itself, then Universal is in a position to pick up that business as well. Effective account penetration has to use a two-pronged approach: Get specified on all the new applications, and be ready to take away the old applications with good performance, good prices, and good salesmanship.

I have a client that sells electronic equipment to airframe manufacturers. Its number one customer is Boeing, whose line includes the 737, 747, 757, 767, and the latest, the 777. My client gets all the 737 and 757 business. Recently it was able to compete successfully on the new widebody 777. The aviation business is interesting in that production for these models can last for 20 years or more. Once you get specified for a particular aircraft, the business rolls in *year after year,* provided you live up to the terms of your agreements with the customer, for example, price, delivery, quality, and reliability.

The downside of this situation is that you have to wait for another plane to be introduced if you are to increase your account penetration. The importance of getting specified on a new application cannot be overstressed. Without that, you get shut out *for the next generation.* Still, hope springs eternal, and there's always the chance that another supplier will drop the ball and you can pick up the business on an existing application. The only way that can happen is if your people are always there to make their presence known and remind customers of how well you've been doing on the business they give you.

5

CARING FOR CUSTOMERS

I didn't want to write another book about customer service or customer satisfaction. There are more than enough of those around to satisfy anyone's demand for the do's and don'ts of nurturing customers. But I do have some thoughts on specific items that contribute to the success of your marketing program.

In general, customers are demanding of their vendors but usually indifferent to their vendors' problems. Working with customers is frustrating. It is a pleasure to take their business, but it is a test of your people skills to keep them satisfied. On balance, though, I'd rather have the problems of dealing with *difficult* customers than the problems of not having *enough* customers. So would you.

33 KNOW WHAT THE CUSTOMER WANTS— AND DELIVER

Empathy *n.* Identification with and understanding of another's situation, feelings, and motives.
—American Heritage Dictionary

I assume that everyone who reads this book is a marketer, aspires to be one, or has a curiosity to understand what marketing is all about. Pause with me for a moment or two and I'll tell you. I once went through a company sales campaign that was titled, "Put Yourself in the Customer's Shoes." The purpose of the campaign was to boost sales in the short run. All the salespeople wore tiepins or lapel buttons that looked like a shoe. Cute. If I remember correctly, some of the prizes for meeting or exceeding quota that month were gift certificates for expensive shoes. Cuter. To get us into the spirit of the campaign, management put us through some "group think" programs where we learned that to put ourselves in the customer's shoes really meant that to be effective we had to have *empathy.* Cutest. It isn't just about serving customers. It's about understanding them.

To be a good marketer you have to remember that for most of your waking hours, after work, on weekends and vacations, you are more often a *customer* than a *marketer.* You buy groceries, clothing, furniture, housing, transportation and countless other items in the course of a year. Many of the anecdotes in this book come from my experiences as a *customer,* exactly like you. When you read them, I count on you to nod in agreement that they are similar to your own experiences. Your customers want to be treated by you exactly the way you want to be treated by everyone you buy from during your waking hours. If you believe that, and if you follow that principle, you will never go wrong. To be a good marketer you have to think and act like a *customer.*

What Does the Customer Want?

I can't count the number of times I have searched through retail stores looking for gifts. When the salesperson on the floor approaches me and asks whether she can help me find something, as all good retail salespeople do, I am at a loss to tell her what I am looking for because I don't know myself. "When I see it, I'll know" is my usual reply, not intending to be rude, but because I honestly don't know what I am looking for. Eventually, something will appeal to me and I will make my purchase and be gone. I don't think such behavior is particularly unusual. Customers very often don't know what they want until faced with choices.

We know, of course, that customers want solutions to their problems and fulfillment of their needs. The hard part is knowing what those problems and needs are. It is logical for us to ask them directly. It is illogical for us to expect a definitive answer. Yes, there are things we know are certain to be what every customer wants or actually demands. And, yes, there are things we will not know and have to dig for, not because customers don't want to share them with us. It is just that they themselves don't know.

As marketers, we are obligated to find out. That is what marketing departments do. Although it might be easier if customers knew their exact requirements, the fact that they may not know represents an opportunity for us to help them make up their minds. Customers will always want the general things like best price, on-time delivery, a quality product, a reliable product, conformance to their technical requirements, and superior supplier performance, whatever that means in any given time frame. What they don't know are the specifics.

Take the case of new products. A routine question I ask in every seminar I present is, "What is the best source of new product ideas?" Invariably, the greatest number of answers come back, "the customer." I would like to think that were true, but my experience tells me otherwise. For the most part, customers will stamp their approval or disapproval on a new product, but getting to that point is up to you.

Successful new products come more often from a fine sense of the customer's needs. We gain that need because we try to know as much as we can about customers and their markets. Over time, the best new product ideas come from our designers, engineers, marketers, and salespeople who have built up their knowledge to the point where they anticipate what will or won't work. Marketers can and do test those ideas for marketplace approval and estimate of demand, but the ideas themselves come from within.

34 GIVE THE CUSTOMER THE BENEFIT OF THE DOUBT

We live in a competitive world. The consequences of everything we do in the marketplace have an impact on our ability to keep our customers. If you screw up, a competitor is more than willing to take away the business.

Case in point. There is a car wash facility in the town where I live that I had been going to for a number of years. Like most similar facilities, as you drive in you are greeted by an attendant who asks you what level of service you wish, whether you want today's wax special, wheel cleaning, and so forth. On a recent visit, I gave my usual "just a wash, please," and left the car in their good hands.

I proceeded to the cashier, plunked down my credit card, and leaned over the counter to sign for the charges. Then I noticed the fee was two dollars more than I had expected. When I asked why, the cashier looked at the check-in slip I had handed her and explained that there was an extra charge for trucks. Granted, my aging Beemer doesn't handle like it used to, but to call it a truck is to insult all the Black Forest elves who put the car together.

"No, it is not a truck. The attendant has made a mistake," I explained, expecting a simple correction and I'll-be-on-my-way.

"I'm sorry, you'll have to talk to the manager," I was told. It was clear that she thought I was trying to deceive her by passing off my truck as a car to save the two dollars. No way she was going to let me get away with that.

"Where is the manager?" I asked.

"He's out front helping customers."

"What does that make me," I questioned, "some kind of freeloader?" Besides, "out front" was about a quarter mile away. I wasn't about to go marching all over the landscape looking for him. "Page him," I insisted.

"We can't."
"You can."
"We can't."
"You will."
They did.

I was truly astonished to learn from the manager, when he finally appeared, that the cashier had acted correctly, as far as he was concerned. In situations like this, only he as manager could make the decision to give money back. Ultimately, of course, the manager realized that I was right and cheerfully (?) returned not only the two dollars but refunded the entire amount as a gesture of goodwill.

Big deal. Ten dollars.

What amazes me about this incident is not that the cashier was rude or the manager patronizing. As a born and bred New Yorker I have no problem mixing it up with the rudest of the rude, even in California. No, what amazes me is that the cashier was not empowered (there's that buzzword for the nineties) to rectify a situation over a measly two bucks. It was not worth two dollars for them to give a customer the benefit of the doubt.

Guess how many times I've been back to that particular car wash.

As marketers we are certain that our company would never, ever let such a thing happen. It always happens to the other guy. But as consumers, we all see it almost every day. I have seen supermarket customers complain that they received the wrong change. Maybe they did. Maybe they didn't. But wouldn't it be better to concede the dollar or two than to make the customer wait overnight until the cash is reconciled in the register? By the time the store manager gets back to the customer, she's probably lost for good. For two bucks they've lost a customer that spends fifty or a hundred dollars a week. Where is the economics in that?

Empowerment of People to Make Decisions

The problem is often that "empowered" workers don't always get the backup from managers when they make a decision in favor of the customer. For instance, in the supermarket situation, if the checker is going to return two dollars on the customer's say-so, management has to reimburse the checker, even if she is wrong. If the employee doesn't think she has the support of management, then she will not be so willing to give the customer the benefit of the doubt. This is another case of policy getting in the way of strategy. Think of it this way. Will some customers take advantage of you if you give in? Probably. Will the business fail because of this practice? Not very likely. Contrast this type of behavior with the Nordstrom way, where the only important thing is to make sure the customer goes away satisfied.

Summary: Business is adversarial only among competitors. When you are dealing with customers, it isn't "us versus them." When you treat customers like they are out to steal from you, you *deserve* to lose them. And you will.

35 BUILD CUSTOMER LOYALTY

Everyone wants satisfied customers. But everyone needs *loyal* customers, customers who are *more* than just satisfied, they are *thrilled* and *delighted* to do business with you. It's just too hard to do business without some percentage of your customer base locked up because they love working with you. If you are having trouble achieving this utopian state, you are not alone. For most of us it is a recurring problem. Thus it has become fashionable to talk of loyalty these days. In a recent issue of *Marketing Management,* a magazine published by the American Marketing Association, the book review section discussed no fewer than three books, each of which included the word *loyalty* in its title. Loyalty is fast approaching buzzword status.

My cellular phone carrier, like others across the country, is in a struggle for new customers. Not only are new customers few and far between, they are also expensive to find and sign up. It costs my carrier, I've been told, about $440 to acquire each new customer. It stands to reason that the more customers they can hold on to, the less they have to spend to bring in new ones.

In the cellular industry, just about all of the obvious big users have by now been signed up by one carrier or another. For the carriers to grow, they are turning over rocks, figuratively speaking (although if worms could talk, the cellular industry would be signing them up, too), to find new accounts. To complicate the situation, customers are taking advantage of the promotions to switch carriers whenever they can. Operators are locked in a competitive struggle to offer additional services, new plans with even lower base prices, free phones for both new and existing customers, and so forth, to keep or attract as many of those potential switchers as possible. This customer "churning" is costing the industry a fortune and there isn't much relief in sight. Customer loyalty is not only elusive, it scarcely exists.

Loyalty comes and goes. Even long-standing customers can't be taken for granted. Scandinavian Airlines (SAS) was probably McDonnell Douglas's most "loyal" customer. For years, the entire SAS fleet of planes, from DC-8s to MD-11s, all came from Douglas. On the last big buy, to replace aging DC-9s, SAS went with the Boeing 737. So much for loyalty. United Airlines was probably Boeing's most loyal customer. At least until they made a major purchase from Airbus. Sears and Whirlpool always had that classic arrangement where all the major appliances sold under the Sears brand name, for example, refrigerators, washers, dryers, were made by Whirlpool. That is still true, but Sears has changed its policy and now sells all the major brand names, including Whirlpool. Where Whirlpool once got all the business, they now share. Sharing is something you learned in kindergarten but it isn't something you want to carry over to your marketing strategy if you can help it.

There is a difference between loyalty and satisfaction. I am *satisfied* with many products and services but loyal to much fewer. I am *loyal* to USAA auto and household insurance, Kodak film, Gillette razors, BMW, Federal Express, and the Apple Macintosh. Whether it is because of the quality of the product or service, or the way they treat me as a customer, I have never seriously considered switching. It isn't that they are always perfect, either. It could very well be the way they perform when they aren't that impresses me most. Federal Express once misdirected an important shipment to me. Bad things do happen once in a while, I suppose. By the time the shipment was located and delivered, and for a week afterward, I got more apology calls from vice presidents and regional managers than I thought would be possible, and enough certificates for complimentary shipments to take care of my needs for a long time. I was impressed.

For the time being, at least, I use and am *satisfied* with Sprint, AT&T Wireless, Microsoft, America Online, Marriott hotels, and American Express. For these services, satisfaction notwithstanding, I am not particularly *loyal*. I may or may not switch to one of their competitors sometime in the future, either for good reason or on a whim. Like most of us, I belong to several frequent flyer programs, but I find flying one particular airline speeds up getting me to important award levels, even if it doesn't particularly speed up getting me to important places. I am a repeat customer, but not only am I *not* loyal, I am very often not even satisfied. What keeps me with this airline is more personal gain or inertia than loyalty. I got good service from my Michelin tires but I switched to Bridgestone when I thought I got a better deal. Besides, how do you fall in love with a rubber tire? I drink Coke until Pepsi runs a promotion, then I drink Pepsi. Which gets to the point. I will continue to purchase from these companies as long as there is an *economic* reason to stay. If I get a better deal somewhere else, or I think another product or service will help my business, then I might switch, satisfaction notwithstanding.

As the cost of finding new cellular customers points out, it's got to be more economical to keep *existing customers* than to be continually searching for *new ones* to replace the ones you lost. All business counts, but *repeat* business is what really counts. Whether they are loyal, or merely satisfied, customers who buy again and again make your business survive and grow.

36 BUILD AND STRENGTHEN RELATIONSHIPS

Relationship marketing is a well-established business principle. Buyers don't like to buy from strangers. It is up to us to see that we don't remain strangers for very long. In the good old days it might mean regular lunches, an occasional dinner, a generous Christmas present, theater tickets with the spouses, and box seats behind first base for a World Series game. Those things might still count for something, but in today's downsized and rightsized business world, the generous vendor might find the recipient just too busy to give you the time and too much afraid for his or her job to accept gifts. Besides, most of those practices are less about relationships than about currying favor with tax-deductible expenditures. I'm sure they still work, but more and more, today's marketer has to be more subtle.

Above everything else, the best form of relationship marketing is to deliver good products and services on time at a fair price. That's what customers are really looking for. Without coming through on quality, you will never be more than just another vendor "we have to hassle with all the time."

That said, if quality is a given, we can get on with the details of enhancing those relationships and turning customers into business partners, even friends. One way to establish that relationship is to bring customers and prospects into the decision-making process. I don't mean the self-serving "customer satisfaction" surveys that are sent out from time to time. Most of them are filled with loaded questions that are transparent attempts to get the customer to buy more or serve merely to collect market research data. I also don't mean focus groups, which are great tools for getting inside the customer's head, but involve too few customers at sessions too few and far between to win any long-term or far-reaching relationships. What I mean is genuine *one-on-one,* even one-on-many, *discussions* to find out what the customer is thinking and to let the customer know what *you* are thinking.

When I worked for Texas Instruments, we would invite 30 or 40 engineers from our biggest customers to a seminar and conference specially designed for them. Since our division of TI was located in Massachusetts, we would set up the seminar at a resort on Cape Cod or in nearby Newport, Rhode Island. Over a two- or three-day period our engineers would answer all their technical questions, we would discuss applications and solutions, and find time during the program to let them in on our new product plans. There was good food and wine, time for play and rest, and plenty of opportunity for supplier and customer to get to know each other on a personal basis. When the program ended and all our guests returned to their regular jobs, guess which vendor they called when there was a new application to discuss?

Another experience. Coming from a lunch meeting with a prospective client at an Anaheim hotel, I was amazed at the number of people in the lobby, even for this popular resort area. It turned out to be a Digital Equipment VAX computer users' conference. Hundreds of engineers and MIS people from all over the world had come together, apparently on a regular basis, to discuss areas of mutual interest and find out what's new and in the pipeline from DEC. They might not have been 100% satisfied users, but I would guess you would have to search far and wide to find a more *loyal* group of customers for one company under one roof. That is what I call successful relationship marketing.

And there are regular Macintosh "expos" where customers come and see the latest Mac hardware and software from Apple and third-party vendors. Also, Apple encourages the ubiquitous Mac User Groups around the country and overseas, where grassroots users get together to swap ideas and techniques and help each other get the most out of their computers and software. Apple, in spite of its problems in the fight for computer market share, still has one of the most loyal customer bases of any product, anywhere, anytime. It is one reason they have historically been able to sell almost everything they could make, most of the time at premium prices. That is what I call successful relationship marketing.

So when was the last time you went to a Chevrolet Caprice Users Conference? How about an AT&T Long Distance Customers Support Group? Just asking.

Running Good Meetings

If you are putting together a meeting or seminar or conference to help get your customers or prospects on your wagon, here are a few things you might want to consider or look out for.

First, a good meeting isn't just a data dump. No one enjoys sitting and listening or being a captive audience for very long while the company goes through an endless lineup of speakers droning on about product and company virtues. To do it right, you've got to identify the issues of *concern* to the audience and draw them into the discussion almost *immediately.* "Interactive" is as good a word as any to describe what a well-put-together meeting is all about.

Second, avoid the blatant sales pitch. When these people go back to their companies, they want to tell their bosses what they *learned,* not how much you tried to get them to buy whatever it is you are selling. Of course, the purpose of the whole exercise is to get more business. But you have to be a little bit—no, a lot—more clever about it.

Third, consider the "take homes." I refer not to the little gifts or bound set of technical papers. I consider a meeting or conference I've attended to be worthwhile if there is something I learned or was presented that I can put to immediate use when I get back to my office. That means that you must consider the *content* of the program very carefully. Err on the side of practical considerations rather than the abstract.

Fourth, get as much feedback as you can both at the meeting and a week or two after it has ended. Assuming you would like to do it again, find out from the attendees what they liked or didn't like about the sessions. Don't make the same mistakes twice. If you do, there will never be a third time with those customers or prospects.

Remember, we are talking about *relationships*. A well-organized conference will do wonders in building relationships with people who count—your customers.

37 SEND MANAGERS OUT TO TALK TO CUSTOMERS

There is a television commercial that you may recall from a few years ago that shows a marketing executive addressing his staff and bemoaning the fact that business is down and customers are complaining they don't see the company's people anymore. Determined that this has got to stop, the manager picks up a stack of United Airlines ticket wallets and hands them out to his people. Message: Get on the next plane out (United Airlines, of course) and go win back your customers' hearts, minds, and business. It is implied that the troops march out, fly off to their customers, succeed beyond expectations, and live happily ever after.

I don't know if this particular spot helped United's sales but it did make an impression on me. It reinforced my belief that you don't help your cause by sitting in the office. Managers should spend as much time as they can in front of customers. That's where the action is.

I learned this lesson as a sales manager years before from my CEO at the time who directed me to stay away from the office. "You can't sell *me* anything. I have more product than I know what to do with. Out *there* is where the customers are." The man indeed had a point. I can understand why individuals may spend their time in the office. The usual excuses are things like catching up on paperwork, making telephone appointments from the office, checking up on customers' orders, attending a meeting, and any other number of "valid" reasons to stay home.

What I can't understand is why managers are sometimes *discouraged* from getting out in the field. At a client company, the VP of Marketing recognized a need to get out in the field, but the CEO founder and owner of this small company was reluctant to let him go. He needed him in the plant, he was told, to help in the strategic decision making. I suspect that the real reason was that the engineering-oriented CEO needed someone at his side "in case anything came up." Besides, it was one of those companies that grew up thinking the technology was so good it sold itself. Wrong.

Benefits

The need to spend time in the field is obvious for sales and marketing people. Their role is not only to find new customers but also to support the ones they have. You can't do that effectively from behind a desk. But it may be equally important for *nonmarketers* to get out in the field and interface with customers. For those without direct sales and marketing responsibility, the benefits are less apparent. The way I see these benefits is threefold:

- The *company* benefits because key staff members get a better appreciation of customer needs.
- The *customer* benefits because he has an opportunity to get his message through to his supplier's management without the filter of a salesperson. That isn't meant to be a negative. My regard for salespeople is second to none, and I make this abundantly clear in Chapter 11. But passing requests and inquiries through a third party is always subject to errors and miscommunications.
- Both benefit because the relationship between the two is enhanced. The customer gets a better product or service. The vendor gets a more satisfied customer.

Engineers and designers get firsthand information about customer needs and how they respond to proposed solutions. Customers meet their technical counterparts face-to-face and come away feeling their message has been correctly received. Technical details can be worked out directly.

Operations managers can learn about the customer's own production process and how your product integrates into theirs. From that time on, there will be no misunderstanding regarding the need for on-time delivery, quality, or any similar "abstract" concept.

Finance managers can resolve terms, conditions, credit and payment policies, and eliminate in advance a major source of friction between seller and buyer.

Regardless of functional role, those who visit a customer's plant are representatives of the company and can put the company in the best light possible. For themselves, it gives them a renewed appreciation of why the company is in business in the first place. It more often than not improves the relationships between the two organizations, improves each manager's perspective, and ultimately improves the company's total performance. Everybody wins.

38 MAKE IT UNECONOMICAL FOR CUSTOMERS TO SWITCH

You've worked hard to bring in your customers. You are working hard to keep them. Work a little harder and make them customers *forever.* How? Money is always appropriate. Not bribery, but economic incentive. If your customer finds it's just not worth it to find another supplier, you've done your job.

Earlier in this chapter I discussed customer loyalty. Not for a moment do I believe economic incentive is a prerequisite to loyalty. Loyalty comes from doing a job so well the customer can't *imagine* living without you. I believe in my heart, however, that an economic incentive can keep the customer with you until experience wins you that loyalty. Cynical, perhaps, but reasonably accurate as a description of how things are.

Frequent Flyers

For example, I have no confidence that all the frequent flyers who go out of their way to patronize a particular airline in order to collect their points would continue to do so if those programs were to be discontinued. I suspect the airlines understand this very well and are resigned, if not comfortable with it. If frequent flyer "loyalty" was a fact, these programs would have been dropped years ago. Each carrier, in its own unique way, would have gathered in a collection of loyal customers who had chosen them for the superior performance or special services they could get nowhere else, whatever the price on the ticket. No, the programs continue year after year because the airlines have first of all amassed an enormous legal obligation to pay off on their incentives, but equally important, they can't risk losing their captive passengers when the programs end.

The incentive is economic. As long as I can look forward to free tickets to exotic vacation locales, free upgrades, and so forth, I can't afford to spread my business around. Provided they fly where I want to go, Indifferent Airlines gets my money every time, even though the last time one of their flight attendants smiled at me was when she told me the only meal choice left was "pork stew and brussels sprouts, and thank you for flying Indifferent."

Few of you can run frequent buyer programs, so it is important to look for ways to keep your customers from being lured away by the competition. Whatever the method or methods you choose, your most important consideration is giving the customer an *obvious* economic reason for staying with you. In Chapter 7 on pricing we will consider the value concept. But at this juncture, there is no room for subtlety. The customer has to see it for himself, without the aid of one of your salespeople trying to bang it into his head. Let's look at a few methods that have stood the test of time.

If it is applicable to your specific business, you might consider that all-time favorite, *the quantity discount:* The more the customer buys, the lower the unit price. The customer ends up thinking there is no point in splitting the business between you and your competitor if it means losing the best price for going with one vendor.

Again, if it applies to your particular business, special *financing incentives* are in order. In the air transport business, Boeing, McDonnell Douglas, and Airbus compete on the advantages of their particular designs. When all is said and done, however, the real competition takes place when the airlines narrow down their selections. That happens when they get to the specifics of the financial deal. When you read about one of the big three taking a billion dollar order, you can be pretty sure a major deciding factor was the financial terms.

Training is another incentive, two ways. First, offering training in operation or servicing as a routine part of the business relationship can be a genuine incentive. The second way occurs when the customer considers the added costs of training employees on different products or platforms. It just may not be worth it.

The best financial incentive is to provide the *most reliable, best-performing* product or service humanly possible. Until you get there, you can at least have won the customer's mind. When you finally do get there, you have the customer's mind *and* heart.

39 CUSTOMER SERVICE ISN'T LIP SERVICE

Lip service *n.* Verbal expression of agreement or allegiance, unsupported by real conviction or action; hypocritical respect.

—American Heritage Dictionary

Suppose you are my customer and ask me a question on a matter of importance to you. Being only human I may not have the answer immediately available, so I promise to call you right back with the information. Two weeks later you still haven't heard from me. If there is still time, you should cancel the order and take your business somewhere else. If it's too late for that, get through it as best you can, but you have every right never to do business with me again.

I just bought a scanner for my office computer system. I read all the reviews in the computer magazines and one particular product stood out from the pack. The magazine articles were universally glowing with praise, a product for the times. So I picked up the phone, called the 800 number for my usual telephone/mail order supplier, and placed the order. The next day I eagerly opened the package and went through the prescribed installation process. It wan't as easy as I thought. It turned out that with my computer and communications software, I could use my scanner only if I disabled my printer and modem, not very practical since one of the scanner's virtues was that I could immediately send off the scanned document via my fax/modem or print it out at will.

After a call or two to the manufacturer's technical support line and a few sessions scrolling through the complaint messages on their forums on CompuServe and America Online (something I should have done *before* I ordered), I learned that there was indeed a fix available for this problem, a different method of hardware installation that would only require another $70 investment on my part. Well, in for a penny, in for a pound, in for $82 more with tax and shipping. I hurriedly called their order entry desk and joyfully passed over my credit card number. "When will I have it?" I asked. "Five to seven days working days," I was assured.

Like our early western settlers anticipating the Wells Fargo wagon, I eagerly awaited the delivery. When I thought it might be due, I spent my time checking all the hiding places the carrier might leave the package when I wasn't there to receive it. In the meantime, the scanner itself wasn't scanning. By the time the week or so had passed I was almost salivating to get my hands on this adapter kit, feeling that, at an initial investment of $300, my scanner was overqualified for a career as a doorstop.

When I could bear it no longer, I called the manufacturer's order line and asked when it was shipped and when I could expect delivery. "Five to seven working days," I was told. When I reminded the clerk that that was what I had been told "five to seven working days" ago, she went on to say that she couldn't comment on what someone else might have told me. The demand had exceeded their supplies; they were out of stock but were getting the kits in any day now.

A week later I called again. This time, at least, no one told me five to seven days. "Within the next two weeks," I was assured. By now my usual relaxed demeanor was beginning to undergo a change or two for the worse, so I insisted on talking to the customer service manager. That was in a different location so she gave me his number—not toll-free, you might have guessed—and off I went. Ring. Ring. "Hi, this is Keith. I'm away from my desk right now. Leave your name and number and I'll call you back," or something to that effect. Curious, isn't it, that of all departments, Customer Service wouldn't have a live body answering the phone? Eventually, Keith got back to me. I explained my case with only the slightest bit of irritation and Keith, a pleasant-sounding young man, was nice enough to reassure me that they were doing everything possible to satisfy customer demand, that I would get delivery at the earliest possible time and, just to be sure, he would check on my order and call me right back. He never did.

You can be sure there were at least two more shipping promises never kept. I got hold of Keith one more time. When he said he'd call me back, I couldn't resist reminding him that's what he had told me two weeks earlier. After a brief moment of stuttering, hemming, and hawing, he apologized for not doing so, even re-membered my earlier call, and promised he would do everything possible for me. Within a day or two I got my kit delivered by overnight express, and the truth is, the installation was a snap and the scanner has been working like a charm ever since.

Is all forgiven? Will I do business with them again? Probably not. In the first place, if you run into a situation where you have a pop-ular product that needs a modification, don't announce the avail-ability of a mod kit until you are *absolutely, positively sure* you can meet demand. If the demand swamps you, as these people claimed, it's your fault for not forecasting properly. Until you can give a realistic and accurate shipping date, don't give any dates at all. Your people may be acting in good faith when they say "five to seven working days," but it sounds like lip service, something you think customers want to hear, something that will get them off the phone so you can get back to more important things. When you are consistently inaccurate in your delivery schedules, it sounds like you are either lying or stupid or both. Finally, there is *never* an excuse for not calling a customer when you have promised to do so. If you aren't going to call back, don't say you will. Lip service is not compatible with customer service.

40 KNOW HOW YOUR CUSTOMER USES YOUR PRODUCT OR SERVICE

And more.

As a consultant I find it painful to ask a client how her product is used and get back only a shrug or a vague answer. It is *easy* to get caught up in the excitement of closing a sale. Considering that the most successful salespeople don't close 100% of their prospects, it is understandable for one to shrug "It doesn't matter as long as we got the order." Understandable but *wrong*.

I was trained differently. One of the first lessons I learned as a sales engineer was how important it was to know how the customer used the product I sold. I was expected to know *how* the product was used, and understand and describe the application. If it was an OEM sale, I was expected to know as much as I could about the customer's model numbers, production schedules, who his or her customers were, who the competitors were, and if possible, it seemed, the customer's favorite breakfast cereal. In other words, *every* piece of information we could gather was important. It seemed like a lot of work to gather a lot of information that might not be any of my business.

But it *was* my business. Our company's sales philosophy was that the more you know about your customer's business *today,* the easier it is to sell in the *future.* We were a team. What I found out from my customer might be useful for another salesperson on the other side of the country. In my best sales engineering mode, if I found out the customer was having trouble applying my product, I might be able to suggest something else we had that would do the job better. If I knew more about the application, I might be able to suggest a change in use that could improve the customer's bottom line. Presto, I'm a hero!

One of the more practical methods of staying aware of customer use is the establishment of a customer advisory panel. Bring together representatives from any number of customers and review with them how they *feel* about your products and services. Customers may be very flattered to be asked to serve on a panel of this nature. Use them to understand the best ways of applying your product. Use them as a *sounding board* to find out what may be wrong or what may be right with your product.

In summary:

- If you know how the customer is using your product, you can expect that there are other prospects, the customer's competitors perhaps, that would have a similar need. Unless you have an exclusive arrangement with your customer, it is perfectly all right to sell to their competition.
- If you know all the customer's model numbers, you have a built-in checklist for determining how well you are doing with account penetration.
- Awareness lets you anticipate future trends in the market and the technology. It provides clues to new product opportunities.
- Awareness lets you anticipate future customer needs.
- It lets you do a better job of sales forecasting.

As a salesperson, I always believed in the adage, "there's no substitute for product knowledge." Over time I have added another adage, "there's no substitute for *customer* knowledge."

6

THERE'S NOTHING LIKE A GOOD PRODUCT

The only way that your customers will get that warm and fuzzy feeling from dealing with you is to give them *good products* and services that first, last, and *always* meet their needs. A cheerful smile, bend-over-backward service, and a total dedication to customer satisfaction will get you absolutely *nowhere* if your product doesn't meet customer needs.

Customers are first, last, and always interested in PRODUCTS. They want quality PRODUCTS, on-time delivery of PRODUCTS, reliable PRODUCTS, useful PRODUCTS. Customers are interested in what products can do for them. Nothing more. Nothing less. The primary decision is made to purchase a product or service. Whether the Department of Defense is purchasing a new stealth bomber or you are looking to replace your videotape player, a decision is made to buy *something*. The overwhelming number of purchases are made because buyers decide they need or want a product. It will be very tough to sell me a car if I don't want one, or if I cannot afford one, or if I don't need one. Show me a car buyer and I'll show you someone who wants or needs one and hopes he or she can afford one. By ignoring this simple fact, though, salespeople waste their time, marketers waste resources, and companies lose their direction.

Now it is all well and true that people buy more than the physical product. They buy what academicians lovingly call the *augmented* product: the *whole package,* which includes, of course, the package, warranty, service, the salesperson's smile, spare parts, and all the other goodies that go along. But none of the augmentation counts for anything if the product or service itself doesn't measure up.

Here are some thoughts on getting a handle on your product line.

41 GET NEW PRODUCTS TO MARKET FASTER

Who was the second person to fly solo across the Atlantic?
Who was the second person to climb Mt. Everest?
Who came in second in last year's Boston Marathon?
What horse came in second in last year's Kentucky Derby?
Who cares?

With apologies to the people (and horse) who will forever remain answers to these trivia questions, there isn't much name recognition attached to coming in second. To the victor go the spoils.

OK, you've got a great new product idea, something that promises to end poverty, reverse global warming, bring lasting peace on earth. What are you waiting for? Until you get that product to market, two things remain possible. First, someone else with the same or a similar idea will get to market *before* you, preempt your message, and skim off the cream. Example: By the time the U.S. auto industry woke up to the idea that the market for economy cars was growing rapidly, the Japanese had established themselves as market leaders, leaving even the Europeans in the dust. Second, something else will come along that will steer the market *away* from your innovation and in a completely different direction. Example: For watching movies at home, laser discs are technologically superior to videotape, but by the time Philips got its act together and brought the system to market, videotape had become the technology of choice. Laser discs will forever be a minor player in the huge home entertainment market.

Time to Market Is Critical

Here are a few reasons it is so important to speed up your new product introductions:

1. Getting to market first gives you a jump on your competition. If they want to keep up, they will have to move faster to make up for lost time. All the time they are scrambling to catch up, you are out there in the marketplace building

up a presence that every day gets more difficult to overcome. Someday they may mount an effective challenge, but in the meantime you are laughing all the way to the bank.

2. The technology that gets to market first is the one everyone remembers and adopts, regardless of whether it's the best technology or not. See my previous laser disc example.

3. Early market entry gives you first choice in getting to key customers. Find 'em and close 'em before the competition knows what hit 'em.

4. Getting to market first gives you first crack at the distribution network of choice. Late entries will have trouble gaining access to the market with inferior distribution.

5. First in the market gets to be first and best in the mind of the customer.

6. Since you are not playing catch up, you can focus your marketing expenses on growth rather than gaining awareness. A subtle distinction but real in terms of lower out-of-pocket costs.

Effect of Late to Market

Consider the effects of being late to market. You've missed all that business that you could have closed if you had been there. The selling process takes time. You can't even begin that process until your sales force has a reasonably good idea when the product is available. There are many sad stories about companies that announced new products and saw their existing business go in the tank while customers waited for new rather than buy old—from Osborne Computer in the early 1980s to any number of PC makers today who announce new product introductions, then don't introduce. Osborne's existing business went to zero, a level they maintained long enough that they ended up turning off the lights and locking the front door for good. At the time of this writing, Apple Computer is a year late with a new operating system called Copeland that is supposed to turn its business around. Meanwhile

Apple is fast becoming a footnote in PC history books. Delays in product launches are so common in the software business a new word, *vaporware,* has entered our vocabulary.

Late to market, of course, doesn't have to mean going out of business. It does mean, however, that *you lose momentum and market share.* When you finally get there, chances are you will have to enter at lower prices than originally intended. Poof! Lower sales volume and lower profit margins. As for image, you will have your work cut out for you trying to reposition yourself from being an also-ran.

Getting to market first isn't a guarantee of success. You still have to have a good product and put together a winning marketing mix. Still, on balance, I'd rather be first than second. As writer Damon Runyon said a long time ago, "The race is not always to the swift, nor the battle to the strong, but that's the way to bet."

42 INNOVATE

Some day you may find yourself bolting upright in your bed in the middle of the night, eyes wide open like saucers, mind clear and alert, shaking with the realization that you have thought up a truly great product. If you don't think such things are possible, understand that someone invented the computer, the laser, the transistor, pantyhose, toenail clippers, cellular phones, Big Macs, mutual funds, food processors, and word processors. It could happen to you.

If there is *ever* any truth to the old saying that necessity is the mother of invention, then it just goes to prove that successful, innovative products are invented to satisfy *real needs* (although one could make arguments about Big Macs and pantyhose).

Innovation takes several forms. There is the innovation that results in lasers or satellite communications or the cure for a horrible disease. These are not only new ways to do things but new things altogether, once-in-a-lifetime developments that come from massive investment of time, money, and human intellect. Then there is another kind of innovation that is more modest but equally important. These are advances that take existing technology and put a new slant on it to do a task cheaper, better, or faster, or all three. For example . . .

A Quick Scan

The paradox of modern business life is that the more we use our computers and the deeper we get into electronic communication (e.g., E-mail, file transfers, fax/modems, and so forth), the more it seems that paper piles up on our desks, so much so that we spend significant parts of our working day doing what we promised ourselves we would never do, that is, shuffle papers. Will there ever be a solution to this problem?

Partially, at least. I am sitting at my desk wondering what to do with a piece of paper I think I might need for reference sometime in the future. Whatever the reason, I know I don't want to discard it. In days gone by I would put it in an out basket and, eventually, either an assistant or I would bury it away in a folder in a file cabinet, when naturally enough I would soon forget I even had it. Over time my file drawers fill up with more and more of these "important" papers until I am forced to buy more cabinets filled with more drawers, and the cycle continues—more paper, more drawers, more cabinets, and on and on.

But today I can do something different. I have just acquired a piece of equipment for my computer system that not only eliminates the clutter on my desk but is actually fun to play with. I can feed a document into this device on my desk and watch as it instantly shows up on my computer screen. From there I can move it into a folder somewhere on my computer's hard disk where it will stay the rest of its days (or the rest of my days, at least). Should I ever want to look at it again, a little pointing and clicking and it's back up on my screen, where I review it, print out a copy, fax it to my editor, or eliminate it, or even—now this is the beauty of it—*edit* it. This is truly an innovative product. No, not another semiconductor or laser, but innovative in the sense that the manufacturer has taken an *existing* technology, applied some clever packaging, bundled in some software that makes it work easily and quickly, and priced it reasonably enough so that I didn't think I could do without it. It won't bring permanent peace or end famine, and it will never actually get us to the paperless office, but it does get rid of lots of paper, and it makes document retrieval *a breeze.*

Someone has seen a way to take a bulky, slow, expensive process called scanning and bring it to the masses, solving one of the office's severest problems, the crushing burden of more and more paper. That is what I call *innovation*—breakthrough products that carve out a market where there never was one before. And even if it *was* there, it was never served well enough to satisfy customers. Now it is. The software industry calls it *the killer app,* nerdspeak for the application that makes the chosen few millionaires many times over. It doesn't matter whether it's high tech, low tech, or no tech, whether it's a product or a service, whether the intended customers are consumers or business users. The only thing that matters is you get there to solve a real problem in an innovative—and cost-effective—way.

Innovative products give you a jump on the market, allow you to establish a firm position before competitors can catch up, allow you to keep prices high enough to start paying back your investment before competition forces the prices down, make your company name recognized all over the world. Try it. You'll like it.

43 IF YOU CAN'T INNOVATE, COPY

In a perfect world, every new product will be innovative and revolutionary. But we don't live in a perfect world, and there are many companies out there that just follow the pack. If imitation is the sincerest form of flattery, lots of people are blushing. Flattery, however, isn't the motivation, *profit* is.

Although manufacturers may claim unique features and radical new designs, we still see products that look remarkably like other offerings. Take the PC as a case in point. Once IBM opened up its architecture for all to copy, the flood began. The differences today have more to do with sales and marketing skills than they do with technology. Most PCs use the same microprocessor and are driven by the same operating system software and run the same application software. The innovation in personal computers comes from everywhere but the computer makers themselves.

Go into Circuit City or Best Buy and count the number of VCRs on the shelves, then ask a salesperson to explain the differences among them. Assuming that he knows something about the products he is selling, and assuming he isn't getting a "spif," which is a modest bonus from the manufacturer for every one of its products the salesperson sells (a common practice in electronics retailing), there's a good chance it will be *impossible* to explain why one product is any better than another. Try it out on TVs, stereos, or any other home appliance. Doesn't matter. They all look pretty much alike. And when one TV network offers a sitcom about yuppie singles in the big city, pretty soon they all do. Who was first? Who knows?

Some very substantial companies out there do very well by imitating the market leader. Sony has the well-deserved reputation for being a great innovator, but how long does it take after Sony comes out with a new concept before Panasonic (Matsushita) or Hitachi or Toshiba is right there with its copy? It happened with the Sony Walkman and the Discman, and it will probably happen again the next time Sony brings out something new. Whether it's high tech or low tech, consumer or business-to-business, as soon as an innovation hits the market, the copiers come right behind. There will *always* be followers that leverage on the development investment of others to get imitative products to market.

Why Reinvent the Wheel?

Michael Porter, the Harvard strategy guru, called it *a followership strategy*. You take advantage of all that your competitor has done before you. Before you get *your* product to market, the competitor has invested not only in product development but also in the heavy promotion required to get market acceptance. The competitor's sales force has been out on the street making presentations and demonstrations. Early entry customers have evaluated the product and reported back where they found it wanting. You have learned from those early mistakes that someone made for you. It turns out to be cheaper and faster, if not better.

This is an excellent strategy for anyone who does not aspire to leadership, or for anyone who would rather keep costs down than risk an untried approach to the market. Still, with a one-for-one copy, you will always be positioned as a follower, and you will always *be* a follower, for all the reasons I pointed out in the last section.

In the real world, you probably will want to differentiate your offering to *some* degree in order to carve out a niche for yourself. It doesn't have to be, nor will it be, profound. The products will still be similar, but yours will probably have fewer features and sell for a lower price. You might also differentiate in approach to market, such as a different distribution method. This has been a common form of differentiation in the personal computer industry. Packard Bell, considering the PC just another appliance, went big into mass merchandisers like Circuit City and Office Depot, nontraditional computer retailers. Dell, on the other hand, eschewed retailing entirely, concentrating on telephone and mail order sales. The products are virtually identical as far as the buyer is concerned. The difference is in how the companies approach the market.

44 OFFER REAL PRODUCTS THAT SATISFY REAL NEEDS

Here are a few reasons for bringing a product or service to market that will put you well on the road to failure:

- We have the technology to do it.
- We have unused capacity.
- It's a by-product from making another product we already sell. ·
- We need it to fill out our product line.
- Why shouldn't we?

Of these five reasons, and there are probably countless others, only the last one, "Why shouldn't we?" has any merit at all. Not to say that you should go ahead without answering the question—you shouldn't—but at least it holds out the possibility of a positive answer. You may yet come up with a correct rationalization.

Let's look at the others one by one.

- *We have the technology to do it.* If the product isn't needed to start with, an elegant technical approach won't enhance its utility very much. Peter Drucker told us that customers don't buy technology; they buy what technology can do for them. I make my case with home banking, navigation systems for automobiles, telephone/video conferencing, clear beer, and nonrefrigerated milk in sealed cartons. Yuk. My mind is not yet made up on direct satellite TV, home bread machines, and digital audio tape. These are all elegant products that advance their respective technologies. Unfortunately, I don't think they make great long-term businesses because they are mostly *solutions looking for problems.*

Remember the old TV cartoon *The Jetsons?* This was a kids' comedy based in the future with robots for pets and an entire automated household. We're not there yet. A computer in every home has been the dream of computer makers since the first Apple II fell from the tree. A computer in every home turning lights on and off, planning meals, handling the family finances, educating the children, you name it. The reality was that the personal computer did very little that could benefit most people outside a working environment. If it was games you wanted, there was always Nintendo, a dedicated—and cheaper—solution. Except for use in home-based businesses, the home computer was a tough sell. Today, it is finally a growing market. There is enough software around to do useful things, and the entertainment aspect has been expanded with CD-ROMs and multimedia capability. Hardware costs have dropped as manufacturers introduced systems dedicated to the home market. Things are looking up because they finally are offering real products that satisfy real needs.

- *We have unused capacity.* For this, think of Ford's Edsel, history's classic lesson in what comes from bringing out a product to take advantage of unused plant capacity. Turned out to be the wrong car for the wrong market at the wrong time. Otherwise it was perfect.

- *It's a by-product.* Who wants your old junk? I will admit that many products in the petrochemical industry come about as part of the process of making something else. But they are offered to the market because they are *needed,* not because they are part of the inventory. It isn't only by-products, either. Spin-off products or products obtained through a merger or acquisition sometimes get you into businesses you have no business being in.

- *We need to fill out our product line.* Business isn't poker. You don't need a full deck to play the game. Unless there is suffi- cient demand for an add-on product, why would you want it? What are you going to do with it? For a while, at least, Apple Computer had so many different models for different markets it was inevitable that sooner or later it would miscalculate demand. Sure enough, one year Apple stocked up on certain units for the Christmas season and ended up taking a major hit when it overes- timated demand. The company's been in trouble *ever* since.

At the end of *every* successful new product development pro- gram is one common denominator—a customer willing to buy or, rather, enough customers to make the product a success. If your product isn't designed to attract that customer and provide a solu- tion to a perceived problem, or satisfy a need, *you don't have a prayer* of a successful product.

45 KNOW WHEN AND HOW TO DROP OBSOLETE PRODUCTS

News item from *Electronics News,* April 11, 1996:

Digital Ends PDP-11 Line

Maynard, Mass.—Digital Equipment is discontinuing its PDP11 computer line which dates to 1970. PDP11 products have been used in a wide range of applications, including copiers and telecommunications equipment since 1970, when the PDP 1120 was introduced. Digital will take final orders for the product in the fall of 1997 and will make last shipments through December of 1997.

The short article goes on to say that Digital has shipped more than 600,000 units over the life of the product. For a high-tech product this sounds like a remarkable ride. Twenty-seven years!

But the interesting part of this is the way Digital tried to ease its customers into the world as it will have to be. First, the time of the announcement to final product cutoff spans almost two years. Even for a big-ticket item, that is a reasonable time to give customers the chance to change over to another product. Then Digital established a "consulting program" designed to aid customers in moving to current products and further developed a full set of emulation tools to ease the transition.

How long are you going to hold on to products that few customers want to buy anymore? If no one is buying, then the decision is easy. They're gone. But if you are producing obsolete products for only a small number of customers, you are probably losing money keeping those products alive. You have to think about getting rid of them.

The process is sometimes known as pruning, that is, cutting back the product line "tree" to get rid of the dead wood and nonproductive branches. By getting rid of dead and dying products *you free up resources* that could be best employed on *newer products* with more promising futures. Those resources include money spent on advertising and promotional material, storage space for parts inventory and finished goods, product and market managers, manufacturing space, and so forth.

When Is It Time?

How do you know when it's time to let a product go? I venture to say it's more intuitive than the result of any clear definitions. But there are certain criteria that will make it obvious:

- The number of customers has dwindled to a precious few.

- Other products in the line or on the market will do the job "cheaper, faster, or better."
- Cost of production is rising and margins are falling. Older products can be extremely profitable, but when there is no longer sufficient volume to cover fixed and variable costs and leave an acceptable profit margin, it's time to go.
- The product has become a management afterthought because it is increasingly far removed from the company's core business.

The Customer Is Still the Key

All those things are important to you, but the most important consideration is how you treat your customer. Treat your customer badly and *you* will be pruned as a vendor. Product elimination calls for a delicate approach. Customers get very upset when you tell them they can't have something they've grown accustomed to getting. If your product goes into your customer's product, there are added complications. Those customers may have to redesign their product to accommodate a replacement part.

There is no all-encompassing strategy for pruning old products, but I offer a few suggestions:

- Raise the price of the offending product to encourage customers to seek alternate solutions. This can be delicate. You don't want to leave an impression of price gouging.
- Do as Digital has done—announce the termination and give customers a reasonable amount of time to change over.
- Sell the product line to a third party. Your anchor may be someone else's parachute. Software programs often get shopped around. WordPerfect is on its third or fourth owner by now.
- Stay the course. You may not have a choice. I have a client who makes products for commercial airliners. It is understood that getting your product specified on a particular platform is usually good for the life of that airplane model, so long as you supply a good product at a fair price. Some of those planes stay in production for 20 years or more. The

good news is that you can look forward to 20-plus years worth of business for the product. The bad news is that you have to keep the line going for as long as Boeing, Airbus, or whomever wants to buy it. It would not be politically astute to tell them that you don't want their business on this item anymore although you'd love to sell them other things.

No one wants to be stuck with products that lose money or make little or none. Still, getting rid of them can be almost as much trouble as holding on. It is a decision you can only make with careful and deliberate thought. It isn't just about you. It is about your customers.

46 KEEP UP WITH CHANGING TECHNOLOGY

Myopia   *n.* Lack of discernment or long-range perspective in thinking or planning.
> —*American Heritage Dictionary*

It is intriguing to me that the newest breakthroughs and advances in technology most often come from companies that either were minor players in the market or who come from the outside. Is there something about advancing technology that puts most market leaders to sleep?

History is full of examples. Where were the railroads when the aviation industry started its growth? Where were the makers of vacuum tubes when it became clear the semiconductor was no longer a laboratory curiosity? With the obvious exception of IBM, where were all the typewriter people when word processors came along? How come Goodyear and Firestone let Michelin, a European niche marketer better known for its restaurant guides than for its tires, become the market leader in radial tires?

Innovation is a wonderful thing. For the innovator. For you who are wedded to the established technology, the risk of ignoring changes is the risk of seeing your business fail without ever knowing what hit you. Theodore Levitt called it marketing myopia. Companies don't see approaching major market changes soon enough, overestimate their relations with their customers, or underestimate the significance of new and innovative products. With little or no warning, a new set of competitors promoting new products using new technology takes over the market completely. For example, with the exception of the giant Dutch company Philips, no company that was a major player in electronic vacuum tubes in the 1960s is a major producer of integrated circuits, the analogous technology, today. Philips isn't even in today's top five.

Staying with Old Technology Too Long

It is apparent that managers of companies with a vested, long-term interest in an existing technology resist, consciously or unconsciously, any changes that would imperil that investment. As human beings, we lack the ability to see into the future. We can *guess* what might be coming along, but then only in our own narrow perspective. We do not acknowledge what we do not want to know. We do not *want* to know that the investment we have poured our heart and soul into to become successful is now threatened by a new order, a new way of doing the same thing, only cheaper or better or faster, or all of the above. Hoping against all hope, we fight to the end to preserve the status quo. Inevitably, we lose. It may not happen overnight, but eventually the new technology takes over.

I've been talking in this section about breakthrough changes in technology. But if anything, this is a book about *details* and success or failure from the little things. Keeping up with technological change can also be about hitting or missing those little things. For instance, there will *always* be evolutionary changes to products. The first competitor to modify its products and get to market ends up with a temporary competitive edge. These are more than "bells and whistles," which are essentially cosmetic changes that allow you to charge more. They are, rather, *minibreakthroughs,* technical or operational advantages that make the product truly more useful or desirable. For instance, the cellular phone makers are in a race for smaller and smaller pocket-sized phones. If you can't keep up with the miniaturization, you can't stay in that business. When I bought a desktop computer in 1988, it came with a 20-megabyte hard drive. Today, you wouldn't consider a computer with less than a gigabyte. That's 50 times my 1988 capacity.

If you want to remain competitive you must *continue* to upgrade your product with advances that make it more useful.

47 CANNIBALIZE—EAT YOUR YOUNG AND NOT SO YOUNG

Lower forms of animal life eat their young. Anyone who has ever had a tropical fish tank at home knows you have to separate the newborns from the mother or she will have them for lunch. Only the fittest, fleetest, and luckiest will survive. Maybe she knows what she's doing. In the natural order of things, that's the way it is.

From time to time I do a speech called "What Have You Done Lately to Obsolete Your Product Line?" The essence of the talk is that if you don't do something about your future, your competition will do it for you. Doing something about your future includes bringing out new products that will supersede what you already have. Bringing out a new product that you know will take sales away from one already out there is a form of cannibalization, one product feeding off another. Normally you might want to avoid doing something like that. You have enough trouble with outside competitors. Why compete with yourself?

Not an illogical position, but *wrong*. The correct thinking on this subject is, "The customer will be attracted to the new features and benefits of new products coming into the market. Switchovers are inevitable. If they do switch, I want them to switch to another one of *my* products."

Intel has brought out a steady stream of new microprocessors from the 8080 series to the Pentium in all its variations and, as I sit here at my computer, I suspect that they are busily working on the next two or three generations of processors. These, no doubt, will compare with the Pentium like rabbits compare with snails. Today's Pentium does a perfectly fine job for what it was intended to do. Chances are it will perform well long into the future. It isn't that Intel is *dissatisfied* with the performance of any one particular processor. The company recognizes, however, that customers demand change and improvement. If Intel doesn't improve on it, *someone else will.* Better to lose business to *yourself* than the competition. That's the way it should be, continuous improvement in the entire product line, even if it means competing with yourself.

Don't relate this to planned obsolescence, which has a definite negative ring to it. The phrase implies that change is for its own sake, more marketing hype than response to market need. When Procter & Gamble or Lever Brothers comes out with a "new and improved" version of an existing brand, the cynic in us says that is just hype. We've always accused the auto companies of excessive model changes, prodding consumers into trading in their cars for something newer or better, which may not actually be. Environmentalists would call this wretched excess.

Yet I can imagine a society where all products are strictly functional, where cars are cars and soap is soap, a society that is supply driven rather than market driven. I have never been there but I suspect that is what North Korea is like. Not a lot of customer demand being satisfied. In a customer-driven society, however, even if customers may not always demand change, they usually respond to it. If you don't keep your product line on the cutting edge, customers will go elsewhere.

48 UNDERSTAND THE PRODUCT LIFE CYCLE— THEN FORGET ABOUT IT

If you have ever taken an academic course in marketing, or browsed through a marketing textbook, you have been exposed to the product life cycle (PLC) concept. You know that the PLC describes the stages in the life of a product, from its introduction, through growth, maturity, and inevitable decline. The instantly recognizable S-curve (Figure 6.1), often shown with a profit curve superimposed, has been with us for years. It has become an act of faith to consider it, ponder it, and, unfortunately, dwell on it.

Figure 6.1

THE PRODUCT LIFE CYCLE

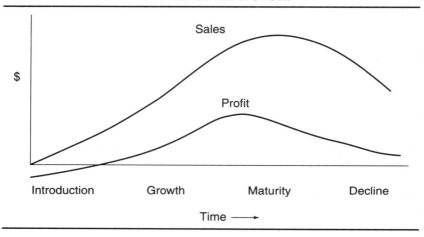

Theory versus Reality

Having said that, I cannot think of a single practical use for the product life cycle curve. Yes, it is *interesting* to be reminded that products have finite lives, but we knew that already. In theory, PLC analysis is supposed to point out different marketing strategies at different stages. I am not sure how many other analysis tools there are that would do the same thing, but I would put common sense at the top of the list.

What's Wrong with the PLC

First, the typical product life cycle curve *isn't typical* for any product I know. Is there any product that follows a curve so beautifully sloped and balanced as the one we always see? Maybe, but I've never seen one. If you were to plot real-world, real-product life cycle curves, they would vary from a horizontal line with no perceptible slope to the very short life high-tech product whose curve looks more like an inverted V than an S.

Second, there is the question, just what is the "product" you are talking about? Are we talking about automobiles, sedans, Buicks, or Le Sabres? Are we talking about computers, desktop computers, Compaq, or the Presario model? Cars and computers will be here for a long time. Sedans and desktop computers are also here for the long run. Compaq and General Motors, Buick's parent, will be cranking out products for as long as we can imagine. So we are down to the individual models. Eventually, Buick will retire the Le Sabre model or might just put a different name to a vehicle with similar characteristics. Compaq will come out with another model with a faster microprocessor or a bigger hard drive and give it another meaningless name ending in a vowel. When you get down to the brand or model, there isn't much mystery behind how long it is going to last. So what else is product life cycle analysis supposed to tell us? I give up.

Third, there is no real-time *practical* role for PLC analysis. There is no way to tell what stage the product is in until it has passed on to the next stage. "Sales have slowed down, so I think I just left the growth stage." Is the slowdown just a short-term anomaly, or does it mean a *fundamental strategy change is* in order? Don't count on the PLC to tell you.

Fourth, the model doesn't account for the role of *management* in altering the shape of the curve. Show me a product manager who doesn't think the product has plenty of growth left in it and I'll show you someone who should be brushing up a resume. That's the way product managers are supposed to think. Their job is to avoid downturns whenever humanly possible.

Fifth, products aren't like aging ballplayers. They *can* be given new legs. Again, that's what product managers do. Jell-O has been a popular dessert since before I was born, and that is a long time, I assure you. The model implies that once your product is in the mature or decline stage, you would be better served by shifting your investment to something that promises more growth. But suppose you invest more to promote the product. There is every good reason to expect that it can be rejuvenated.

And, finally, product life cycle analysis is *too simplistic* to be of any use to managers caught up in the daily struggle to move a business to a higher level of performance.

49 DIFFERENTIATE, DIFFERENTIATE, DIFFERENTIATE

I said it three times for emphasis. I can't overemphasize how important this basic marketing strategy really is. It is a simple concept that can be difficult to implement. It is important to give your customers a reason to buy from you rather than from your competition. It isn't just about *price,* although that can be important. It isn't just about *great customer service,* although falling down in that category will undoubtedly cost you business. It is critically important to give customers a chance to single you out from the pack. Differentiation is still one of the most important principles of marketing strategy.

In its simplest form, differentiation means adding something to your product that sets you apart from competitors. You can "augment" the product with special services, packaging, warranties, postsales support, and whatever else it takes to say, "Look at me. I'm different. I'm better."

Or you can differentiate based on the individual markets you serve. Most big consumer package goods companies offer variations of their core products to their various market segments. That's why Coca-Cola makes Coke, Classic Coke, Diet Coke, Caffeine-free Diet Coke, and who knows what else. That's why the catalog of a major semiconductor producer might be as thick as the Manhattan telephone directory. Different products for different applications. That's why General Motors has Chevrolet, Saturn, Pontiac, Oldsmobile, Buick, and Cadillac, not to mention trucks and buses. Different transportation for different transportation needs.

Consider Eltron International, in Simi Valley, California. It has been one of the hottest new companies of the decade. Started up in 1990, the company has been experiencing triple-digit growth since its founding. From first-year sales in 1991 of about $400,000 the company finished 1995 at $42.4 million. Between 1994 and 1995 it increased sales by 143%. Eltron makes bar code label printers, a fast-growing, booming business. Don Skinner, Eltron's founder and CEO believes that, prevailing strategy theory notwithstanding, it isn't a matter of choosing among quality, cost leadership, or differentiation. Success in his market calls for *all three.* Skinner decided he could meet cost objectives and still put out a quality product that does less but does it better. Rather than build the large, sophisticated, high-speed, high-priced printers that dominated the market, Skinner saw a need for smaller, less pricey units, with fewer features, that ran slower than high-end products but ran fast enough to get the job done. To meet its price objectives, Eltron tooled for high-volume production and designed its printers with very few parts. The manufacturing objective was, and is, to deliver high-quality products without incurring the cost of adjustments or of handling field repairs. Hitting those price objectives has opened up a new world of customers who can now afford to take advantage of bar coding.

For example, many hospitals—one of the company's "marquis" customers is the Mayo Clinic—have adopted bar coding for blood or specimen samples. Instead of the one big printer serving many stations and requiring nurses to walk their samples down to the central processor, each nursing station now has its own bar code printer. The advantage is smoother and faster handling of the samples and much less chance for error.

Although the core of Eltron's differentiation is in its product design, the company doesn't stop there. Where others give a 90-day warranty, Eltron gives *a full year.* Where others promise delivery in 60 to 90 days, Eltron normally ships *within five days.* Eltron's biggest customer is United Parcel Service. UPS puts Eltron's printers in the offices of their biggest customers for package addressing and labeling. According to Skinner, Eltron is the only company *ever* to be singled out by UPS for a supplier excellence award. That's proof in and of itself that *differentiation pays off.*

7

IT ALL GETS DOWN TO PRICE

In the Garden of Eden of Pricing, companies intent on bringing out new products found out first what customers were willing to pay for such offerings, then designed their products to meet the cost requirements. When the results were in, *customers* were satisfied with cost-effective products, *suppliers* were satisfied with profitable products, and *investors* were satisfied with increased earnings. But of course the serpent lured Eve into eating the forbidden fruit, she and her spouse were evicted, and the Garden of Eden of Pricing remains to this day undeveloped real estate.

No issue is more emotional or agonizing than setting price for your products or services. Should we "skim" with a high price or go for quick market penetration with a low price? Quantity discounts? Price breaks for special customers? Can we be sure that our price is competitive? Will our prices give us the margins we need to satisfy our investors? The questions go on and on.

If it were just a matter of establishing a fair and reasonable level, pricing would be a breeze. What complicates the pricing process is that there are always *customers* to consider. And competitors.

In spite of all the textbook discussions about pricing, all the articles in academic journals, and all the formulas, graphs, and charts explaining pricing techniques and customer response to various pricing scenarios, pricing is still more art than science. Perhaps even black art.

50 KEEP YOUR EYE ON YOUR COMPETITORS' PRICES

When you set prices or develop pricing strategies, you should know as much about how your competitors handle the pricing issue as you possibly can. I can't think of any subject for competitive intelligence more important than pricing information. Here are a few situations where this could come in handy, and perhaps save you from a terrible marketing mistake:

• Your margins are a little thin so you want to bump up your price a couple of percentage points, just enough to generate some welcome additional profit without slowing demand. If you really had a good handle on the competitors' prices, you would realize their prices are already lower than yours. But you go ahead anyway, and one day you wake up and see that your revenue is actually down, not up.

• You are putting together a proposal that, if successful, will bring in hundreds of thousands of dollars in revenue for your company. When you get to the moment of truth, you find you haven't a clue as to what any of the other major bidders might be asking. Instead, you submit your bid based on acceptable markups over cost, reduced somewhat by what you guess your competition will come in at. You guess wrong, bid too high, and lose the job.

• A buyer tells you your price is too high but won't tell you how high. You don't know whether he is being straight with you or just squeezing you for a better deal. You assume the squeeze is on because last time you looked, the competitor and you were pretty close in price. You come down as much you think you have to to keep the buyer happy (you're not *that* stupid). During the postmortem, you learn that those dirty dogs at the competition bought the business with a price you could have matched if only you had known early enough. It doesn't matter anymore. The business is gone.

• Even though you are playing catch-up with your competitors, you are counting heavily that the latest new product is going to take the market by storm. You are looking to win an important share of the market. You work up a "fair" price but find out later that customers balk. Eventually you learn that the competitors lowered their prices in anticipation of your market entry. Customers saw too big a price differential to give your new product a try. While not an out-and-out failure, it was a long way from a market winner. If only you had been aware of the competitors' price changes.

Get the picture? Pricing is hard enough as it is, without working in an information vacuum. If you want to make good pricing decisions that will give you the best chance to win the business and still make a little money, you have to know more than just your own cost structure, or even what the customer is willing to pay. You have to know where the competition sits.

Customers are a particularly unreliable source for pricing information and decision making. If you rely on customers to tell you what they want to pay, you will be sadly disappointed. You ask a customer if she thinks ten dollars is a fair price for your new widget and she says, "Sure, it sounds fair to me." You get enough feedback from other prospects answering the question the same way to convince you that ten bucks is a winning price. As soon as you are ready to enter the market, you enter at ten dollars and sit back and wait for the orders to roll in. When they don't, you get back to those reassuring customers and find out that ten dollars is too high for them. They can get the same thing from XYZ for eight and a half.

Customers aren't trying to be deceitful, they just have little or no sense of what a fair price should be until they are faced with options. If your competitor is at a lower level, the burden is on *you* to justify to customers why they should pay more. If you don't know up front what your competitor is charging, how can you present a rational and reasonable case?

How do you get competitive pricing information? There is no one-size-fits-all way to find out, of course, but here are a few that may start you in the right direction:

1. The best source for me has always been the competitor's staff. Pick up the phone and call them and ask how much they get for the product in question. If you get to the right person, you can ask not only what the selling price is but also their discount structure, delivery schedules, terms and conditions, and just about anything else you might want to know, pricing or otherwise.

Does this require deception? Not at all. Tell the party on the phone exactly who you are. Chances are he will tell you all you want to know anyway. While you are at it, ask for a price sheet if it is available. Chances are you'll get that, too. If calling competitors makes you uncomfortable, try visiting their booth at the next major trade show. Again, by asking the right questions, there is little that poor soul manning the booth won't give up willingly.

2. On the off chance that the party on the phone actually recognizes you as a potential threat, you will have to look to another source. Try a distributor. Many distributors handle products from competing companies. Offering competing products creates a certain degree of ambivalence when it comes to protecting what could be construed as proprietary information. Salespeople who are conscientious about serving their distributors and have established winning relationships are more likely to get what they are looking for from a grateful channel member. All you have to do is ask. Nothing to lose. Everything to gain.

3. Try asking a customer. If you have the right relationship, customers will share competitive information with you or conveniently leave a competitive quote lying on their desk in plain view. There may be sensibility and ethics questions here. Back off at the first sign. It isn't worth risking your relationship or putting your customer in an uncomfortable position.

The sources of information vary. What matters most is that you explore all you can to find out what your competitor's pricing strategy has been, is, and will be. The fate of your own company depends on it.

51 USE PRICE AS A MARKETING TOOL

By now very few out there believe price is just a matter of figuring out costs and applying a markup that will give a reasonable profit.

For those who do, we will leave you to your fantasies and concentrate on the rest of us who live in the real end-of-twentieth-century world.

Like distant cousins, price and cost are only remotely related. Customers don't care too much about *your costs,* they only care about what *they have to pay* for your products and services. Note: I am talking about consumers and commercial customers. Selling to government is another matter entirely. Government, it seems, often assumes the right to look at your costs and determine for itself what is a fair profit margin for you to make on any given contract. If you want to sell to the government, you have to accept these conditions.

Pricing strategy is one of the most important tools you have in your marketing bag. It can be a powerful competitive weapon. How you price says a lot about how you are perceived in the marketplace and your marketplace success. Here are a few considerations.

Price as a Positioning Tool

Whether you wear a Rolex or a Seiko on your wrist, you can be pretty sure that either one will keep time well enough that you won't miss a meeting or a flight because of your watch. Yet one sells for $3,000 and up and one for $100 and up. If it's utility you're looking for, no one seriously thinks you get 30 times more utility with a Rolex. Rolex uses its high selling price to say its watches are big-ticket luxury items and status symbols. They are for those who want the world to know they've "arrived." Seiko, on the other hand, just wants to sell a lot of watches. The same goes for Mercedes, Godiva Chocolates, Montblanc writing instruments (you can tell they are expensive because they are writing instruments; if they were cheap, they would be pens or pencils), Sony, Hartmann luggage, and the list goes on.

If you want to be known as a low-end, no-frills, high-volume house, price accordingly. The retail business is full of them. Marshall's, Price/Costco, Ross, and the like. Looking for a car in that category? How about Hyundai or KIA? Hyundai and BMW will both get you to work in the morning, if that's what you care about. It depends on *how* you want to get to work. The choice is between you and your wallet.

Positioning on price for an industrial product is the same idea, except a bit more subtle. Subtlety is required because conventional wisdom says that industrial buyers are more rational than consumers and not swayed by seller machinations. (This is a concept I don't believe in for a moment, by the way. In their own ways, industrial buyers can be just as emotional and irrational as consumers.) Hewlett-Packard products usually run a little more than those of their competitors. In better times, the watchword was that no one ever got fired for buying IBM, even if they were more expensive. For the longest time, probably too long, Apple kept its prices high and positioned the Macintosh as worth the price difference. To emphasize the point, they made sure that the product was technically different from the run-of-the-mill PC.

Pricing as a Selling Tool

Breathes there a salesperson in the entire world who doesn't feel more comfortable and confident when she knows she has the lowest price around? Of course not. Price is a wonderful tool for the sales department. All other things being equal, lower price means more units sold, more market share. And if you give salespeople some margin to play with, you'll see how much better they do in a competitive situation when they have to give in a little on price to win the business.

Want to build up sales on a new product as quickly as possible? Come in with the lowest price you can live with, and watch the customers line up. Not only that, but it discourages competitors from chasing after you because they have to set their price even lower than you to get customers interested.

Do you have a unique product or a technological breakthrough? Price it *high* to get your investment back as quickly as you can. Just don't keep the price up too long, or you are sure to get burned. Do you remember how high the Sony Betamax videocassette recorder was when it first came out? I'll tell you—more than $2,000. Sony, unfortunately, overestimated the difficulty of bringing out a competitive product. When the VHS format was introduced, it was not only cheaper but also more widely promoted and ultimately more successful. It is interesting to speculate on what might have happened if Sony had dropped its prices fast enough to boost up its sales before VHS took hold.

Price, Value, and Quality

For better or worse, customers will equate price with quality. The higher your price, the higher your *perceived* quality. In some respects this is most often true, that is, the higher-priced item is considered of higher quality. You set your price high to take advantage of that concept, hoping that the customer will go for quality in spite of the price difference. Of course, when it comes right down to it, neither price nor quality are the burning issues. The real issue is *value.*

There are countless experts who will explain the meaning of value in the context of customer expectations. There are also countless experts who will be happy to define quality in any context you would care to know about. Notwithstanding any or all of the collective expertise of academia or the consulting profession on how to define value, I submit that people equate price with quality and quality with value and therefore, logically, price with value. The higher the price, the greater the quality, and the better is the value of the offering.

Ironically, a higher-priced item, implying higher quality, may actually be of *lesser* value to the buyer. Some people buy personal computers with blazingly fast microprocessors, extra RAM, endless storage, multimedia, 20-inch color monitors, and fax/modems to communicate with the world, then use them for little more than turning on America Online to check their stock prices. They paid a lot of money for high-quality products with very little value to them.

"There's a sucker born every minute," said P. T. Barnum.

52 DON'T EXPECT THE CUSTOMER TO PAY FOR YOUR MISTAKES

One of the most difficult things I run into is trying to get clients to understand that the most important factors in setting price have to do with customers and markets, *not* the client's own internal conditions.

Late to Market

Whether luxury or economy, any car will get you where you want to go in about the same amount of time. Mercedes gets its high price because of its perceived benefits and value, not because the manufacturer couldn't keep its costs down and had to charge more money. For a product to succeed at a higher price than its competition, the customer has to perceive greater value. In other words, customers who plunk down hard-earned cash have to believe they're getting more than just wheels.

A company I know was hoping to short-circuit a major development effort by private labeling a finished design. The company had a good market presence with a major component but was aching to move up to the total system. Unfortunately it had neither the resources nor the time it would take to invest in developing a product of its own. The company was in luck to find a European manufacturer who was just dying to get into the U.S. market but didn't want to invest in setting up its own sales and distribution network. A marriage made in heaven.

Well, not really. Technical problems caused delay after delay in getting the product to the market. In the meantime, established competitors were fighting hard for market share, causing the street price to plummet. Economies of scale and design innovations cut what was originally a typical selling price of about $5,000 to no more than $3,000, and the trend was pointing to $2,000 and below.

Based on the agreement he had with his supplier, the client found himself between a rock and a hard place. If the product had been available on time, he could have gone to market with a competitive price of about $3,500, giving him a small but acceptable profit margin. Now he was seeing street prices below his actual landed costs.

I'm no psychologist but it seems that when managers are faced with an impossible situation, more often than not their rationalizing mode kicks in. In this case, management decided to go to market with the higher price and position the product as a higher-quality product with more desirable features. In fairness, they really believed that to be the truth. In truth, they were *wrong*.

The strategy didn't work. For one thing, even if the product was of higher quality, which it was not, the marketplace wasn't prepared to reward it as such. There were too many good systems out there from established suppliers. Competitors had set the standard and this latecomer couldn't make a convincing case that there were enough additional benefits to justify the higher price. When prospective dealers and distributors were apprised of the prices they would have to sell the product for, they turned away in droves. Why take up shelf space with an expensive line that had nothing going for it except its high price? Without a distribution network, there was no practical way the company could get to the market.

Because management couldn't offset its mistakes by pricing higher than prevailing levels, the product died. The company, older and wiser, returned to its core business in which it made a lot of money and from which it should never have strayed. A lesson learned, though bitter and costly, especially for those managers who found themselves on the street.

Moral: The correct price has to do with the current market conditions. It is virtually impossible for you to make up for extraordinary costs by pricing higher than the competition.

53 GET MORE MONEY WITHOUT RAISING PRICE

Suppose that times are tough and you feel you have to increase margins. You have taken as much cost out of the product as you can do safely; now it's time to look at the revenue side. You consider an across-the-board price increase but dismiss it as being suicidal. You doubt whether your competitors would go along, and a unilateral price increase would have an opposite effect to what you want. Customers will bolt. What to do? You might try looking for ways to get more money from customers from other, more acceptable sources.

A company I used to work for sold a very expensive electronic system that ran between $75,000 and $100,000 per unit. We thought of ways to increase the price but were locked in with an intense competitive situation. One idea we came up with was to encourage the customer to buy a full set of spare parts. In exchange, we would extend the warranty from one year to two. Our rationalization was that we could save on warranty expenses if the customer would attempt repair first using the available spares, before calling for factory service. This wasn't a bad deal for the customer, either. The product ended up all over the world in some pretty remote places. An extra year without paying the expenses of service calls could save the customer the cost of the spares and then some. For us, it was a gamble that the added revenue from the parts purchase wouldn't get eaten up by additional warranty expenses later on. In any case, we were able to increase the revenue from the sale 5 to 10% with a much smaller percentage increase in cost. Win-win.

Every product or service is different and the approach to increase revenue from other sources will vary with product and industry. Nevertheless, there are a few things to look at:

1. *Change the discount structure.* Increase the purchase quantities required for each price break or eliminate altogether the deep discount breaks at maximum quantity levels. As long as you don't deviate too far from industry norms and previous customer expectations, this should work.

2. *Charge for warranties* or extended warranties. This is becoming common with consumer products such as automobiles and major appliances. For an additional fee the customer can get years of "peace of mind" knowing that anything major going wrong with the equipment will be covered for all or most of the repair costs. A good deal for the selling parties, too. More revenue for the producer, the dealer, and the insurance company backing up the policy.

3. *Charge for technical support.* This became increasingly popular within the computer industry in the 1990's. When the consumer end of the business exploded, the number of calls from new hardware and software users for support—for everything from how to turn on the machine to how to load in the program—exploded as well. Companies increased the size of their technical support staffs, but costs rose far out of proportion to the increased sales volume. The solution was to charge in one way or another for the service.

The first thing to go for some suppliers was the toll-free number to call for help. Now the customer paid for the call, no small expense considering the waiting time for some calls was a half hour or more at daytime long-distance rates. Multiply that by many thousands for a popular program or piece of hardware and you can see how much money is saved. This, of course, cuts costs, *but it doesn't add revenue.* To do that the industry considered, and at the time of this writing has begun, asking for credit card numbers before a technician will begin work on your problem. The controversy generated by these actions goes on. The industry says it can no longer afford to provide free service. Customers claim poor quality or poorly written manuals are the cause for most of the calls. Whatever the true cause, it has led to a degree of acceptability for a company to get more money for telling a customer how to use its product.

4. *Charge for packaging and handling.* When I filled out the order blank for a software upgrade, I was pleased that it would only cost me $49.95 to be fully up to date with the latest and greatest. The sales tax added another $3.62 to the cost, and finally there was a whopping $7.50 for shipping and handling. My nominal $50 item ended up costing me more than $60. Did I argue the charge? No. Did I even give it a second thought? Not really. By now I am used to seeing handling charges added to the total price, although I've never been able to figure out what "handling" was all about. Does this mean I pay for the product, pay for them to put it in a box, and pay for them to send it to me? Probably. Though I have never been given a satisfactory explanation of what handling actually covered, it seems to be an acceptable item for most customers. I know it didn't cost $7.50 for the software publisher to send an eight-ounce package via first-class mail less than 400 miles. No doubt a good source of additional revenue.

Finally, you *might* consider reducing the warranty period. Not a good idea. In these days when quality is king, anything that indicates reduced quality or hints that the producer is not standing behind the product is dangerous.

54 BE FLEXIBLE; MARGIN ISN'T EVERYTHING

Everybody likes a big margin. The bigger the margin, the bigger the ultimate profit. But what happens when you get caught in a price squeeze? Do you want the business or don't you? If you do, you will rethink whatever gross margin guidelines you had set down in happier times. Simple math: A 20% gross margin on something is infinitely more profitable than a 50% margin on nothing.

A few years ago I was working on a market study for a segment of the global telecommunications business. To make the study more meaningful my associates and I decided to interview as many of the equipment suppliers as we could, face-to-face. Which brought me across the desk of the managing director of a British company, based in a London suburb. In addition to a standard set of questions I always asked, I usually tossed in a few open-enders I hoped would give me some insights into the industry.

To a general question concerning the overall health of his business, the managing director replied something like this. "Good, but we are facing a problem in that our system has been on the market for several years and the design is obsolete. Rather than spend money on a stopgap rework, what I really would like to do is private label a good system that is already out there. Then I could spend my engineering and development money on the next generation design."

Private labeling, we all know, is buying someone else's product, having them put your name on it, and you selling it as your own. Companies do this all the time to fill in gaps in their product lines or save themselves the cost of an expensive development program.

Fair enough, I thought. By coincidence, there was a small company in California I knew that had just the product for him. Even though they were a struggling little business, their system was a good design and would do very nicely. When the managing director mentioned a quantity requirement and a price he was willing to pay, a little mental arithmetic told me there was a potential for at least a million dollars in business for the U.S. company. That could be more than a third of its annual sales revenue. Smelling a five-figure finder's fee, I sent a long fax to California that evening outlining the situation. When I returned home later that week, we began a series of discussions between the two parties with me acting as the go-between.

Cut to the chase. The deal never went through. For starters, no one in the American company, including the CEO, ever got deeply involved in the prospect's requirements. After a first-glance evaluation, the CEO came up with a price that was a good deal greater than the customer had expected to pay. The prospect balked at the initial offer, and that was about it. Instead of recognizing the customer's hesitation for the starting point for negotiation, the company just let it go. Take it or leave it. It was a matter of costs and profit margins, they said. Phone calls went unreturned, personal visits from management were promised but never scheduled, and no serious effort was made to establish a relationship with the prospect. As the months dragged on, the customer became less and less interested in the relationship (if there ever was one), and the project gradually faded away.

In trying to analyze what went wrong, I came to the conclusion that there were two overriding mistakes that doomed the program. First, the CEO dropped the ball by not appreciating the potential and acting upon it. In his capacity as chief marketer as well as CEO, he should have been on the next plane to London as soon as he knew of the project. The relationship building would have—and should have—started right there. Instead, he got bogged down with other things, failed to delegate the authority to act to others, and the opportunity just drifted away. Second was the lack of flexibility on what was and what was not an acceptable margin. The prospective customer was a savvy businessperson. He above all others would have appreciated a frank talk about about what was a realistic price to pay. That talk never materialized because the CEO never brought it up. Successful negotiation means compromise. This ended up a lose-lose situation because the supplier never got the business and the customer never got the break he needed to avoid a costly development program.

I heard the CEO of a client company tell his sales and marketing staff that he never wanted them to lose business on price unless he knew about it in advance. He told them that he was the final authority in his company for turning away business on price. If they could find out the price they needed to get the business, then he would decide whether it was attractive enough to go after it. Right of final refusal was his and his alone. I like that attitude.

Last thought: You can't spend the profit margin you protected if you never get the order.

55 AVOID PRICE WARS

War is hell, said Willam Tecumseh Sherman, Union general during the American Civil War. In three short words he said everything there is to say about a subject that has been plaguing us since the beginning of civilization and for the century and a half since he said it. I have always taken exception to using war as a metaphor for business because to me it trivializes human tragedy. The similarities between war and business are too superficial to be taken seriously.

Unfortunately for my philosophy, however, certain phrases have crept into our language that have become acceptable because they are catchy and descriptive. Price War is one of them.

I would prefer not to compete on price. It says to me I have failed to differentiate my product properly. Sometimes customers will see the difference in quality or service. Sometimes they won't. When they won't, we have an unhappy situation in which the only way we can hold on to our customers is to lower our price. When the competitor then does the same, we are right back to the beginning, only with a lower starting point. Then the cycle begins again. That is known as a price war. A price war is an event inspired by intense competition. Generally, it comes about because someone is trying to gain a short-term competitive edge. Dropping price below the prevailing level is a way to get it. Sometimes, but usually not.

What Causes a Price War?

Competition intensifies when the customer can see few or no differences among suppliers. The buyer figures that he or she might just as well buy from the lowest-priced supplier. Unless you are that supplier, your business slips. "We can't let them get away with that," you say, so you drop your price a little below the competition, who drops his price, so a third one drops hers, and so it goes. Before you know it, profit margins have gone up in smoke, and prices are getting so low you can barely cover your fixed costs, if that.

For a while, customers are having a wonderful time enjoying the cost savings. Then eventually you all get back to your senses. Over a period of time, prices stabilize and, if you're lucky, they creep back up again to acceptable margins.

The paradox of price wars is that they are usually started by one of the weaker suppliers but are most often won by the strongest competitor. The strong can tolerate reduced margins for as long as it takes for a market to return to its orderly past. They have the staying power. This happens on a regular basis in the airline industry. A weaker carrier will try to fill empty seats on a particularly important route by running a "sale" to lure vacationers, or business travelers looking to reduce their expense budgets. Even with certain restrictions it's still a bargain, so customers start to move to the cheaper carrier. Well, an empty seat on any particular flight is revenue lost forever, so the stronger carriers can't sit back and allow this to go too far. When they announce they will match price *without* some of the restrictions—this is a subtle form of price decrease—the hordes shift back. Back and forth. Back and forth.

Whatever happened to brand loyalty? Brand loyalty only exists when the customer sees a *benefit* in staying with a supplier. Except for frequent flyer members, those who have a stake in upgrades and free vacation travel, most travelers figure the best way to get from A to B is also the cheapest way, regardless of whose logo is on the tail.

SyQuest and Iomega

Nowadays just about everyone in business uses a personal computer and every computer comes with a hard drive for storing all those files. Still, storage space fills up fast and there is always a need to back up what you have, that is, create duplicates so that a loss of your main hard drive won't put you out of business. Removable storage drives have an advantage in that they provide an endless source of capacity, whether you use them for storage of files and data or for backup, or most likely for both. If the drive fills up, you remove the cartridge and put in another. When you want to check files on the first cartridge, take out whatever cartridge is in the drive and replace it in a few seconds with the one you want. Additional capacity is just a cartridge away.

SyQuest Technology and Iomega both produce portable, removable hard drives for the personal computer market. When Iomega introduced the Zip drive, it knew it was competing head-to-head with Syquest's EZ-135 drive. The Zip drive used a cartridge that looked very much like the ubiquitous 3.5-inch floppy disks we are so familiar with, except it had almost 100 times the storage capacity. SyQuest has been the standard setter for removable drives for many years, and its EZ-135 was in the market first. It was somewhat faster than Iomega's Zip, and each cartridge had 30% more storage capacity than the Zip. Still, Iomega had one advantage. It sold for just a little over $200, considerably less than the EZ-135. The product got a lot of good press and Iomega became the darling of the securities analysts.

SyQuest decided to fight back. To protect its market share, it lowered its prices even though it didn't have the cost structure that could sustain a long-term price war. The results were inevitable. SyQuest lost money by the bucketful and Iomega pretty much won the war of the small removable drives. With 20-20 hindsight, SyQuest management admits it shouldn't have participated in a price war with Iomega. It left the company financially devastated. It seriously affected its ability to market its new product lines that, if promoted effectively, could restore the company's market position.

This was actually an unusual kind of price war. Iomega designed its product to be sold at the level it knew the market would accept. SyQuest had designed its product to be sold at a higher point but had to come down to remain competitive. The only one that got hurt was SyQuest. They started the war. They lost it. War is hell.

Summary: Price wars are to be avoided. It is rare that anyone ever benefits from them. Even the ultimate winner isn't really a winner. He gets the business at a lower margin, maybe so low that the more he sells, the more he loses. More often than not, everyone loses.

56 KNOW WHEN AND HOW TO RAISE YOUR PRICE

After much thought, experience, and empirical evidence, I have concluded that there is no really good time to increase prices, so the title of this section is a little misleading. I hope you don't infer that I have a secret way of raising price that makes buyers immediately agree with you and reach for their order pads. Not so. Raising price is *never easy* and, I believe, should be avoided at all costs (excuse the pun). However, if your costs are starting to put a squeeze on your pricing structure, you won't listen to me anyway, so let's at least talk about it.

The best you can say is that some times are not as bad as others. During inflationary periods, you will generate resentment in some of your customers, but since everybody is doing it—including your customers—the resentment will no doubt be short-lived. During recessionary times, you may need the additional revenue, but everyone is running at reduced capacity, and raising price may just begin an exodus of customers running to your competitors. Your only hope is that your competitors are probably in as much trouble as you are. In most cases, though, raising prices in a down economy is like shooting yourself in the foot.

Price Leadership Issues

Unless you are the price leader in your category, raising price unilaterally is a chancy practice. Price leaders are usually the dominant producers and if they don't go along, you are left out there high and dry with no choice but to back down. For example, in the U.S. airline business, United and American are the price leaders in the long-haul market. As the two dominant companies, what they do with the price of an airline ticket pretty much sets the tone for the entire industry. If TWA should announce a price increase, unless United or American follows along, TWA is left holding the bag.

If the price leader raises price before you, you have a golden opportunity to raise yours accordingly. As a matter of fact, you can almost count on the leader expecting you to. If you don't, you're just leaving money on the table.

Price and Strategic Advantage

Raising price at the wrong time shifts the strategic advantage to your competition. Suppose, for example, you are locked in a competitive struggle with a company located in Germany. Then suppose the relationship between the dollar and the deutsche mark is acting in your favor, that is, the increasing value of the mark is making your competitor's costs go up. Rather than raise price and lose business to you, the German company maintains price for as long as it can to protect its market share, willing to sacrifice some short-term profit in hopes that it can hold out until the currency values shift.

If you raise price now, the German company will undoubtedly raise price, too. But look at what you've done. You had an advantage over your competitor when you could sell at an acceptable price and still make a reasonable profit. For the German company to stay competitive, it had to lose money or sell at very low margins. Now, you've given your competitor a chance to return to profitability without working for it. You have ceded an important strategic advantage.

This actually happened a few years ago, except it was Detroit versus the Japanese automobile industry. In the eighties, the value of the dollar had taken a big dip in relation to the yen. The Japanese were desperately trying to hold on to their share of the American market. Profits were going out the window. Then GM, Ford, and Chrysler did the unexpected and uncalled for. They raised their prices and let the Japanese off the hook. If you stood on a California beach, you could almost hear the collective sighs of relief blowing across the Pacific Ocean. Up went price. Up went margin. And since their competitors had already raised their prices, Toyota, Nissan, and others, didn't have to lose business because of public outrage. Not a good time for Detroit to get greedy.

Actually the best way I know to raise price without suffering too much customer resentment is what I call the "new and improved" strategy. Add a feature or two to your existing product, change the package, change the color, do *anything* you have to do to change it without incurring much added cost, and take it to the marketplace as a new product at a higher price. Then discontinue the older product as quickly as you can get away with it. It has worked with soap powder and computers, cars and orange juice. It might work for you.

Raising Prices for Your Top Customers

If you are committed to getting more money for your product or service, the most delicate part of the price increase exercise is presenting it to your top customers. If you have to raise price, you have to level with them. You have to tell them *why*. You have to lay out the numbers. Make a case.

If you pin down a reputable buyer from a reputable company, she probably will admit under duress that it isn't always in her company's best interests to force suppliers to hold prices at artificially low levels. Suppliers that lose money are likely to cut corners on features and quality. It isn't worth taking that risk just to keep squeezing the vendor.

Be honest with your customers about why you have to raise prices. It is the only way you can get them to accept the increases willingly.

57 WHEN IN DOUBT, GO WITH A LOW PRICE

A client once asked me, as part of an overall market analysis, to determine what price customers were willing to pay for a new product. While we eventually were able to get our arms around an answer, some interesting things came up as a result of this effort:

- First, it confirmed in my mind that, when it comes to a new product, at least, customers have no basis for comparison and therefore no valid way to state what price they are willing to pay.
- Second, when the first is true, customers will tell you whatever they think you want to hear.
- Third, when the time comes to place the order, anything customers have told you previously about acceptable prices no longer applies.

Published surveys usually show price way down the list when business-to-business buyers state their preferences. I once saw the results of a survey that listed price as low as *25th* on a list of factors in a purchase decision. Pardon my skepticism, cynicism, and pessimism, but those are usually the same buyers who will tell you your price was too high and they had to go with your competitor.

Now picture this scene. You've submitted your quotation and you find out your price is higher than a competitive bid. Your good salesmanship mode kicks in and you call for a meeting with the buyer. You make your pitch about superior service, quality, reliability, the whole nine yards. The buyer listens respectfully, tells you the company will give you every consideration, the decision hasn't yet been made. He says you will hear from them in a week or so.

In your heart you know the order is lost. And it is.

What went wrong?

Well, surprise, surprise! No matter what those textbooks and *Harvard Business Review* articles have said, price is still *very* important. You haven't made a case that any of the other factors you presented makes up for the price difference. And the competitor convinced the buyer (not too difficult a task) that the only important difference between his offer and yours is price. Goodbye order.

What could you have done about it? You might have offered to meet the competitive price, assuming the buyer would have given you the opportunity. Again, given the opportunity, you might undercut the competition. Of course, you don't want to get into a price war and neither does anyone else. Except for the buyer. In my experience there is nothing—nothing—buyers love more than some good price competition among suppliers, so they can end up with the lowest price.

The problem here is that price is tangible, solid, concrete. *Value,* on the other hand, is difficult to define. To sell *value* you can't just point out your superior service. Your competitor probably does a pretty good job at service also. Subtract service from both sides of the equation and *x* still equals price. To prove *better value* you must show that, in spite of your higher price, there is an *economic* advantage in buying from you. You must prove there is an advantage when the customer considers *all* the costs involved in purchase and long-term use. If you can't do that, you'd better sharpen your pencil.

8

PROMOTING YOUR BUSINESS: GETTING OUT THE WORD

Promotion means getting out the word. It is about making customers aware of your company, your product line, and what you can do to help them. It is about why they should come to *you* for these solutions, rather than listen to your competitors. Once they are doing business with you, it is about reassuring them that they made the right decision by coming to you in the first place.

How you get the word out is the challenge. It depends on scores of factors, like who you are, how much money you have, who and where your customers are, how many there are, who and where your competitors are, the nature of the product or service, and so on and so on and so on.

The Boeing Company probably knows every prospective buyer for its aircraft on a first-name basis, anywhere in the world. I seriously doubt that United Airlines would be induced to looking into a 747 purchase from a Boeing advertisement in *Aviation Week*. But you can bet there's a Boeing executive camped on United's front lawn wheeling and dealing like the good salesman he is supposed to be. Down the road from Boeing's big plant in Everett, Washington, is Redmond, home of Microsoft. It is safe to suggest that there are probably more Microsoft customers right at home in

Redmond than Boeing has in the entire world. Different products, different markets, different price levels, different solutions to reaching customers. Two successful companies with completely different promotion requirements.

There is no "one-size-fits-all" promotion strategy. There is no permanent strategy. What worked yesterday may not work *today*. What works today may not work *tomorrow*.

A further thought. It is fashionable to use the word *communication* for *promotion*. I do not see the two as synonyms. I concede that communication is a more elegant word, but it isn't elegance I'm looking for, it's business. To me it begs the issue of what you are really trying to do. If you want to *communicate*, send an E-mail. If you want to *sell*, promote.

In this chapter I'll deal with a few things you should consider when getting out the word, including tailoring a promotion mix that fits.

58 PUT YOUR PROMOTION DOLLARS WHERE THEY WILL DO THE MOST GOOD

Willie Sutton, one of history's most notorious holdup men, was asked why he robbed banks. "Because that's where the money is," was his candid reply. An honest answer from a dishonest person. When it comes to promoting your business, going where the money is, is what it's all about. In this case, *money* means customers. You spend money on events, activities, or media because you expect that's where you'll reach your customers and prospects. Whether it's print or TV/radio advertising, direct mail, trade shows, or pumping up the sales force, your first priority is what will get you the *most exposure* with prospective and existing customers. Like any other issue in your business, cost is important. Certainly you want to be sure that whatever methods you use are cost effective. But nobody wants to select a promotion strategy because it's cheap. If it doesn't present your message to enough prospective customers, it is too expensive.

When a giant company like Boeing places a two-page full color advertisement in *Business Week* extolling the virtues of flight, for example, there is little or no expectation that someone will be influenced to buy a fleet of 777s by the ad. The purpose of these so-called institutional ads is more to spread goodwill or lure potential investors than sell planes. If you are Boeing, GE, IBM, or someone of that size, of course, you can afford the luxury of an institutional ad designed to make the world feel good about you and you feel good about yourself. Most of us don't have that luxury. The money we spend on advertising or any other part of the promotion mix, must get us to our customers as quickly and efficiently as possible.

Where Do We Go?

Choosing the most effective way to reach your customers is entirely industry specific. Whatever works for you. If the best way to reach your customers is with print advertising, then that is the way to go. Then again, why advertise in a high circulation general business magazine when the customers you want to reach are more likely to be reading a trade journal focusing on your industry? Why spend money on print advertising at all if personal selling is a better way to reach them? Or, why have a high-paid, high-cost sales force when most of your customers phone or mail in their orders?

On more than one occasion I have worked with clients on their marketing plans, and I have asked to see what they've put together for promotion expenses. One client had a list of about ten domestic and international trade shows scheduled out over the year. When I asked what experience they had with results from any particular show in previous years, no one could tell me. When I asked if they were sure if their most likely prospects even attended the show or conference, no one could tell me. My question to them was "Why are you going back this year?" They couldn't give me any objective reason for doing so, other than they go every year. Staying away would cost them their place in line for space selection for the following year. I posed similar questions about their media advertising and the answers were just as vague. "Why are you in that magazine? How many leads have these ads generated for you in the past? Can you trace any leads directly or indirectly to any particular ad? Can you trace any orders?

Here are some typical questions you should be asking before you submit or sign off on a promotion plan:

- What is the best way to communicate with the ultimate buyer of the product or service?
- What are the alternative ways that might also be effective?
- What has been the success rate for previous promotion methods?
- What are the most likely publications read by your prospects?
- What are the most likely trade shows and conferences attended by your key buying influences? (Note: This is an extremely important issue. It isn't enough that representatives from your prospect attend and visit your booth. Those representatives have to be in a position to make or influence

the buying decision. See Number 60 for more on this subject.)
- Can you reach your potential customers with your existing sales force?

Summary: If the promotion mix you've put together doesn't reach the prospects you want it to reach—and help convert them to customers—you are wasting your time and money.

59 ALL PROMOTION HAS A PURPOSE

When I see how much money companies spend on promotion to reach the consumer side of the market, I am filled with admiration and a little bit of awe. To spend hundreds of thousands of dollars to show one's stuff for a few seconds of a Super Bowl telecast, or millions to get the corporate name closely tied in to the Olympic Games tells me they must be very confident that the returns from these promotions justify the huge sums. Either that or they have more money than they know what to do with. Which one it is, is still a toss-up.

Coca-Cola and Budweiser have been around for a long time. I guess they know what they are doing. As for me, if I had that much money on the line and was relying on the rational and predictable behavior of consumers for a return on my investment, I would never stop shaking.

Smaller companies, take heart. There is more to effective promotion than pouring money into the bottomless well of media advertising.

Thinking Objectives and Strategies

Good promotion starts with objectives and strategies. What *results* do you want to achieve with your promotion dollar? The answer is company specific and time dependent. By the latter I mean your strategy and promotion mix will change over the life of your product.

Moving prospects along the selling cycle is the most obvious objective. Any good marketing textbook will give you more than you ever thought you wanted to know about motivating buyers. Philip Kotler uses terms like *cognitive, affective, behavioral,* and *response hierarchy models.* And there's the old standby, AIDA— *awareness, interest, desire,* and *action.* (In the words of Casey Stengel, "You can look it up.")

Another objective might be to position or reposition the company. Consider the challenge for Church & Dwight to take an ordinary commodity like sodium bicarbonate and market it as an indispensable multiuse product. What is Arm & Hammer Baking Soda, anyway? Antacid? Deodorant? Food additive? Fire extinguisher? Apparently, it is anything C&D wants it to be and everything it *can* be.

Or maybe you want your promotion to precondition the customer for a salesperson's visit. Or a price increase. Or anything else.

Criteria for Promo Selection

Whatever you decide as your objective, putting together the best promotion mix to satisfy that objective is the next step. It's easier to figure out if you know *where* your customers are. The reason Coke and Pepsi spend so much on advertising is because that's the only way to get to their end customers. If you want to sell to consumers, you have to consider how big an ad budget you can afford, because some form of broad promotion is in order.

Industrial marketers spend most of their promo money, even though they might not regard it as such, on the sales force. Better to hire an extra person for the Midwest territory than spend the equivalent amount on advertising. It's faster and more direct. Better to give the salesperson good brochures and data sheets. They are of more immediate use than print ads. Better to put money into selling tools like presentation software and laptop computers. Better to invite key customers to a private demonstration and presentation than go to one more marginal trade show.

Summary: You see how it is. No generalities, just what works for you to accomplish your objectives.

60 SELECT THE RIGHT TRADE SHOWS FOR THE RIGHT REASONS

Trade shows can be fun. Sure, they are hard on your feet, whether you are an exhibitor or a patron. But they are usually a welcome change from routine. They give us a chance to get away from the office. We get to spend a few nights in a city far from home, get out on the town and sample the night life, even get to meet some of our customers. If we're really sharp—maybe lucky—we might even sell some product.

They are also *expensive*. Consider the cost of exhibit space, producing, shipping, setting up and tearing down the booth, travel expenses for the people staffing the booth, and the opportunity cost of tying them down to the exhibit hall for four days or so when they could be out doing something that turns directly into more business. Add to those factors the costs of special treatment for customers, the expense of get-togethers with distributors or independent sales representatives, and you have quite a bit of cash tied up in the event. It would be well worth some thoughts in advance to ensure you get out of trade shows what you hope for. Ultimately, of course, that means booking business either at the show or as a result of it.

Choosing the Right Ones

If your budget is limited—and whose isn't?—you want to be very careful choosing which shows to spend your money on. The choice should rest mainly with return on investment. Since you are betting on long-run results, that isn't so easy with trade shows. Some considerations:

- Take into account your past experience. Can you trace any business from past participation? Was it worthwhile?

- How well attended have they been? Do the right people show up? By right people, I mean prospects and customers from your target market, not merely catalog collectors. Big numbers don't necessarily mean the right numbers.
- How much will it cost? Consider *all* the costs.

What Kind of a Place Is This to Introduce New Products?

One of the great rationalizations for trade shows is that they are ideal times to introduce your new products. But are they so ideal?

Let's say you are ready to take your new product to market. It has been tested and retested. You are convinced it's a winner. You are proud of the results of the development and gratified by the feedback from the first field tests. Now you want to get *maximum exposure* to prospective new customers.

So here's what you do. You find a time and location for your new product introduction that coincides with the timing of introduction of 5 competitive products, 35 related products, and probably 300 or 400 products that aren't even remotely connected to what you do. At this same time and location, you will expose the product to 25,000 or so individuals, among whom may be the key 25 who you really want to get to see it, but you aren't sure where they are or when they are coming by your booth to see it or how much time they can spend. Further, the trade press will give you at least one-half a column inch of "free" publicity that will tell the world of your innovation.

To draw attention to your product, you may go out and hire someone to do magic tricks, or use ever-smiling models, who haven't a clue to what your product is or does. They will hand out key chains or plastic bags with your corporate logo, or make luggage tags from laminated business cards. The magic tricks work like magic and draw big crowds to your booth. The models draw the usual oglers and self-deluding Romeos. Most of the giveaways go to individuals who don't care what you are selling or what your blockbuster new product can do for them. And to make it all just perfect, about a hundred other companies are doing the same thing.

Get the point? Trade shows and exhibitions can be *lousy* places to introduce new products. The bigger the event, the more you risk getting lost in the noise and hoopla.

"We Always Go" Is Not a Reason

New product introduction isn't the only reason companies go to shows. Here are some others that marketing people usually give to justify the time and the expense of exhibiting.

- We go because the industry expects it of us.
- We go so our competitors won't spread rumors about us going out of business.
- We go because it's a good place to meet customers.
- We go because it's a good place to get qualified leads.
- We go because it's a good place to meet our reps and distributors.
- And the real reason, inertia. We go because we've always done it.

The only *good* reason I can think of is that your experience has proved the trade show results in business you wouldn't have received any other way. Trade shows are wearying. Standing on one's feet for eight to ten hours a day for four days, all the while trying to be charming, professional, and alert can take its toll. At least get something worthwhile out of it.

61 USE PUBLICITY TO BLOW YOUR OWN HORN

Modesty will get you nowhere. Everyone has heard of IBM and General Electric. How many people have heard of *you?* How many prospective customers know you even exist? In Hollywood they say any publicity is good publicity. Getting your name in the paper is what counts. That may be too cynical, even for me. Although I am as pure as the driven snow, I can imagine some things about me I wouldn't want to get into newspapers. The trick as I see it is to get your name mentioned in the most favorable light possible. Advertising will do that, but it comes from you. Your customers know it comes from you so your message is discounted for being obviously self-serving. Your sales force will do its best to get your message across. But that's what they get paid to do, and everyone knows that, too.

Besides, advertising and maintaining a sales force are expensive. Let each do what it was intended to do without muddying up its mission. The smart marketer looks for other ways to increase exposure without costing the company vast sums of money. The answer is publicity.

Publicity, sometimes used interchangeably with the term public relations, is a component of a good promotion mix. It means getting credible exposure without appearing self-serving.

I do not know exactly how much money Microsoft spent when they introduced their PC operating system, Windows 95. I wouldn't even want to guess. Buying a whole day's edition of the *Times* of London doesn't come cheap. What I found more interesting than what they spent is how much publicity they got without having to pay for it. The introduction of Windows 95 became a *news story,* like the birth of sextuplets, only more so. Less important, but more of a story. Every TV station and newspaper in the country, and much of the world, ran pieces about the coming of this cybermessiah. As rich as Microsoft chairman Bill Gates is, he couldn't afford to buy the kind of positive press coverage this generated. Now *that's* what publicity is all about.

Getting the Most from Public Relations

Effective public relations is a bargain. Much of it you can do yourself. Much of it you already do or should be doing. For example, every time you bring out a new product you should have a press release announcement going to all the trade journals and business media. It isn't intended to replace space advertising, but a printed new product announcement in a trade magazine can be a major source for new prospect inquiries. And it's usually free. Here are some PR situations and ideas:

- Every time you promote someone to a new position or hire a new manager, you should let the world know.
- Every time you bring in a major contract, you should issue a joint announcement with your customer. If nothing else, it will upset your competitor, which would be just fine with you.
- Are you participating on an industry standards committee? Let everyone know.
- Did you have better than anticipated financial results this past quarter? Let everyone know.
- Did someone in the company receive an award?
- Did the company make a donation to the local school district?
- Was there a breakthrough discovery in your labs?
- When one of your people presents a paper at an industry conference, she comes off as an expert, but the company comes off as an industry leader. That's good PR.

Behind every company profile in *Fortune, Forbes, Business Week,* or the business section of your local newspaper, there was probably a public relations effort to get the editor to do the story.

Whether you use an outside PR firm or do the job in-house depends on budget and the extent to which you are willing to go. I have known Don Skinner at Eltron International for several years, so I was much impressed when I saw a short piece on him and his company in *Forbes.* When I asked Don how it came about, he told me one of his board members had got the ball rolling.

While good PR isn't astrophysics or brain surgery, you are probably better off with a professional firm, all things considered. All things considered includes whether anyone in the company can write a decent press release or knows how to distribute it, whether anyone can write a good feature article, or prepare a speech.

Summary: In-house or outside firm, PR is still a bargain. It gives you a level of credibility and prestige you could *never* get with advertising.

62 MAKE YOURSELF LOOK BIGGER OR SMALLER— WHATEVER IT TAKES

It is very frustrating to know you have the capabilities to do a fine job for a major customer and lose the order because the customer thinks your company is too small. Customers, especially big companies, are more comfortable when the suppliers they deal with can handle the job and are solvent enough to be around for the long haul. If you are a small company competing with the big boys and girls, you are at a competitive disadvantage.

You can't make yourself bigger than you are, not overnight. You hope that if you get the order and dozens like it, someday you'll be much bigger. But until that day, you'll have to settle for appearance. I don't mean appearance without substance. That is deception, and it guarantees that you get in trouble. Trouble means law suits and bankruptcy. But there are things you can do to reassure your customer without going over the edge, legally or ethically.

Big Enough to Do the Job . . .

Eltron International's Don Skinner told me that from the very beginning of its corporate life, the company has made a special point to appear bigger that it actually is. At trade shows, its people always wear conservative, professional clothes. The company's main offices aren't posh but they are tastefully decorated in subdued colors and quality furnishings. Eltron's original proposal to United Parcel Service was so professionally done, so slick, the UPS buyers who visited Eltron's plant before placing the order were amazed at how small the company was at the time. The company's message was that it was indeed small but it was *big enough to do the job*. UPS believed them and Eltron does very well today, thank you.

. . . Yet Small Enough to Care

Whenever I was competing against a major company, one of my sales tactics was to try to impress on the customer the idea that the competitor was too big to really care about the customer's own special needs. I, on the other hand, was with a small company very much like the customer's. I was in a *better* position to understand the customer's needs and, more importantly, act on them *quickly*. That was why we enjoyed a bigger share of the market than even our giant competitors (IBM was one of them). We were small but our market leadership was proof that we would do the job. The tactic usually worked. Customers are human, too. They empathize with the little guy over the big guy. David had more fans than Goliath.

In today's service-conscious business world, that tactic might not work as well. Large companies have learned to be responsive to the needs of their customers, plus they have the overwhelming advantage of greater resources and staying power. That's just the way it is.

Example: Hewlett-Packard supplied a large computer system to the Ventura County (California) Municipal and Superior Court. The hope was that the new system would go a long way to streamlining their operations and paperwork. This was a high-profile installation, and sister agencies all over the state and country were looking at the improved system as a way of dealing with similar issues.

The system was all it was supposed to be, except for a nagging habit of shutting down unexpectedly and losing data. At first there was the usual finger-pointing. "It's a hardware problem," said the software vendor. "It must be a software problem," said the HP service people. Finally, the problem was isolated to a hardware fault that wasn't being corrected quickly enough to suit the customer. An irate call to HP's president resulted in an immediate visit by a company official. HP, it was learned, had recognized that problems happen. At the time of this incident, it had set up what they called "Customer Escalation Centers" in strategic locations all over the world. The managers in these offices, at the vice president level in HP's hierarchy, have absolute authority to get things done, cut through corporate bureaucracy and get the customer back on-line again. In this case, the HP representative was able to cross divisional lines and get the right people and material on the job. In a short time the system was up and running, and they all lived happily ever after. The resources of a *big* company, the care and responsiveness of a *small* company. The best of all worlds.

Sometimes you may be bigger than you actually think you are. EG&G, based in Wellesley, Massachusetts, is a $1.4 billion company with divisions in technical services, instrumentation, mechanical components, and optoelectronics. It employs about 25,000 people all over the world. EG&G Flow Technology, in Phoenix, Arizona, on the other hand, grosses about $10 million and employs fewer than 100 people.

In 1995 Flow Technology developed an ultrasonic flow meter to measure automobile hydrocarbon emissions. According to Ron Madison, Flow Technology's Director of Marketing and Sales, the low levels of emissions achieved in American automobiles today—and mandated by the Environmental Protection Agency—were too low for conventional equipment to measure. Something was needed to measure emissions and prove the cars met EPA standards before the manufacturer could ship its cars to the dealers.

Working with one of the major car manufacturers, Flow Technology developed a meter that did the job better than anything then available. But FT is a very small company, and giants like the big three automakers are reluctant to rely on companies so small for equipment of this importance. However, FT's pitch to the industry included representatives from other EG&G divisions that served the automotive market. The presentation proved to the major players that EG&G knew the industry, knew gas vapors, knew shake tests, knew road tests, knew all about flow measurement. No longer was it a pitch from a tiny $10 million company. It was now a pitch from a major organization with major resources and major knowledge of its customers' problems and requirements. Again, resources of a *big* company, the care and responsiveness of a *small* company. The best of all worlds. Incidentally, the last time I talked to Ron, the orders were starting to flow their way.

Summary: Adjust your image to meet the needs of the customer. Whether you are big or small, what customers *really* care about is your ability to satisfy their needs.

63 TAKE CHARGE OF YOUR OWN PROMOTION

When prospective clients ask me what I do, I go through my usual elevator speech, but I carefully point out that I don't get into the detailed execution of advertising and public relations programs. These issues, I point out, should be left to professionals who deal with them every day. Thus I have some misgivings when I see clients execute their own PR programs or prepare their own ads and ad campaigns. True, if you have the skills in-house, there may be some substantial cost savings involved. But if you don't know what you are doing, you'll very soon have an expensive mess on your hands.

For the sake of argument, let us say that you recognize your shortcomings. Or, if they are not shortcomings, then you believe your time and your people's time is better spent doing things that have a more direct impact on your business. So you finagle the budget, come up with some money, and turn the details over to a local ad agency and a public relations firm that came highly recommended. You send them on their respective ways and get on with running your business.

Guess what. You've messed up. You've forgotten that it's your company and you are in charge. Whether you work with agencies or not, it's your money. Giving outsiders carte blanche to do what they think you want is a recipe for disappointment. At best.

Working with Agencies

Advertising agencies make some money when they produce your ads and collateral literature. In that sense they act like consulting firms. You pay them and they perform. Where they make their *real* money, however, is in placing your ads in the print and electronic media. They make a little from you on producing the ad and a lot from the media on placing the ad.

If you are a very large company with a large advertising budget, the agencies grovel for your business. Should you be less than happy with the performance of your current firm you "put the account up for review," as they say in the business. You invite a representative number of firms to "pitch the account." The biggest firms are headquartered in New York, but branch offices and very good independent firms can be found in every major city in the country. If you are big, there will be no shortage of firms chasing you down wherever you are. After their presentations, you make a selection based on your assessment of their creativity and the quality of their pitch. Out with the old. In with the new. Things get back to normal until you lose faith with the new firm, and the process starts all over again.

On the other hand, you probably aren't a very large company and your advertising budget is small, if it exists at all. Chances are you've been getting along with new product announcements and technical articles in *Modern Widgets,* your industry trade magazine. One day the publisher hints rather broadly that he loves to run your announcements but wouldn't it be nice if you took advantage of their special industry overview edition with a full-page, four-color advertisement? The inside front cover is yours for the taking.

Trade magazines will tell you that their editorial and advertising departments not only don't compare notes, their offices are on different continents. Sure. But they are businesses just like you. Most of their readership get complimentary copies. They make their money on advertising revenue. No ads, no money, no magazine.

So you go out looking for an agency. Soon you realize that the guys who do Miller Lite aren't terribly interested in you as an account. You end up with a small shop in the neighborhood that handles some other companies in your industrial park. Good people who know absolutely zilch about your business. Is this the kind of firm you want to let move out on its own with your money? (In fairness to small agencies everywhere, the big firms will know zilch about your business, too. In fact, there's a better chance that the local guys will learn more about your business in a shorter time than you could ever hope from a major agency.)

Putting Someone in Charge

Although it will never be a substitute for senior management oversight, an important step in ensuring good promotion strategy implementation is to have a qualified person on your staff to manage the marketing support functions. Most people who employ such an individual call her the marketing communications manager or marketing services manager. Either way, she's in charge of the advertising and promotion efforts. She puts together the trade shows from start to finish. She works directly with the outside agencies and makes certain that they comply with the company's objectives. She will either do the market research or oversee an outside firm that does. She's in charge.

Summary: Don't let outsiders perform vital functions without oversight from you or a responsible member of your staff. It's your company; handle it with care.

64 GIVE OUT THE BEST LITERATURE MONEY CAN BUY

"How little do they see what is, who frame their hasty judgments upon that which seems."

—Robert Southey

With all due respect to this eighteenth-century English poet, people make judgments on what they *see*. The burden is on the presenter. You would have a right to be very upset with your salesperson if he called on his customers looking as if he just got out of bed. Unshaven, disheveled, disorganized. He may be the world's greatest closer, but if the first time a prospect sets eyes on him he looks like death warmed over, the odds of success plunge out of sight. You never get a second chance to make a first impression.

But suppose Mr. Bright-and-Shiny, clean and professional, sits himself down in front of a prospect and makes a marvelous presentation. At the conclusion of the meeting the prospect, genuinely impressed, asks for a data sheet or some product information. The salesman, obviously pleased with himself for the job he's done, hands him a sheet of information, promises to get back that afternoon with answers to some questions, shakes hands and leaves. The prospect picks up the sheet, and recoils in horror. In his hands is the business equivalent of ring-around-the-collar. The data sheet was obviously produced on the cheap, printed on ordinary copy paper, poorly laid out, an occasional typo thrown in. What does that say about the company making the presentation? If you scrimp on sales literature, where else will you cut corners?

In an earlier generation, no one could have imagined producing a data sheet or any other sales literature on a typewriter. Today, however, the computer revolution is upon us. Anyone with a Macintosh and Adobe Pagemaker can be a graphics designer, or thinks he can be. Follow the templates, run it off on a laser printer, take it over to Kinko's and you're in business. The results I've seen have been mixed. There is some pretty shoddy stuff out there passing for product literature.

I can understand the other point of view. No one wants to be stuck with 5,000 full-color brochures that are unusable because the product is obsolete. So print fewer brochures. It is also true that the information on data sheets changes often and the customer is more interested in correctness than beauty. But if there's no beauty, they may never get to the substance. Besides, we're not just talking beauty here. We're talking about looking professional, substantial, profitable, and successful. Cheap literature makes you look like none of those.

Summary: Professional-looking literature should be done by professionals. Your product literature should be the best you can possibly afford, and you can't afford anything but the best.

65 USE DIRECT MAIL

Direct mail is one of my favorite marketing tools. I use it in my own business and I recommend the procedure to clients whenever I can, especially in business-to-business markets. I learned the process at the feet of direct marketing pro Shell Alpert, of Mount

Gretna, Pennsylvania. Shell, who has become my good friend as well as my mentor, taught me how to write letters that get *read,* but more important, how to write letters that get *responses.* That's no small accomplishment for a technique that many consider a waste of time and money.

For many of us, direct mail or direct marketing are just other names for junk mail. Our mailboxes fill up with unwanted material from advertisers who get our names from who knows where and make offers we are only too willing to refuse. And toss in the refuse. Junk mail is only slightly less annoying than the telemarketers who call us at dinnertime to get us to change our long-distance carrier or list our house for sale when we don't want to sell.

That is why clients wrinkle up their noses like there was a foul smell in the air when I suggest that a direct marketing program for their new product or service could be in order. The usual responses argue that direct mail isn't worth the effort because there are too few responses. I would agree if the client were to send out 25 or 50 letters and expect half of the addressees to respond and half of that to turn into business. That is unrealistic.

But look at some realistic numbers. You send out 500 pieces of mail to 500 prequalified executives, get five responses (1%) and two of those turn out to be customers, in time giving you $100,000 worth of business each. For that $200,000, you spend a couple of hundred dollars for a well-qualified list (forget buying a list if you have a good database of your own), about $100 for stationery, $150 to $200 for postage, and a day or so of someone's time to produce a good letter, print it out, add the right enclosure, stuff the envelopes, apply postage, and get them in the mail. A thousand dollars, tops. For the thousand you get $200,000 back. Is that an acceptable return on investment? Suppose you only got one customer out of the exercise. Would that be acceptable? Those numbers still look pretty good to me.

Are there any hitches? A few. First, you've got to have a good mailing list to work with. Up-to-date names, addresses, and job titles. No matter how many you send out, you want to keep the undeliverables to a minimum. If you buy a list from a broker, make sure you understand what their policy is with respect to guaranteed deliverability. If it's your own list, ensure that you've brought it up to date recently.

Whatever the source, no matter how good the list, the names are still "suspects," not "prospects." Before you can turn prospects into customers, you have to turn those "suspects" into prospects. The way we make that conversion is to get suspects to respond to our letter. Of course the letter has to be well-written and catchy. You have to get readers' interest in the first paragraph or you've lost them. Even with their interest, nothing can happen unless they respond. The best way to get response is to include in your letter a nonthreatening, no-strings-attached *free* offer they can't refuse, something useful but not blatantly promotional. In my own business, I've offered notebooks from seminars I conduct, or reprints of articles about me and my business. You might offer test reports, product comparisons, or copies of technical papers. When recipients request the piece, you send it to them with your compliments. Now you have a prospect, someone who has communicated with you. How you respond further to eventually make that prospect a customer is not much different from handling any other lead. Follow-ups, appointments, demonstrations, closing. Presto, a *customer.*

How many respond is a function of how well you write that letter. If you do a poor job on the mail piece, you'll never get *any* response. If you do a great job, you will be rewarded handsomely. Typically one could expect a 1% or less response on direct mail; the more obvious the sales pitch, the smaller the return. I get from 5% to 10% response on my suspect letters because the recipients have *nothing to lose* by responding.

Summary: Remember, a good list, a good letter, a nonthreatening offer, and follow-up. Try it. What have *you* got to lose?

9

WORKING WITH DISTRIBUTORS—MORE FEET ON THE STREET

I have a surefire way for you to increase revenue, increase profits, decrease overall selling costs, be more responsive to customer needs, and increase customer satisfaction. The way to this bliss is to set up and maintain a distribution network that works for you.

In my experience, distribution is the most neglected element of the marketing mix. The others are keenly followed and managed. Products are the lifeblood of the company. Top management looks at pricing strategies and policies on a daily basis. Everyone is interested in the effects of the promotion program. But distribution is the stepchild. Everyone takes it for granted. In some companies, managing the distributor network is left to the individual territory or regional managers. Corporate management might not even know the names of the distributor firms, no less the names of their executives. If there is a designated manager of distribution, the job often goes to someone with little or no background in distribution, and little support. It doesn't have to be that way. It *shouldn't* be that way.

Distribution moves product where you can't get to or where you never thought it was feasible to go. A well-oiled distribution network will increase revenue from sales that cost you little or nothing to get. Your sales force is free to pursue other business. If your product line lends itself to distribution sales, and most do, you have an opportunity to increase your sales and profits dramatically. If you don't take advantage of it, you are missing out on something special.

66 KNOW WHEN TO USE DISTRIBUTORS

When Compaq came out with its first line of personal computers, the company made an immediate decision to sell through distributors and dealers. The sales force would call on distributors and dealers. All potential customers would be referred to the dealers.

When IBM came out with its first PCs, the company had never sold *anything* to *anyone* at *anytime* except through its own company sales force. Shortly thereafter, it changed its historic policy and set up a distribution and dealer network to rival that of its other PC competitors.

Obviously, there's a time and a place for distribution.

But selling through a distribution network isn't for everyone or every situation. Here are a few of my "rules of thumb":

- The more potential users of your product or service, the more likely it is that you can only reach them with a good distribution network.
- The more standard the product and the less tailoring required, the more viable it is for selling through distribution.
- The less hand-holding and guidance a customer needs to make a selection, the more favorable a distribution network becomes.
- The less after-sales support required, the more reasonable it is to sell through distribution.

Traditional Reluctance to Use Distribution

In a discussion with a client in the electronic components business, I suggested that he could improve his situation if he were to set up a distribution network. For the 20 years or so the company had existed, it had always sold to its OEM customers through its sales force of independent representatives. His attitude was that his products usually required modifications for individual customer applications. Since everything was a "special," it was impractical to set up a distributor inventory of standard products. There really weren't any standard products. I picked up on the word *usually* and asked if we could look through the product line and see whether any individual parts were sold to more than one customer. As it turned out, a considerable number of them either were sold to several different customers or were so close in specifications that they may as well have been.

The client then put together a parts list and began talking to a number of national and regional electronics distributors, finally coming to an agreement with a major regional group. Working with a few experienced people in the distributor organization, they were able to put together a trial inventory. An initial stocking order was received and parts were put on distributor shelves. The distributor sales force was given some rudimentary training in how to sell the product, and off they went. Within a year, *more than 10%* of the client's revenue, in this case about $3 million, came from distributor sales. Not a bad incremental business from a source they had gone out of their way to overlook.

For the most part, these sales were for small-volume requirements, prototypes, and the like. These were applications that the company's sales and marketing people had never chased before, first because they never knew about them and, second, because they were always too small to want to know about. This was the perfect sale for the distributor. Off-the-shelf products with no application engineering involved. Win-win.

Yes, it required a lot of work from the start of the project to completion. Yes, it was a headache looking for the right distributor, particularly after being turned down by some of the majors. But $3 million goes a long way to offset the extra work, and you can buy a lot of aspirins for that kind of money.

Why Do Companies Avoid Distribution?

The best reasons for *not* using distribution are straightforward. Too few customers to make it worthwhile, too technical a sale, too much support required before, during, and after the sale. Many of my clients, those who sell "big-ticket" items with a *high* degree of engineering for each application, can't delegate such a complex sale to distribution. It isn't practical for the distributor to stock the product, thus it isn't practical for them to get involved in the process. All well and good. Trouble is, companies sometimes have other rationalizations that turn out to be excuses, not reasons.

The most common reason is that the sales force doesn't want to give up good commission sales to third parties. That is why I think it is unwise to leave the oversight of distributors to the local sales representative. There is a potential conflict of interest and a potential for friction, "channel conflict" as we call it, which I discuss later in this chapter.

Then, for some reason, companies are unwilling to commit sufficient resources to maintain a distribution network. Distribution costs money. You have to train the distributors' people, stock their shelves, go with them on calls, make some provision for taking back stock that doesn't move. If the company has no experience with working with distributors, or there is no one on the staff with that experience, distribution through third parties isn't going to get the hearing it deserves. Nevertheless, getting to customers through a well-managed, well-located distribution network can be just what is needed to stay competitive.

Summary: The answer as to when to sell through distribution channels is a simple one for me. Whenever you can. "Our product doesn't lend itself to distribution" may not be a valid excuse.

67 USE CAUTION WHEN SELECTING DISTRIBUTORS

Before you can work effectively with distributors, consider what you want to get out of the relationship. You certainly want increased sales coverage; that's a given. You may want them to take the smaller customers off your hands. You hope that the relationship will hold down your overall marketing costs and give you the chance to concentrate on more profitable accounts.

But you then have to find a distributor whose objectives are compatible with yours. Remember, this is a two-way street. You can't expect an independent business that could get along very well without you to accept your terms if those terms run counter to their own. Some distributors will no doubt give you outstanding sales coverage but may not be content to limit their coverage to your throwaways, for example.

Getting Started

Once you're convinced that you need an expanded distribution network, get yourself ready to go out and sign them up. Good luck. Finding good distributors isn't quite as hard as finding the Holy Grail, but it gets closer all the time.

First of all, you need the good ones more than they need you. Generally, they have more business than they know what to do with. Although some distributor arrangements call for exclusivity, most handle competing lines. If that's the case, the burden is on you to convince them that they can benefit from adding another line.

For each territory, you should interview as many distributors as you can. It's a numbers game. The more you talk with, the more likely it is that you will find the right ones. What you want to understand for each of them is:

- What kind of products do they handle? Are they compatible with yours? Do they compete with yours?
- What markets do they normally serve? Are they the same markets you serve?
- How do you feel about their management? Are they competent? Will you be able to get along with them?
- What is their financial condition? Do they have a good credit rating? Are they solvent? Can they be expected to stay solvent for the foreseeable future?

I remember a former employer of mine who spent a great deal of time setting up an international network of distributors. There was very little attention paid to the preceding points. Some were selected for no better reason than they asked to be selected. Others because they went to the same school as a key customer or two or belonged to the same yacht club. The result was a network that was, for the most part, useless. If we hadn't chased down the business ourselves, we would have starved.

68 GET CLOSE TO THEIR MANAGEMENT

In the beginning I thought distributors were just there to take business away from me and make it harder for me to make my numbers. Why would I be happy to see business go to a third party? Of course, this was pure ignorance. I soon learned what distributors could do for me.

Here is what I found in dealing with distributors over the course of a career. Distributors are real people trying to do a good job and make some decent money. Almost without exception, I have observed that the typical distributor management team is professional, hard-working, and dedicated to the success of the company. The best way to get the most out of distributors, dealers, and other third-party resellers is to work *closely* with them.

Good Distribution Starts with Good Principals

Successful relationships between principals and distributors starts with you, the principal. You have to have realistic expectations of what you can get from any single distributor or the entire network. If distribution is new to you, you must convince their management that *your* line can be sold through *their* channels. You have to make a commitment to support them with time and money. You have to make your people available: outside salespeople to call on them and work closely with their sales force, inside salespeople to take their orders and expedite delivery.

Partners, Not Customers

You have to work with their management to establish mutually acceptable, workable goals. Most of all, you have to treat them as *partners.*

At an industry conference dealing with emerging technologies, I was privileged to speak about specific marketing issues of concern to the group. During the discussion period following the talk, the CEO of a highly respected equipment manufacturer made an impassioned point about customer service. He kept using the term,

175

"my customers," in his description of how his company was able to solve some particular problem. It turned out, as he got deeper into his point, that the "customers" he was referring to were his dealers and distributors.

I totally support giving distributors the highest level of service you can offer, as high as you would give to any direct customer. On the other hand, distributors don't buy your products for their own use, they buy to resell them to *their* customers. Without *their* customers, your products are of no use to anyone. Distributors should be *treated* like customers but *approached* like partners. As a partnership you work together for mutual benefit.

Getting the Partnership to Work

Right from the beginning you need a written agreement that you can both live with. I believe sincerely that good relationships don't work any better with a written agreement than with a handshake. Still, having it in writing saves a lot of misunderstandings down the road. But make it simple. I have seen agreements drawn up by lawyers that are so lengthy and so complicated that they literally scared the other party away. One distributor executive commented that if there was that much distrust up front, how could it ever work?

If you can get past that obstacle and get a signed agreement, the first thing I would recommend is that the two of you develop *a joint marketing plan,* outlining how the two of you are going to work together to get the most out of the territory and the relationship.

The agreement should spell out the coverage area you expect for the distributor. Distributors are independent businesses and once they've bought and paid for the product they are free to resell it anywhere they choose. Practically, however, they usually work in a well-defined area. You want to spell this out because you want to minimize conflict from adjacent territories whenever possible.

Go out to dinner with them once in a while. Play golf. Go to a ball game together. The more time you spend with each other, the better the relationship and the better it will be for business.

69 GET YOUR "UNFAIR" SHARE OF DISTRIBUTORS' TIME

Probably the most common cause of this relationship breakdown is the perception by the principal that the agent or distributor isn't doing the job. And, of course, in some cases, that is probably true. Third-party sellers, in spite of their best intentions, take the path of least resistance. They concentrate on the products in their line that are (1) easier to sell, (2) more profitable to sell, and (3) that they know how to sell. As a principal you have a right to assume that the distributor will spend time pushing your product. If distributors don't think you match (1), (2), or (3) above, they will spend less and less time working for you.

In a perfectly objective world, if your product represented 5% or less of the distributor's revenue, you might expect to receive 5% or less of their attention. That would mean, assuming a 40-hour week, you could count on about 2 hours a week of their time. And that might be about as much time as a distributor would think was justified, or fair.

You can't let them get away with that. You don't want a fair share of their time. You want an *unfair* share, a share of their time out of proportion with the amount of business they would expect out of your product.

How do you get an unfair share of their time? You don't get it by management-to-management letters cajoling them to excel. Or sending cartons of technical material, brochures, samples, price lists, testimonials, or just about anything else you think would make it easier for them to sell. There is only one sure way to get their time, and *that is by being there.* The only time you can be absolutely certain that distributors—or independent sales reps, for that matter—are working specifically for you is when you are with them.

A recent consulting assignment for me involved an evaluation of a client's European distribution system. The client felt that the company wasn't getting enough business out of Europe, and that perhaps some changes were in order. "How could it be," I was asked, "that we are the number one supplier in the United States and we do so poorly in Europe? We think some of these distributors aren't doing the job for us." My role was to find out what was wrong with the distribution network, which distributors were at fault, and what to do about it.

Over a two-week period, I set up appointments and had meetings with the top managers at most of the client's major European distributors. Some I met at a major trade show that coincided with the project schedule. The others I visited at their main facilities, which gave me a chance to check out their business practices and their abilities to support their principals' products. I also had a chance to talk to a few other firms that could be replacements, if necessary.

During the 12-hour flight back home, I had plenty of time to reflect on the assignment—what I thought I would find, and what I actually did find. I had been concerned that my client was so small, its message would be "lost in the noise." That wasn't true. The client enjoyed a reputation in Europe for technological excellence. I was afraid that the distributors in place would be inferior companies with little or no status in their home markets. Not true, either. Without exception, the distributors were professional, well-managed, profitable organizations. Without exception, they were knowledgeable about the industry, the market, and the client's product line. All of them handled complementary products that gained them access to my client's prospective customers. They were all sincerely interested in doing as good a job as possible for the principal. The client had selected distributors wisely and had as good a lineup as they could expect.

Then what was wrong? As it turned out, Europe was a much smaller market than the United States. The overall market potential was less than originally thought. Second, there were several Europe-based competitors in there, all of them bigger than my client. Even though we could make a case for superior technology, the competition had more clout in their home markets than the client could muster.

As good and as sincere as the in-place distributors were, this product line represented a small percentage of their overall business. Although there were a few other industry-specific issues, the essential fact was that the distributors didn't see the *value* of spending a lot of time on this product line. As far as they were concerned, my client *was* getting his "fair" share.

In my final report I had several recommendations, but time in front of the customer was the critical issue. The client had an excellent product line that met all conceivable performance requirements, and it was priced fairly and competitively. With adequate exposure, there was little doubt that European market penetration would increase significantly. But for this to happen the client had to convince the distributors that it was to *their* advantage to focus on this line. To do this, the client had to be there. Without being there, making joint calls, and otherwise convincing the distributors that they could make money with these products, they would not put in the effort, no matter how good their intentions.

The squeaky wheel gets the oil. To move from a "fair" to an "unfair" share of the distributor's time, you have to spend *more time* and put *more pressure* on them. Remember, the customers out there are *your* customers, not the distributor's. The responsibility is yours. If you want the distributor to help your business, *you* have to lead the way.

70 PROVIDE ALL THE SUPPORT THEY NEED

Look at your distributor network as an extension of your own direct selling effort. Just as you would take the time to train and support your own sales force, so should you take the same time—or more—to make sure your third-party sellers are well qualified to sell for you.

Remember that the distributor sales force has many different lines to sell, some of them may even compete with your own products. You have to give them a reason to work for you. The guiding principle is that you must make it as easy as possible for them to sell your line.

It's the Little Things That Count

It starts with simple things. Make sure your distributors have enough catalogs on hand to give out to their customers. Keep replenishing them. Don't let them run out. Out of sight, out of mind. If you are not giving the distributor the entire line, then prepare a special distributor catalog that includes only the products it handles. Make sure there's a place on the catalog cover for the distributor to imprint his or her own name and address. To the distributor, that's more important than your corporate signature.

If it's applicable to your product line, provide samples or sample kits that distributors can use to give out to their customers. Whether you charge for these or not depends on their value. If the distributor takes samples from stock, then replace them as quickly as possible.

Joint advertising may be appropriate. This includes sharing the costs, "co-op advertising," so to speak. Similarly, other joint promotions usually are well received, like dealer trade shows or direct mail campaigns. Again, sharing in the costs is important. Remember that the more you participate jointly with your distributors, the more you have obtained their share of mind. The greater the share of mind, the more time they spend on your products.

Training is undoubtedly the most important of all the distributor support functions. Training the distributor sales force in product knowledge and the fine points of selling the product can only improve performance. I recommend that the training be structured but not stiflingly formal. I see the most successful training sessions take place in the early evening after normal working hours have ended. The "teacher" is usually the company's local salesperson, but a technical expert from the home office may be there for backup. From the distributor's side, as many of its salespeople, inside and outside, as possible should attend, as well as responsible managers. In addition to the technical training, these sessions are good times to talk about customer requirements, competitive activity, market trends, and anything else of mutual interest and importance. Again, it's a question of share of mind.

In the long run, there should be enough well-trained people at the distributor so that they can eventually train themselves. Looking forward to that day, ensure that you've given them enough training aids and materials to make it happen.

Communicate with Your Distributors

Another major aspect of distributor support is the communication link between them and your sales office. As you grow and expand your distribution network, it makes sense to add a distributor desk to your order entry section. A dedicated inside sales desk gives the network additional support and focus it needs. Until then, see that the inside people who deal with distributors recognize the importance of servicing those accounts, especially that the nature of distributor sales requires quick response and turnaround.

Financial Issues

On the financial side, distributor support requires careful attention to prices and discount structures. It's hard for me to generalize on what that means because every industry is different and has its own sets of norms. But this I *can* say. One of the touchiest subjects in dealer/principal relations is the discount structure. When is it more economical for a customer to buy directly from the company? Is there a danger that the company will undercut the distributor's prices? Is there a danger that the distributor will undercut the company's prices? Get the financial issues resolved early in the relationship, otherwise they will come back to haunt you.

Customer Issues

Finally, there is the question, which customers belong to which partner? It is usually understood that the principal will take the high-volume customers and leave the low-volume customers to the distributor. That's a good deal for the principal, but the distributor hates it. Then there is the matter of house accounts. Which specific customers are off-limits to the distributor? These are questions that should be decided as early in the relationship as possible. They can be a continuing source of friction.

71 DON'T COMPETE WITH YOUR DEALERS AND DISTRIBUTORS

I don't know anything more disturbing to distributors than to find out that they're competing with their supplier for customer business. Whatever happened to the old partnership theory? Take the following example.

Managers at a major software publisher were convinced that their distributors weren't working hard enough for them. In this company, a handful of key distributors controlled a vast network of local dealers. To overcome this problem, the company put together a telemarketing effort designed to bypass the distributors and put the company in contact with the dealers directly. The telemarketers would call the individual dealers, introduce themselves, and solicit business. For the most part, they were successful. Many of the dealers, who previously had no contact with the principal, were receptive to doing business directly, hoping for better prices, faster delivery, more service.

The distributors were livid—and who could blame them? They were the ones who put the network together. They were the ones who had the burden of managing the dealers. For the principal to come in and bypass the distributors was, in their minds, a breach of faith. Eventually cooler heads prevailed. The company discontinued its telemarketing campaign, but not before receiving assurances from the distributors that they would do a better job of working with the dealers.

The company had a valid case. The company was looking at the numbers and not seeing what they wanted. The distributors had a case, too. Although the company may have had a contractual right to go to the dealers directly, it was an affront that cut the distributors out of the loop and out of the revenue stream.

In technical terms, it is called *channel conflict*. It is when one channel member is unhappy with another. In this case, both parties ended up unhappy with each other. To make it slightly worse, the third member of the channel, the dealers, weren't happy to be caught in the middle and forced to choose.

Channel conflict comes in a variety of sizes and shapes. Some of it may be caused by pricing decisions, territory alignments, or multichannel members vying for the same business. Whatever the cause, it is the principal's responsibility to ensure that conflicts don't crop up, and if they do, to get them resolved.

Not only is there a potential conflict when principal and distributor chase the same customer, but conflict exists when there is more than one channel member involved in the hunt. As we'll see in the next section, there are valid reasons why companies select different types of distribution methods. Most often, the primary reason is that different channels are strongest with different market segments. For instance, an appliance manufacturer may sell through independent retail stores, major department stores, national chains (e.g., Circuit City), or discount warehouse clubs. A computer manufacturer will sell through computer stores, mail order houses, office equipment superstores, or directly to large customers with its own sales force. There may or may not be product differences, and if there are, they may only be cosmetic. It's when the differences are so subtle they disappear that conflicts build up.

72 CHANGE CHANNELS WITH CHANGING TIMES

Channels should change with changing market conditions. Nothing is forever. Just as your customers may change over time, your path to your customers will change also. The first personal computers were sold through high-tech hobby stores or in kit form from hobby catalog companies. As the industry grew, the distribution changed. Early on, the computer retailer was able to provide all the service the customer could want or need. Then came the computer superstore, still providing service but offering a bigger line of products and a lot less of the personal touch. Today you can buy a computer via phone from a catalog store or direct from certain manufacturers. You can buy one from a warehouse club or an office supply superstore. The more you know what you want and the less servicing you need, the more likely it is that you can just pick one up from a mass merchandiser, bring it home, and get right to work.

Example: Magellan Systems

Magellan Systems of San Dimas, California, manufactures Global Positioning System (GPS) receivers. The Global Positioning System, developed by the U.S. Defense Department, provides users with precise position location anywhere in the world at any time. The completed system consists of 24 orbiting satellites. The user turns on his receiver and reads his exact position to within a few meters.

For the many years the system was in development, civilians were allowed to use it at their own risk, and use it they did. In the beginning, only a few satellites were in orbit, thus the system was usable for only brief periods of the day, and then not throughout the entire world. Paralleling most other technological developments, the first receivers were large cumbersome boxes. The market for these receivers was restricted to those who could afford to wait for as long as it took to get a position fix. These turned out to be land surveyors, oceanographers, or academics experimenting with the technology. As the system grew and more satellites were put in orbit, it became more useful for more people.

When Randy Hoffman and Rick Sill founded Magellan in 1987, they knew exactly where they wanted to take their company, both to what market and at what price point. The only thing holding them back was the technology. Specifically, the company saw a huge market for a handheld GPS receiver among hikers, campers, backpackers, and other people who spend their recreation or business hours in remote places. That market, they assumed, wouldn't take off until they could build a receiver to sell in the

$200 price range. There was no way that the technology of the time would allow that.

At the time, the GPS satellite constellation was only available for a maximum of six hours a day. After careful study Hoffman and Sill determined that the best market for them under those conditions was in recreational boating. Boating enthusiasts traditionally spend generously on their hobby. Magellan set the price of its receivers at $3,000 and sold them through marine electronics dealers located in and around yacht harbors and marinas all over the world.

The market took off rapidly. As more and more people bought GPS receivers, the price for individual units plummeted. Technology changed so fast you could hardly catch your breath. Eventually, the selling price of a handheld receiver came within range of Magellan's dream price point; Magellan started to promote itself heavily to the land outdoor market. Today the company is one of the leading suppliers of GPS receivers for this market.

But changing market emphasis demanded changing channels. As new technology helped drive down the selling price, the total market for the company's products expanded exponentially. There are many large, multioutlet marine electronics dealers, but the industry is still mainly local businesses run largely as "mom-and-pop" operations. As Magellan's market grew and changed focus, a different type of distribution system became necessary. Hikers don't go to boating equipment dealers for their gear. They go to the big sporting goods stores, department stores, and mass merchandisers. That's why Magellan now sells through the likes of Wal-Mart and the major outdoor recreation specialist chains.

Changing channels also means changing one's approach. As anyone who has ever worked through the giant retailers will tell you, they can and do exercise all the pressure and clout they can muster. It's as dog-eat-dog a business as you could imagine. With $200 to $300 selling prices, there is little margin available—and no margin for error. You have to move a lot of product at that price to make it a viable business. To handle the task and keep up with channel demands, Magellan has built up a specialized sales force and marketing staff that work the retailers, train their salespeople, and provide all the service and support necessary.

Magellan still has a professional product that it sells to surveyors and mappers through a different network of dealers. It also sells to the aviation market via another set of dealers, and it still has a stake in the boating market, again through different dealers. Whatever it takes.

73 CLEAN OUT THE DEAD WOOD

Bad distributors are worse than no distributors. When distributors do a good job for you, the benefits are obvious. When they don't, not only are there no benefits, but there can be actual harm. By the time you recognize the need for change, you may have lost business that could have been yours. You might also have lost stature with your customers and, if the distributor handles competitive lines, your loss has been the competition's gain.

Under the best of conditions, maintaining a distribution network is expensive. Each individual distributor adds to the cost, whether or not they do the job for you. Sales training, joint sales calls, maintaining inventory, handling returns, sales literature, demonstration kits. The list goes on and on. If a distributor doesn't move the product, all those costs become a major burden that isn't offset by revenue.

Obviously, you are better off making good distributor choices from the very beginning. At times, however, you have to face the fact that all or some of your channel partners just aren't pulling their weight. Then it's time to reevaluate the relationship. If it isn't salvageable, it's time to get out.

In anticipation of this possibility, your agreement with the distributor should have provisions for termination. You should spell out and get agreement on the number of days, weeks, or months for advance notice, and what your obligations are as far as taking back stock, and at what price. These are sticky points if they aren't spelled out carefully in the agreement.

Evaluate Distributor Performance

Seeing the necessity to replace a distributor isn't something that should catch you by surprise. The smart marketer keeps a running evaluation of distributor performance and knows early on what has to be done. Here are a few guidelines you might use:

- How well have distributors exploited the potential in their trading area? Are they getting a reasonable share of the business? How much business have they brought in, either on their own or with your help?
- How well do they demonstrate competence in selling your product? Do they understand the line and know its applications?
- How well do they work with you? Are they cooperative? Do they respect your policies and procedures? Is it easy or hard to deal with them?
- What is the quality of their sales force? Are they aggressive? Passive? Order takers or order chasers?
- Do they really care about you as a supplier?
- Are you getting your "unfair" share of their time?

No one likes to see a relationship like this end. You would just as soon not have to take back their inventory. Negative sales don't look so great on the income statement.

10

MANAGING THE MARKETING TEAM

Good technology can only get you so far. It isn't only about technology. It's also about people. Good people—well motivated, well trained, well managed. If it's a matter of strategy, it all comes down to implementation. Implementation of strategies demands putting all the skills and knowledge together in a concerted effort to do the absolutely very best.

It's about many other things, too. At Spellman High Voltage Electronics in Hauppauge, New York, the company tries to live by a six-letter acronym, SWETTT (pronounced just like the result of hard work). As explained to me by CEO Merrill Skeist, SWETTT is what it takes for them to win and breaks down to:

S—Skill, including smart, well-trained people.

W—Will, the motivation to succeed.

E—Energy and enthusiasm that comes from healthy, hard-working, and deeply committed people.

T—Tools, including money and the things you can buy with it; giving people the tools to do the job.

T—Time and timeliness. Doing what has to be done in a timely manner; meeting commitments to customers and self.

T—Truth. What is the real truth? What is the core customer problem?

In this chapter we deal with the issues that differentiate between a *good* marketing department and a *great* marketing department.

74 ORGANIZING FOR EFFECTIVE MARKETING

Marketing is about products and services, but it will always be about people. Good marketers are good people who know how to deal with other people, whether they are customers, prospects, or those within their own organization. Whatever the organization chart looks like, if you don't fill the blocks with people who know their jobs and do them without constant supervision, the whole system breaks down. The first step is to have the right marketing manager (I'll deal with that in the next section). After that you have to put together a marketing organization that can get the job done.

The Functional Organization

In an era of quality circles, new product development teams, and reengineered organizations, it is both unfashionable and risky to make a case for the functional organization. I accept the risk. I favor the traditional organization, at least the traditional marketing organization, because it has always worked for me. There are specific jobs that have to be done, and you need to fill those jobs with people who can do them. For example, you will participate in trade shows, send out press releases, work with ad agencies. Whether you have a marketing communications manager or not, someone's got to look after those functions. So as long as you have to take care of them, you ought to have the position named and, budget permitting, assigned.

Typical Functions

I never try to spend my clients' money for them. On the contrary, I am a strong advocate of the "get by for less" school of business management. That's the way I run my own business, that's the way most of my clients run theirs. So I list the following positions, not because I think you will sink without hiring someone to perform each function, but because I strongly believe these are functions that must be accounted for. I learned many years ago that you can eliminate a position, but you can never eliminate the *function* performed.

Depending on your approach to the market and the nature of your product line, you should have product managers or market managers, or both. Product managers, or brand managers as they are called in the consumer package goods world, do just that— manage the product line. They are the product champions. They work closely with the design people to keep the product current and respond to customer needs. They may also act as application engineers if appropriate.

Market managers are the industry experts. They know all there is to know about the markets served, and what it takes to get your product or service into those segments, whether you segment by application or by geography. In a multiproduct, multimarket company, the market manager ensures that the market is served with everything the company has to offer.

Then, of course, there is sales management. The sales manager is one of the most vital cogs in the marketing wheel. I refer you to Chapter 11 for a closer look at sales management and sales issues.

I like to think of sales, product, and market management as line functions. They deal with customers and work with internal departments. They have a direct bearing on success or failure. In addition, there are the staff functions. These are the supporting functions that don't necessarily interface with customers but serve important roles in the overall marketing program. None of these functions is necessarily a job unto itself, but as companies grow from start-ups to giants, along the way these roles become separate positions. There may be any number of them, but I narrow it down to three critical disciplines: advertising, public relations, and market research. Someone has to take care of the trade shows, deal with the ad and PR agencies, and conduct or contract for market research.

Vested Interests

There are no "turf wars" in a well-run, well-organized marketing department. It's a team effort. The only payoff is the bottom line.

The payoff comes when the customer buys. Rivalry between sales and marketing is nonproductive and immature. Yes, some competition among serious, hard-working professionals is healthy. As long as it doesn't go too far.

Summary: Instead of competition, there should be a well-orchestrated concerted effort to bring all the skills to bear on the only thing that really counts, getting the customer to sign on the dotted line.

75 HIRE THE RIGHT MARKETING MANAGER

When it comes to executing a successful marketing program, there is no substitute for leadership. You have to have someone in charge of the organization's marketing activities who can get the job done by getting others to get *their* jobs done.

To my way of thinking, the role of the marketing manager is the most difficult to define of the entire business organization. First off, there is ambiguity, because different companies have different names for the job. A short list of titles I've seen used include Vice President for Marketing, Vice President for Sales and Marketing, Vice President for Sales, Marketing Manager, Sales Manager, Vice President for Business Development, Product Manager, and Vice President and General Manager for Sales and Marketing, which is quite a mouthful when someone asks you what you do for a living. Thus the problem with the Marketing Manager title is that it can refer to the big boss or the most junior person in the company. Since most of you believe that titles aren't important anyway (sure), I use Marketing Manager to describe the one who is in overall charge of the marketing function or, even more to the point, the one who gets fired when the company misses its numbers for the year.

In more than 30 years in sales and marketing jobs, I have seen my share of marketing managers. In that time I have drawn some conclusions about what it takes to do that job effectively. When going out to hire someone to fill the position or when you are evaluating someone already filling the position, you might do well to consider some of the following points and issues.

Good Sales Managers Don't Always Make Good Marketing Managers

There's an old saying in business that companies sometimes promote their best salesperson to sales manager, often ending up with a lousy sales manager and losing the services of their best salesperson at the same time. The same applies when thinking that the sales manager can seamlessly take over the top marketing job. You risk losing a good sales manager without getting the marketing manager you had hoped for.

The characteristics required to be successful in these two positions are not necessarily the same. Sales managers focus on *personal selling* and the ability to *motivate* a sales organization. They look to fulfill *short-term* sales goals and execute *tactical* programs. Marketing managers are concerned with immediate sales, too, but are forced to look at *broader* issues. They must understand the importance of planning for the future and must consider a wide range of factors that impact on the profitability of the firm.

Ambiguity in Perceptions

Not only is there an ambiguity in terms of job title, there is a more important ambiguity in terms of what the job is about and how it gets done. Although it is true that in organizations of any reasonable size, the marketing manager has some people to help, the real role of marketing managers is to get things done from people who are not directly responsible to them. When there is no line authority to back up your requests, you have to have the personality and leadership skills to get people to do the right things because they are right, not because someone told them to.

The most common ambiguity is in what is expected. What should be the focus of effort? Short-term sales? Long-range strategic planning? Product and market development? Meeting sales quotas? All of the above? *All of the above.*

Short-Term Sales and Long-Term Market Success

There will always be marketing managers who bear the title but are anything but. These individuals are totally focused on short-term sales. Perhaps it's because they came out of the sales force. Perhaps it's because the CEO is exerting the pressure for quick results. Whatever the reason, sales is everything and precious little marketing ever gets done. Consider Bill, Vice President for Marketing at a midsize manufacturing company. Regardless of the title, Bill is a great salesman and loves to be out in the field talking to his customers, working with his sales staff. Too bad for the company that Bill never looks beyond the next quote or the next order. Sure, the product literature is up-to-date and the advertising, what little there is, is under control. The company even has a home page on the World Wide Web. Of course, Bill has an assistant to take care of all that. Otherwise it would interfere with his sales management role, his first love. In effect, Bill is the de facto sales manager. The other marketing management roles, like planning, new product development, pricing, and so forth, are kicked upstairs to the president, who conveniently enjoys those roles as much as Bill enjoys his. The president has become the de facto marketing manager. You might call it a marriage made in heaven. Well, not exactly. The president has other functions to play, like overseeing the company's operations and finances and holding hands with the board of directors. Pressing marketing issues have slipped to secondary importance. As long as the numbers are OK, Bill will be a hero. When the numbers slip, as they must without any professional marketing in place, Bill is going to be mud. And the president isn't going to come off looking so well either.

Then there is the other side of the coin. There will always be the marketing manager who refuses to acknowledge that he or she has a role to play in sales. When John took over as Vice President for Marketing at an electronic components company, he came with the best credentials, including product and industry experience. On the sales side, the company had a sales manager who reported to John, plus three field regional managers who supervised a network of independent representatives. John decided he was a "big picture" guy and preferred to leave the sales function to the sales manager. Rather then get himself out in the field to meet his key customers or accompany his managers and reps on sales calls, John stayed home and planned for the future. His distance, figurative and literal, from his people gradually turned into resentment, then outright hostility.

Things might have turned out well anyway, but John had the bad luck to preside during a business downturn. Guess who caught the flack for the falloff in sales. Not the sales manager, for he was considered an old pro who could do no wrong. Not the reps or regional managers. They were digging up the applications. It wasn't their fault if the company wasn't responsive enough to come up with winning quotations. No, things were better before John got there. Things would be better if he were to go. Which he did soon enough.

What Should the Marketing Manager Do?

If you are about to hire a marketing manager, you ought to at least be able to tell him or her what's expected. The best way to answer the question "What does a marketing manager do?" is to show you a job description passed on to me many years ago by my old friend Roger Lockwood-Taylor when he was marketing manager for Arma-Brown in England. (See Figure 10.1.)

Arma-Brown was a manufacturing company but you can easily adapt this to service companies or nonprofit organizations as well. Use it with my compliments.

Qualifications

When it comes to qualifications, it's the norm to expect that good candidates for marketing manager are familiar with the company's business and its markets. Second, they should be familiar with the company's technology or, in a nontechnology company, at least know and understand what the company offers the marketplace.

Figure 10.1

SAMPLE JOB DESCRIPTION FOR MARKETING MANAGER

Job Description: MARKETING MANAGER

The Marketing Manager is responsible for developing and implementing marketing policy and plans; promoting and coordinating sales, market research and publicity activities; developing an effective marketing mix for the company's various product and market opportunities; and fostering good customer relations. The following specific duties are included:

1. Planning and putting into effect methods for assessing markets and customer demand.
2. Keeping abreast of professional, technical, and trade developments essential to the selling of the firm's products, and insuring that marketing and sales personnel and outside representatives are well trained and acquire a similar knowledge.
3. Forecasting sales subdivided as appropriate between products and markets. Establishing quotas, based on overall forecasts, for individual sales territories and sales personnel. Reporting to management periodically on sales performance vs. forecast.
4. Preparing, when appropriate or required, expense budgets for marketing, sales, advertising, and other promotional activities and insuring that budgets are not exceeded without prior approval.
5. Directing the activities of marketing and sales personnel to insure maximum contact with customers and market exposure for the company's products.
6. Developing promotional plans including advertising, trade shows, press releases, etc. (and coordinating these activities with other divisions and corporate headquarters for maximum effectiveness).
7. Collaborating with the technical staff in evaluating product specifications from the standpoint of marketability.
8. Selecting, with management approval, marketing and sales personnel and/or outside sales representatives for specific territories.
9. Determining possibilities for new applications and markets for the firm's products.
10. Evaluating customer and market requirements for determining new product specifications, and submitting properly documented justifications for any new product development.
11. Developing pricing policies in support of the company's objectives and strategies for specific product and market requirements.

(continued)

Figure 10.1
(CONTINUED)

12. Maintaining effective channels of distribution, overseeing the selection of distributors, and preparing and implementing the company's distribution policy.
13. Planning and taking part in visits to customers in conjunction with the appropriate sales personnel or alone, if necessary, to make sales presentations, determine customer needs, submit quotations, and follow up to obtain the orders.

In carrying out his/her duties, the Marketing Manager has authority to take any reasonable action necessary, provided such action is consistent with sound business judgment and the established policies of the company and its management. The Marketing Manager may delegate appropriate parts of these duties to subordinates with necessary authority to carry them out but shall retain responsibility for the outcome.

This is a safe practice, and I couldn't argue it any other way if industry and technical knowledge was the only discriminator among the leading candidates for the job. But hiring the right marketing manager is also a matter of chemistry. How well do all the parties get along and how well do they work together? Don't be a slave to industry experience. Product knowledge can be learned very quickly. It's like falling in love. When the right person comes along, you'll know, and background won't count for as much as you think.

76 MEASURE MARKETING PERFORMANCE REGULARLY

When Ed Koch was mayor of New York City, he was noted for how well he worked the crowds. Koch was the consummate politician and his ego was nine yards long. Even so, he still needed that reassurance you could only get from voter enthusiasm. Whenever he was out there with his voters, he would ask, "How am I doin'?" The crowds would respond with cheers and encouragement. Koch would move on, shaking hands, hugging, kissing, his ego stroked once again. Sadly for hizzoner, as with most political figures, time took its toll on voter enthusiasm. Either Koch stopped asking the question or he wasn't listening carefully enough for the answer. Eventually he lost a reelection bid. (Don't feel sad, though. He makes a good living now as a political commentator and radio talk show host.)

So how are you doing, and what are you doing to find out and keep track? I am talking about *keeping score*. Scores count in bridge, baseball, billiards, and business. I am talking about measuring your performance against what you thought you could do, what your competitors are doing, what your customers think of you, and how good you are at serving those customers.

What you thought you could do is a measure of how well you are meeting plan or forecast. You should have procedures in place for comparing actual performance with planned or forecasted performance. You should have procedures in place that examine variances and provide the mechanism for getting back on track.

Keeping track of competitive performance requires an organized effort to gather and evaluate competitive information. Understanding what your customers think of you is an ongoing effort.

Understanding how you stack up with your customers can be a trying task.

Customer Satisfaction Surveys

Many companies periodically conduct customer satisfaction surveys. It's their way of giving the customer a voice, encouraging feedback, and finding out from them what you can do to make their lives better. Surveys range anywhere from the mail-in warranty cards included with new purchases to the guest questionnaires found in every hotel room to structured surveys mailed or phoned to customers soliciting their response to questions of quality, service, performance, and so on.

My problem with customer satisfaction surveys is that what you learn from them is mostly that there is nothing to learn from them. Unless they are done by professional, qualified third parties using carefully designed questionnaires posed to a statistically valid sample of the entire universe of customers, the information gathered is suspect. Customers, God bless them, will tell you what they think you want to hear.

I am as guilty as anyone. On a business trip recently I spent an evening chatting with the bartender in a hotel lounge. He was friendly and efficient and we had a very pleasant conversation in a convivial environment. Somehow or other the discussion got around to how hotel employees were rated. I am a marketing person and these things interest me, you know, especially after a glass or two. He told me that the survey forms in the rooms were an important vehicle for him. Having his name singled out on the form was very helpful. When I checked out the next morning I made sure I handed in the completed form, making particular reference to his skills as a bartender and his congeniality as a representative of the hotel. Within a week I got a letter from the hotel management thanking me for my comments, especially what I said about Ted, the bartender. A day or two after that, Ted telephoned me—you were asked to put your name and phone number on the form—and thanked me. I was touched.

Was Ted a great bartender? Yes, by all means. Would I have filled out the form if the subject hadn't come up the evening before? Probably not. I have always considered such forms snitch sheets, useful only to complain without confronting the guilty party or management face-to-face. I am ashamed to admit that I am much more tuned in to poor service than outstanding service. Outstanding service is transparent. Poor service is painfully visible.

Audit Yourself

Although not mutually exclusive with the customer satisfaction survey, a much more realistic and useful method of evaluating your marketing performance is the *marketing audit*. This was a term coined by Philip Kotler, the renowned marketing scholar from Northwestern University. By the way, if you ever took a marketing course and didn't use a textbook written by Kotler, you were shortchanged.

The marketing audit is a comprehensive look at the way you conduct your marketing affairs, from the marketing mix to internal procedures, and on to customer and third-party sellers. It should be every bit as thorough as a financial audit. Like a financial audit, it should be conducted by an outsider, someone with no special ax to grind, so to speak, and no preconceived ideas about the company and its business. Once an audit has been conducted, subsequent checkups can be performed by inside personnel, but you really want that objectivity the first time around.

Summary: Whatever method you use, it's vital to know how your performance stacks up in the minds of your customers.

77 PUT PROFIT BEFORE VOLUME

Or is it the other way around? That may sound like a facetious question, but it wasn't intended to be. Everyone running a "for profit" business wants to make money. That's what it is all about. From profits come the funds for new products, new plant and equipment, shareholder dividends, and the annual Christmas party. Without volume, however, there's not enough profit to pay for any of them.

It is a conundrum. Like "Which came first, the chicken or the egg?"

My solution to the dilemma: *You* worry about profits. Let your *salespeople* concentrate on volume. Each does what it can do best. Every multiproduct company has variations in profitability among various products. Management understandably wants to see greater emphasis on those that make more money. The way *not* to do it is to leave it up to the sales force. I am all for making the sales force as professional as possible. That includes selling skills, of course, but also growth in business knowledge that will make them more useful as future managers in the company. But giving salespeople, or even sales management, the burden of choosing which items to sell on the basis of individual profitability is bad business.

This issue poses two questions in my mind. First, how does the staff know which products are profitable or not, or which is more profitable than another? Second, and more fundamental to your marketing strategy is, why are you carrying unprofitable products to start with?

Neither question is hypothetical. Time and again I see companies enjoin their sales force to sell profitable products, forget the others. This isn't just a request. Oftentimes, the salespeople get rated on the profitability of their sales. Or their commission plan is structured to steer them toward more profitable products. I think this is patently unfair, because it is almost entirely out of their control. It goes against my grain because it tells salespeople their first priority isn't fitting the customer with the best product for their needs, it's doing what's best for the seller. This is very much like the spifs I mentioned back in Chapter 6. The motivation for offering the product is suspect.

In the perfect world we strive to achieve, all our products are profitable and they are sold in sufficient volume to please all connected to us. There is the special case of new products. One of the principles of successful new product development is that you design products to make an acceptable profit at the price at which it can be sold. To do that is the essence of good marketing. There are times, however, when the margins on new products are below expectations. Is there anyone who seriously thinks that the sales force should be steered away from selling the new product because it doesn't make as much money as the product it replaces? If you didn't want to sell it, why would you bring it out in the first place?

If a product is unprofitable, raise the price, lower the cost, or drop it from the line. Salespeople should be free to sell anything in the line to meet the needs of the customer. And sell as much as they can. For the sales force, the name of the game is *volume*. Move product.

78 TRAINING THE STAFF IS A HIGH-PRIORITY TASK

I never heard anyone say that training wasn't a good thing, so this point shouldn't be too hard for you to accept. Nevertheless, I think it's an issue important enough to stress. My reason is that *marketing* training is not nearly as prevalent as *sales* training. I have no problem with training salespeople, but I am disturbed at how often marketing training is left as an afterthought—or never thought.

Improve Marketing Skills

Your inside marketers must have a sufficient level of product knowledge to do their jobs well, even if that's only to steer the customer toward the right person. You can do this with a series of product familiarization presentations by product managers or engineers that will give them an overview of what the product does, who the customers are, how they use it. Order entry clerks, expediters, and sales correspondents all should have enough familiarity with the product line to engage the customer or prospect in an intelligent conversation. Although this gets more difficult with more technical products and services, it's really the easy part because the level of product knowledge doesn't have to be very deep.

The most important skills, however, are the marketing skills required for people who make day-to-day decisions. The junior staff members are the ones who will move up to managerial positions, ultimately taking over the company's marketing direction. If that's a scary thought, it's either because you don't have the right people or they don't have the necessary skills.

If you don't have the right people, you have bigger problems than I can help with. But the right people can be trained to do a better job and ensure the success of the company. Here are some topics that I think are important enough to merit formal training programs:

- *Planning*—Have you ever seen marketing people sit down to write a marketing plan and not have the vaguest idea how to get started? I have. Not a pretty sight. I've given you a start on planning earlier in this book, in Chapter 3. Planning is a team activity. CEOs or marketing managers can't do it on their own.

- *Pricing*—I would never expect major pricing decisions to be made at a junior level. The more the staff knows about the pricing process, however, the better the information you will have to work with.
- *Forecasting*—Forecasting is an arcane subject and no one likes to do it. Unfortunately, everyone has to. Give your people the skills to make forecasting more meaningful than merely projecting trend lines.
- *Competitive Analysis*—It's a competitive world. Your people should be collecting and analyzing competitive information all the time. Give them the skills to do the best job possible.

Who Does the Training?

Here you have choices. Do it yourself, if you have to. I have seen self-training work well. Different staff members are assigned individual topics, learn all there is to know, and conduct the training for the rest of the group when their turn comes. It can be very effective, or it can be a disaster, depending on the individual effort or the source material. If you want to keep training in-house but aren't too keen on handing it over to the people who need it, you can use a member of the corporate staff or a counterpart from another division. If these options exist in your organization, you would be wise to take advantage of them.

Of course, you may consider bringing in a marketing trainer from the outside. Outside trainers bring a fresh perspective to the company. They've been around, seen how others do it, know what works and doesn't work. They are professional. They know the discipline and how to present it.

On the downside, outside trainers couldn't possibly know your company and its issues as well as you do. They may or may not understand your product line, your technology, or your market. The bad ones will deliver a canned presentation that may have little or no meaning or applicability to your special problems. The good ones will take the time to learn as much about your business as they can. They will interview you and probe for issues and answers. Their recently acquired knowledge about your company will be reflected in the quality of their presentation.

Outside Seminars

You can choose to send your people to public seminars. Most of my daily mail is taken up with announcements of training seminars for every discipline under the sun. The American Management Association has a comprehensive catalog of sales and marketing seminars. There should be one for you. These programs are generally presented by authoritative people experienced in the discipline. From what I know about AMA, for example, the material is under continuous review, so it is always up to date. Downside? First, as public seminars, they are still meant to be all things to all people. Only remarkable coincidence would cause you to get out of the program exactly what you were looking for. Second, they are expensive. Send one person and it is acceptable. Send more than that and you begin to concern yourself with total costs.

Summary: The choice is yours. Each option has its advantages and each has its problems. The important thing is to make sure your people have the skills to do the job correctly.

79 GIVE KEY ACCOUNTS SPECIAL TREATMENT

I grew up in the business world thinking that a customer was a customer. Any business at all was to be greatly appreciated. It has always struck me as bad policy to treat some customers better than others. The size of the order and the annual volume should have no bearing on our commitment. Besides, the big-volume customers probably started out small and grew with us. It is likely that one of our smaller customers could grow into a major, also. Not only is it a question of good business policy to be evenhanded with all of your customers, it's also a question of business ethics and business law. But . . .

The 80-20 Rule

Yes, all customers are equal. In the real world, however, some customers are more equal than others. You can expect that 80% of your business comes from 20% of your customers. This rule, by the way, is attributed to Vilfredo Pareto, an Italian sociologist and economist and a professor of political economy at the University of Lausaunne. Pareto wasn't really talking about marketing and customers when he thought this up; he died in 1923, long before someone articulated the marketing concept. But the analogy seems to apply well enough to marketing and other business situations. Your business probably follows a similar distribution. Whatever the split, it's obvious you have some customers that have become very important to you. Those are the ones you go to extraordinary lengths to serve. Whether it's fair to your other customers or not, you should do it anyway. Life isn't always fair.

Getting the Inside Track

In the product group I worked in at Texas Instruments, we had one customer who was so important we would do anything to make them happy. Their every wish was our command. In the normal course of business, whenever the customer introduced a new model, we worked with them to come up with correct electrical and mechanical specifications of our component to fit the new application. There was considerable testing on both sides, a lot of trial-and-error sampling, and significant time delay between concept and final specifications. As the customer's product line expanded, it became clear to both parties that the application engineering load was getting too heavy for us to continue with these procedures.

The most important thing we did was set up an application engineer in the customer's plant on a full-time basis. Rather than have their engineers call us to go over technical specifications for new components, they would talk directly with our man in their shop. His responsibility was to get all the application data and pass it on to our plant. Back home we set up a product specialist whose sole responsibility was to work with his counterpart at the customer location. Between the two, there was very little the customer could ask for that wasn't taken care of immediately. But should the system ever break down, we still had a field salesperson assigned to the customer who could hold their hands whenever necessary. Which it rarely was.

If it isn't practical or appropriate to assign someone to the customer's facility, you might consider appointing an insider marketer as an account specialist as we did at TI for other important customers.

What else can you do to treat top customers with the deference they deserve? Airlines and hotels deal with their top customers as you would expect. For airlines there are usually several levels of frequent flyers. Those at the top level get the extra perks. If you are hoping for an upgrade, you stand by at the gate while the agent fills seats on a priority basis. Guess what customer is at the top of the priority list. And why not? The company has more to lose by annoying a 100,000-mile-per-year passenger than it does with the occasional vacation traveler. Hotels have their frequent guest programs with upgrades to "executive club" floors, suites, and guaranteed reservations when they are sold out for everyone else.

Department stores announce their upcoming sales in advance to their special customers and may even set aside "private sale" hours just for them. American Express has special promotions for their Gold and Platinum Card holders, usually giving them access to theater or sporting event tickets that may not be available to the general public. At any trade show, see who gets invited to the corporate hospitality suites or the "invitation only" receptions and parties. And who gets invited to sit in the private box at the Super Bowl?

Summary: Special treatment for your best customers is an accepted business practice. It's something you have to live with. Customers expect it.

80 SUPPORT THE SALES FORCE

Imagine yourself as a salesperson sitting in front of a buyer and negotiating the order of your life. The buyer thumbs through your written quotation over and over, drums his fingers on his desk, and finally turns to you and says, "I'd like to do business with you but we have a few problems. Your price is too high. I don't like your delivery schedule. The material has to be blue, not black. If you can give me something on the price, get me the goods a week earlier, paint it to our specs, the order could be yours. But I need to have your answer by tomorrow."

You excuse yourself, rush outside, reach in your pocket for your cellular phone, and dial the product manager back at your home office. Ring. Ring. Ring. Ring. "Hi, this is Jeff. I'm not at my desk right now. Leave a message and I'll call you right back. Or press zero for the operator." Ring. Ring. Ring. Ring. Ring. "Operator, may I help you?" "Yes, this is Mike in Timbuktu. Would you page Jeff for me? It's urgent."

And so it goes, the cellular minutes building up and the probability of success crashing down. After a few more tries and an urgent call to your boss, the National Sales Manager, who happens to be out of town, you finally get Jeff on the line. "Sorry I wasn't available when you called earlier. I was at a meeting on customer service issues," he apologizes. You start your pitch. You know you are asking for the moon but what choice do you have? From Jeff you get the following responses:

On the price, he can't adjust price on his own. The empowerment thing hasn't worked its way down to him yet. He'll get a meeting together with the VP of Marketing and the Sales Manager to make a decision, and let you know. Both of them are out of town so it may take a while to get them together for a conference call.

On the delivery, he'll check into it. Depends on backlog, prior commitments, the operations manager's mood, and so on.

As for the paint job, no problem. We do that for lots of customers. Just a $5,000 one-time setup charge. But because it's a nonstandard, it will take about three weeks longer on the delivery schedule. Will that be OK?

Being the great salesperson you are, or ought to be, you don't take those answers as final. More calls, more delays, more involvement by senior executives. At last you get some answers you think the customer can live with and you get back to him. You may or may not get the order. But you know you've spent the better part of a day on the phone with the home office fighting for your customer (and your bonus) and you wonder if there isn't a better way.

Inside Marketing's Major Role

There are several roles for the inside marketing sales staff, but the most important one is to support the sales force in the field. Support in its most everyday manner means being available to answer questions as they come up. It doesn't necessarily mean being tied to one's desk the entire working day. It does mean working out some means of internal paging or call transfers that get inside and outside together as quickly as possible. If you think my point is that sales force support means giving them everything they want regardless of its impact on the business, you are wrong. My point is that support means being there, empowering people to make decisions so that the person in the field can get back to the customer as quickly as possible with an answer, whatever it is.

Here is a short list of things that would go a long way to giving salespeople in the field that warm and fuzzy feeling that the marketing staff really is determined to give them the support they need:

1. Get quotations out on time. Nothing is more frustrating for someone in the field than to promise a customer a quotation in his or her hands by a certain date and have it not happen. If frustration or embarrassment were the only issues, the salesperson might be able to live with it. The

real downer is that it could mean business lost to your competitor.

2. If you can't answer your salespersons' questions immediately, let them know what you are doing and how long it will take to get them an answer. Remember that the question is being asked for a reason, probably because the customer had a need to know. When you don't respond, you aren't just letting down the salesperson; you are letting down the customer.

3. Get your product managers and inside marketers out in the field making calls with the salespeople as often as possible. There is no better way to learn what salespeople go through on a day-to-day basis than to be with them before, during, and after customer visits.

4. The inside marketer should act as the salesperson's internal advocate. If everything is as it should be, being an advocate for the salesperson and an advocate for the customer are one and the same.

5. If you have to deal directly with the customer, let the salesperson know what is going on as quickly as possible. The salesperson deals with the customer on a daily basis. If left out of the loop on important exchanges of information, salespeople can't do their jobs properly.

6. Believe your salespeople. When they tell you they need a faster delivery or lower price or special modification, accept them at their word. Give them the benefit of the doubt that it is the customer's word, too.

7. Keep the literature coming. Salespeople need data sheets, brochures, testimonial letters, and all the printed matter they can use to do the job. Remember, they don't need this stuff to wallpaper their offices. They use it to keep customers informed.

Summary: Supporting the sales force mean just that—support. Be there for them when you are needed. You are both working for the customer.

81 INSIDE PEOPLE SHOULD KNOW HOW TO SELL

All marketers should know how to sell. True story. As a product manager I had set up a visit to an important customer to introduce a new product we were hoping would be adopted for a line of systems the customer was developing. As a matter of company procedure, the local salesperson had set up the appointment for me, picked me up at the airport the night before our meeting, and dropped me off at my hotel.

Early the next morning the salesman phoned to tell me he had become ill during the night and would not be able to accompany me on the call. I was on my own. He suggested I get a taxi to his house, pick up his car, and get over to the customer.

Fortunately, I had been in field sales before I joined this company as an inside marketer. The long and the short of it was that I was able to make the call, present the product, answer questions, handle the objections, and, yes, even try out a close or two. By the time I left the customer's plant, we were well on our way to getting a major order.

Selling isn't just for the sales force. Situations come up like the one above where it is vital for a *nonselling person* to be familiar with the do's and don'ts of the sales call. At trade shows, most companies staff their booths with a combination of technical staff, marketing types, and outside salespeople. When someone comes into the booth, *everyone* should be able to qualify that person as a prospect or not. Each should be able to do the selling thing— probe for needs, identify problems, propose solutions, and so forth.

All Marketers Should Be Aware of Their Impact on Customers

Sales correspondents and order entry clerks should be trained well enough to recognize customer complaints or expressions of need. I have seen and heard clerks give a customer caller a run-down on price and delivery, then smooth as silk, ask for the order. It wasn't luck. They were trained to do that. I have seen field service engineers work their magic, then get the customer to place an order for an equipment upgrade, something the account representative hadn't been able to do for all the times he tried.

Part of the physician's Hippocratic Oath states "First, do no harm." Even if service engineers and sales correspondents can't be expected to do as well as trained sales individuals, they can be trained at least to do no harm.

As I walked through the inside sales office of a client of mine, I overhead a sales correspondent discussing a delivery schedule with what must have been a customer expediter on the other end of the line. I remember her saying with no apparent reservations something like, "No, we won't be able to ship your order for another three weeks. Yes, I know we'll be five weeks late, but if you think that's bad, some orders are more than eight weeks late with no delivery date in sight!" I guess she thought she was making the customer feel better. Within five minutes the customer was on the line to the client's CEO, who spent the better part of the next hour smoothing ruffled feathers and promising superhuman efforts to get the needed parts to the customer. Within three days, the client company was visited by a team of specialists from the customer looking into everything and demanding answers on the when, where, and how of seeing that these delays would never happen again.

Or how about the service engineer working on a system commenting to the customer words to the effect that he sees these problems all the time. Just about every system the company ships needs this kind of service. Not conducive to a warm feeling, is it? How many customers do you know who would feel really good with that tidbit of information?

You don't want to lie to customers, that's for sure, but people who deal with customers in difficult situations should at least be trained in how to talk to them so as not to exacerbate already serious problems.

82 USE TECHNOLOGY TO IMPROVE PERFORMANCE

Luddite *n.* One who opposes technological change [after Ned Ludd, an English laborer who was supposed to have destroyed weaving machinery around 1779.]

—American Heritage Dictionary

Get with it. The world is round. Technology is here to stay. If you haven't accepted that technology can make your life easier and your marketing efforts more efficient, you are living in the past. You are also giving your competitors an edge they didn't work particularly hard for.

Improved performance means doing a better job at identifying and satisfying customer needs. If it means using up-to-date technology to do that job, you must make the investment. That investment includes the right hardware, software, and communications tools.

Technology is a great equalizer. Although I run a small consulting firm, I know I can compete with bigger firms on the basis of skills and experience. All I need is the opportunity to show my stuff. It is technology that gives me that opportunity. My computer and laser printer ensure that my proposals and reports look as professional as any other. My presentations are as good as those of big firms because we probably use the same software to prepare our slides. I carry a cellular phone and a laptop with me, so that when I'm out of the office, I'm not out of touch. I can send and receive E-mail from anywhere in the world. My fax machine and voice mail will take your messages 24 hours a day, seven days a week. I have an Internet address and if you search hard enough, you can even find me on the World Wide Web. Just a twenty-first-century guy!

I assure you that none of the above facilities give me a competitive edge. But I'd be at a disadvantage if I didn't have any one item. Which is fine with me. I would just as soon compete on my own merits.

Here are my ideas on modern equipment and processes that you should be using just to keep up. I consider this list a bare minimum. Without them you slip way behind.

If you have your own sales force, each person in the field should be equipped with a notebook computer. That computer should have the capability of communicating with the home office via fax or E-mail from anywhere in the world. It should be equipped with the fastest fax/modem hardware you can buy. The computer should be loaded with useful software that will help the salesperson keep track of customers and prospects, schedules, call summaries, to-dos, price, delivery, and inventory data. Naturally it should include word processing and spreadsheets. Without the right software, they might just as well be carrying an anchor with them.

Cellular phones are a normal way to do business today. I still hear about companies that set limits on cellular phone usage. Either they make their sales force buy their own phones and set limits on the amount of reimbursement, or they provide the phones but make the salesperson pay for calls in excess of a preset amount. Admittedly, cellular phone use is expensive, but any company policy that makes someone think twice before making a phone call is misguided. If people are abusing their expense accounts, there are other ways to deal with them besides setting arbitrary limits on phone calls. In this case, trust makes better business sense.

Back at the office, you should make laptop computers available to marketers who travel on company business. The longer the trip and time away from the office, the more important it is to have that capability with them. Ditto for cellular phones, although there isn't much point today in taking a cellular phone overseas. The systems aren't compatible. If they need one, they can rent it when they get there.

As for office equipment, someone, somewhere should have a desktop publishing system for data sheets, announcements, brochures, or whatever else is needed. With an in-house capability you can save some money, but, more important, you can respond faster to changing needs.

Voice mail is a necessary evil in today's business climate. Used correctly it can be a wonderful tool for saving time and keeping important messages straight. Used incorrectly, it can be a nightmare. I have more to say about voice mail in Chapter 12.

Your office should have a decent scanner and a fast laser printer. A color printer can be a real plus. You should have an expanding database of customers and prospects that can be accessed by every key person. You can't practice database marketing without a good database and good software to use it properly.

And you will not be allowed into the next millennium without your own Web page. I was originally skeptical about the World Wide Web as a marketing tool. It looked to me like stacks of advertisements with no assurance that customers would ever see them. My original skepticism has now mellowed to ambivalence. If you can get it to work for you, fine. It isn't that expensive to set up and maintain a page. Incremental business will cover your costs and maybe add a little to the bottom line. Can't hurt.

Summary: If you are not using all the technological tools available, you risk slipping behind the competition. Use whatever it takes to make it easier to find and serve customers. Don't be a Luddite.

11

SUCCESS AND THE SALES FORCE

Military experts will argue that you can't bomb the enemy into total submission. There will always be pockets of resistance that survive the blasts and will fight on. In the final analysis, it takes the infantry and its foot soldiers to take and hold the ground. In business, the infantry is the sales force and the foot soldier is the salesperson.

Marketers pick target markets, identify customer needs, develop products, price them for profit, and promote them effectively. But in the end, whether you sell cars, trucks, computers, miracle drugs, or anything in between, someone has to *sell* the product to a real customer. Everything else is abstraction. *Selling is reality.*

Whether you employ a direct sales force or you go the independent representative route, the effective deployment and management of the sales operation is one of the most important marketing functions any company can deal with.

To succeed, you need:

- Good people.
- Motivated people.
- Well-trained people.

- Adequately compensated people.
- Well-managed people.

Not much different from filling any other management position, admittedly. But if putting products or services in the hands of customers is your measure of success, then sales is the critical juncture between success and failure. The performance of the sales force you deploy is directly related to the results you can expect.

83 HIRE THE BEST SALESPEOPLE YOU CAN FIND

Salespeople are treated differently. Most of the time they are out there in the big wide world with little or no supervision. They are on their own and can do what they please, so you have to count on them to do the best job possible without looking over their shoulder all the time.

In some respects, an ineffective salesperson in a territory is worse than no salesperson at all. At least if there's no one in the territory, you can make some provision to cover it from the home office or assign someone in an adjacent area to watch what's going on. If you have someone you think is doing the job and he or she in fact isn't, you get a double whammy. Not only are you not getting the business but you don't even know *why* you are not getting the business. And for a triple whammy, you may not even *know* you're not getting the business.

That says you have to have good people selling for you. No, not just good people, but the *best* people. The burden is on *you* to make sure you acquire the best, the absolute best people money can buy. Accept no substitutes. Compromising on sales talent for whatever reason—cost, experience, availability, and so forth—puts you on the path to disappointment or even disaster.

What constitutes "best"? Richard Pinsker runs Pinsker and Co., an executive search firm based in Saratoga, California. When Dick sits down with a client prior to doing a search for a sales manager or a field salesperson, they work together to come up with a profile of what the right person should look like. Dick's three most important criteria for hiring sales and marketing people are (1) experience in the client's market, (2) knowledge of the product area, and (3) a track record of accomplishments in the client's field or in a related field. Experience in the client's market and product knowledge make for a faster start-up in the assigned territory. A record of accomplishments—verifiable—indicates to the client that prior success might at least lead to future success.

Of course, most companies hire without the aid of a search firm, but in the case of hiring salespeople, the usual pool of talent is probably the same. It is no coincidence that most of the candidates that fit the right profile work for competitors. The pluses for going this route are obvious. You get everything you think you are looking for. The competitor's salesperson knows the market, the customers, and the product category.

Hiring a competitor's sales rep brings on the hope that she can bring her customers over with her, not an unreasonable thought in these days of relationship marketing and selling. My friends in the investment brokerage business tell me that it is very common for a broker to leave one company for a better deal and take all her accounts with her. This makes sense because the relationship between client and broker is very personal. The client's loyalty and warm feelings are for the salesperson who made money for him, not necessarily for the company she worked for.

So it is with many service businesses. It is natural for your loyalty to focus on the person with whom you are doing business. If you trust a particular auto mechanic, you'll follow him wherever he goes. I know women who may have greater loyalty to their hairdressers than they do to their own spouses. (You can always find a husband, I've been told, but a good hairdresser is worth holding on to.)

Those are services. Products are different. The departing salesman finds that taking customers with him isn't as easy as it looks. Customers are loyal up to a point, but that does not necessarily include shifting suppliers. Unless the competitor is doing a poor job for his customers (remember that one of my earlier recommendations was to avoid underestimating the competition), the chances are very good that the customer is reasonably satisfied. At least he's satisfied enough to be unwilling to make a change based on the salesperson's good looks. Further, if it's an OEM product, one that goes in the customer's equipment, there may be problems of form, fit, and function that preclude a quick changeover. Maybe you get some of your competitor's customers, maybe you don't. For whatever reason, bringing over former customers could be beyond the new salesperson's control, so give him or her the benefit of the doubt.

But the compelling issue that I have seen is the person's ability to fit into a different culture. Even with similar product lines and identical markets, companies are different and they do things differently. The longer people have been on the job, the more they have become part of an existing culture. When they change, it's every bit as much a culture shock as if they were set down on another planet.

One time back in the dark ages of my career, I went to work selling a product that I had competed with for a number of years. Coming over from the market leader, it was difficult for me to put aside years of competitive ardor to handle a product I had always thought was not nearly as good as mine. Of course it turned to be just as good. Not better, but just as good. Before I could convince my customers of that, though, I had to convince myself. That took a while and, even today, I am not sure I ever succeeded in that.

Another point: I had to overcome my trepidations that I would lose credibility with customers who remembered all my past discussions comparing products. It turned out that most customers were polite enough not to remind me of my previous statements. Some even bought from me, eventually. Time has a way of clearing up problems. But looking back on that experience objectively, I have a feeling my employers could have been better off had they hired someone from a different business.

Then there are legal issues involved with bringing on someone from the competition. One of my clients hired a sales manager away from a direct competitor. The first thing he knew, the competitor's corporate attorney was on the phone threatening a lawsuit, accusing the departed individual of taking confidential information, plans, customer lists, and so forth. Nothing ever came of it, but it was a distraction no one needed. There are times when people have signed noncompete agreements with their employers. If the "injured" party wants to enforce the provisions of that agreement, you may be a party to the suit, accused of encouraging the employee to violate his or her contractual obligation. Again, it may never come to anything, but it is a distraction you could well do without.

All in all, hiring someone from a direct competitor is a two-edged sword. You may get the best and the brightest, but you may also be getting yourself an armful of problems. Worst of all, you may not be getting the business you were hoping for.

One of the problems in hiring good salespeople, according to Dick Pinsker, is that the person doing the hiring is usually a sales executive, too. Often executives are looking for a particular type of personality they think will make a good sales rep. When they find that trait, they tend to overlook other aspects of the candidate's background and sometimes forgo reference checks. Not a good practice.

A company I once worked for hired a new salesman that looked like he had everything going for him. He was smart, he was articulate, just the kind of guy you would want representing you. He was also a pretty good salesman and, as a bonus, he was a great golfer, freely giving tips and time to the duffers in the company. Everyone thought this guy was too good to be true. He was.

We put him through our training program and sent him out in the field. Eventually someone got around to checking his references and found out he didn't have the university degree he said he had. Not by a long shot. In this company, lying on a job application was an unforgivable sin, so they fired him. The company lost several months of time, hiring costs, relocation expenses, the pending sales he was working on and who-knows-what-else by hiring someone before they looked into his background. References are important. Check them.

84 USE REPS WHENEVER IT MAKES SENSE

It is *expensive* to hire, train, and maintain a sales force. When you add salespeople to your staff or fill vacancies that previously existed, you have to give them enough time to get familiar with the customers and prospects in their territories, find the applications, start the selling process on its way. It may take as much as six months or even a year before they are making a contribution to your total revenues. In the meantime you've paid their salary, or perhaps a draw against commission, included them in the health insurance program and the pension plan, spent money on training, equipped them with selling tools and product literature, picked up expenses in the field. You may even provide a car or a car allowance. All told, you've incurred a substantial cost that's there whether the salesperson produces or not.

Of course, you rationalize away all the expenditure as an investment. You hope that the salesperson will ultimately succeed and bring in much more business and profits than the expenses associated with keeping him or her in the field.

That's one way to do it. But there is another way. You can have at your disposal trained people with access to your customers and prospects. You do not have to pay salary or benefits. You couldn't care less about out-of-pocket expenses. If they want to take a vacation, they are on their own. In most cases you'll pay them as a percentage of their total sales, figures that you and they have agreed on beforehand.

Depending on your business, you may call them independent representatives, manufacturer's reps, agents, brokers, jobbers, or any number of specific terms in specific industries. Whatever the term, they all work pretty much the same way. For our purposes, I'll just call them reps and be done with it. The major characteristic—and benefit—of using reps is that you don't have to pay them until they produce business for you, and then usually only after you've been paid by the customer.

Whenever possible, you should use reps instead of building up your own sales force. Here's why:

1. Reps have the *contacts.* You engage a rep firm because it handles similar products, and its people call on the customers you are interested in reaching. Unless you hire your own salespeople from your competitors, there is always a time-consuming education process that takes place before they know who to call on and are accepted by the prospects.
2. For just the time and the nominal cost it takes to find and select your reps you can have a national sales force *up and running.* If you go with your own force, the cost of hiring and training is anything but nominal, and the time it takes to find and hire them is anything but short.

3. If you go with a reputable firm (and why wouldn't you?), you can count on a *professional sales effort.* These people are motivated to make money and stay in business, just like you.

4. Because these people are professional and knowledgeable about your industry and markets, and need less training, they are capable of doing an effective job for you months before a direct hire can learn the product line and know where the customers are. Remember, all the time your direct hire is learning her craft, you have to give her some income to sustain her, not to mention expenses and benefits.

5. Even if you would prefer to go the direct employee route, there may be some territories with such low potential they wouldn't justify the fixed costs of keeping your own salespeople there. You can tack the territory on to that of your closest direct salesperson or you can ignore it completely. Either way, you're not going to see much revenue. But for reps covering the area for several principals, the incremental business they get by handling your line may be all that they need to justify taking you on. For you, anything they bring in is like found money.

There will always be those who discount the benefits of going the rep route. Perhaps the prejudice is based on experience. Maybe the nature of the product, they think, precludes effective selling by anyone other than highly trained and skilled sales engineers. For whatever reason, there is no shortage of myths regarding the supposed disadvantages of using independent reps:

Myth 1—Reps are just order takers. They won't put in the effort for business that requires extra time and work. They won't take the trouble to learn the product line. If it gets complicated, they'll leave it for the factory people.

Comment: Most reps I've met are eager to learn the product line. But you have to take the time to train them.

Myth 2—Reps will take on your line but they will only work hard on their most profitable items. Reps love to add principals to the "line card." They'll work the new product line for a while until they meet their first resistance, then they'll go back to their favorites. You can't become their favorite if they won't put in the time for you.

Comment: If you want their time, you have to put in time with them as well. The only way you can get their time for sure is by being there.

Myth 3—You do all the work and the rep gets the commission. You find the customer. You work the application. You make the presentation. You close the sale. All the rep does is pick you up at the airport, sit quietly while you go through your paces, and get you back to the airport. Most of the time he'll expect you to pay for the lunch. As soon as you ship the order, he's on the phone looking for his commission check.

Comment: It's training once again, and building up skills to the point where the rep can act on your behalf without your assistance.

Myth 4—Reps won't help with nonselling functions, for example, forecasting, research, and so on. Getting field input for a short-term forecast is almost impossible with reps. Though they won't tell you in so many words, they'll maintain that their job is to sell, not to contribute to your paperwork blizzard. More often than not, they'll just ignore you. But how can you make a realistic forecast when they won't tell you how much business they expect to bring in over the next year?

Comment: There is some validity with this point. But remember that reps are not your employees, and you have no right to take up so much of their time with nonselling functions that you impact on their selling time. Which isn't too bad a philosophy for a direct sales force, either. Their time is no less valuable.

Myth 5—Reps are just interested in making as much money in as short a time as possible, so they don't work on long-term projects. They always take the path of least resistance.

Comment: Not the reps I know. Like all good salespeople, they balance their planning with short-term as well as long-term prospects. Your direct sales force should do the same.

Myth 6—Reps won't look for new business opportunities. Why explore for new business when you're getting good results from existing customers? They will usually leave that kind of effort to the principal. Once a new sales opportunity is identified, they'll go after it, but not before.

Comment: Good marketing, among other things, is about identifying opportunities and developing the strategies and tactics to bring in that business. If your marketers and sales managers are doing their jobs, the rep will be scrambling for all the new business you can identify.

Myth 7—Reps can't sell complex products.

Comment: Baloney! There are reps out there selling every conceivable product line. True, for some reps, shoelaces are a technical sell. But there are others with advanced degrees in the most esoteric sciences selling complex systems and doing every bit as well as their direct counterparts, sometimes even better. They are out there. Every industry has them. All you have to do is find them.

Reps have to be selected and managed, just like they were your own sales force. If you don't take the trouble to do that, you won't have a good experience. Since it's *your* business and *your* customers, a bad experience is not only *your* fault, but totally *your* responsibility. Later in this chapter I'll discuss managing the reps and describe one company's successful efforts to get the most from independents.

85 MAKE SURE YOUR SALESPEOPLE ARE PRODUCT EXPERTS

Would you buy a car from a salesperson who couldn't tell you how to unlatch the hood or didn't know anything about the car's features? Would you buy a clothes dryer from someone who couldn't explain how to turn it on or clean the lint filter? Unless you are a very rare kind of consumer, chances are you want some explanation of the details before you sign on the dotted line. Customers, whether consumers or industrial buyers, expect salespeople to know what they are talking about. It isn't enough to know price and delivery. The customer can get that with a phone call.

Good salespeople aren't good just because they are smooth talkers. The good ones have something to sell and know how to sell it. More and more, with today's fast-paced technological changes, buyers want explanations to justify their purchase decisions. The salesperson who can explain the product's features and benefits on the same plane as the customer's technical expertise is the one who will be the most successful. There is no substitute for product knowledge.

I was once hired to sell a line of marine radars. One of our prime prospects was the tanker department of a major oil company. Eager to get going, I made an appointment to go see the company's engineer in charge of shipboard electronic equipment who, it turned out to be, was a legend in the industry for being somewhat of a curmudgeon.

As I unsuspectingly sat down across the conference room table he began to fire a series of questions at me that made us both painfully aware that I didn't know enough about my product to make a sale with this guy. He had to be convinced that our radar was well designed and reliable enough to be put on his company's ships, and I wasn't doing a very good job convincing him. After a half hour or so of this kind of questioning, I was about as limp as a wet dishrag. When the interview was over, we stood and shook hands and I read in his face the smug satisfaction of having had me for lunch. His look said all too clearly, "Don't come back here until you know what you are talking about." Was I embarrassed? Humiliated would be a better word to describe how I felt.

I would like to tell you that I went back home and learned what I should have known to start with; then returned to this prospect and dazzled him with my expertise, winning a huge order for my company. Alas, that was not the case. Yes, I became very knowledgeable about marine radar and associated equipment very quickly. But with that particular customer, I would remain dead meat for a long time. A painful but valuable lesson.

Management guru Peter Drucker is quoted as saying, "Customers don't buy technology. They buy what technology can do for them." Drucker is one of my business heroes. Even though I've never met him, I think of him as a mentor. Still, I'm not entirely comfortable with this statement. Yes, customers are more interested in what a product does for them than how it does it. But it's a trap to think that customers aren't interested in the technology, especially if the technology or the design has a serious bearing on their confidence that your product can do an adequate and reliable job. My oil company engineer wanted to know all about our design, not because he was nosey but because he wanted to be sure our supposedly new equipment used state-of-the-art techniques that improved on industry reliability and seaworthiness. If it didn't, there was no point in considering it. If the salesperson couldn't convince him from the start that it might meet his needs for long-term performance, there would be no point in going on.

Remember the old-style neighborhood hardware store? When you walked in searching for a solution to a problem that you were convinced was unique, the wizened old proprietor would understand exactly what you needed, then miraculously put his hands on the exact part in a store that looked like semiorganized chaos. Product knowledge was his strong suit. Not only did he understand your application but he also knew *the exact product* that would fix your problem.

The Home Depot chain of warehouse stores is as far removed from the neighborhood hardware store as you can get. But is it? Sure, their major attraction is the size of the operation and the number of items they stock. Chances are they have a solution for any problem. But that isn't their *only* attraction. Like all the warehouse stores that rely on customers serving themselves, Home Depot lets you wander on your own to find what you need. But if you have a question, there is that knowledgeable employee working the aisle in each department who will know just what you are looking for and lead you to it, explain how to use it, and maybe even show you a few alternative solutions. Once, I even had them admit they didn't carry what I needed, but they were quick to recommend another store where I could get it. Technically, they are not salespeople, but if they don't tell me what I need or how to use it, I probably won't buy anything.

Summary: There is no substitute for product knowledge. Customers expect it. Your salespeople have to exhibit it. *No one* wants to talk to salespeople who don't understand the product they are trying to sell.

86 MAKE SURE YOUR SALESPEOPLE KNOW HOW TO SELL

If this isn't a non sequitur, what is? After all, isn't selling what salespeople are supposed to do? Well, yes and no. In some companies, the sales force is hired, pumped full of product knowledge, then sent out into the world to call on customers, establish relationships, and bring in orders. Trouble is, many so-called salespeople don't know how to sell.

Shortly after starting my first sales job, I was sent out for three weeks of product training at the home office. When I returned, I was assigned for a few weeks working with the established salespeople, sitting in quietly on calls while they went through their techniques. Over a quick fast-food lunch one day, my counterpart explained that we weren't really salespeople; our roles were to act as "consultants" or application engineers for our customers. Solve the technical problems, he explained, and the orders will follow right behind. I quickly learned what *nonsense* that was. My boss was not a touchy feely guy. He wanted results. Orders. They could only come from effective selling. Yes, that dirty word, *selling*.

All the product knowledge in the world isn't going to help if the salesperson doesn't understand and practice the art of selling. And art is what it is. In that first sales job, my employer (I was working for a division of Honeywell at the time) put the entire corporation's sales force through a series of training sessions called the Science of Selling. It was a great program and taught me all I ever wanted to know about the selling process. Overcoming objections. Presentation. Closing. Team selling. The whole thing. In the sense of how it was—and is—taught, selling *is* a science. There are tried and true techniques and procedures that must be followed. Certain ways to present the product in its best light. Certain ways to handle objections. Certain ways to ask for the order.

But in how it is practiced, it will always remain an art for me. For those who sell for a living, some of us are Picassos. Some of us paint bullfighters on velvet. Some of us can barely draw stick figures on cocktail napkins. Except for the Picassos among us, we can all use a little boost when it comes to improving our selling skills.

Product Knowledge Isn't Enough

Product knowledge goes a long way. I doubt if any customer feels good knowing more about the product than the salesperson. But product knowledge isn't enough. A good salesperson knows how to sell. The great ones know it instinctively. The good ones learn it either from training or trial and error. If your sales force lacks selling skills, boost them up before it's too late. You can jump-start the process by engaging an outside sales training firm. There are lots of them around. The professional organization I belong to, the Institute of Management Consultants, keeps track of its members' skills in its directory. There are many sales trainers listed in the directory of the National Speakers Association. Or just find one by asking some of your counterparts in other companies you do business with.

87 MOTIVATION AND THE SALES FORCE

What is it about salespeople that produces so many books, articles, and training seminars that deal with motivation? Is there something in the genes of sales professionals that says the only way they will move is if you bait a hook with incentives? Do you have to get them charged up with get-out-there-and-win-this-one-for-the-Gipper pep talks for you to be competitive?

I've never seen a Chief Financial Officer fire up the accounting clerks to produce bigger and better spreadsheets or have the paychecks ready a day or two early. I've never seen a Director of Human Resources push the staff to increase the number of hires or fires per day. The bottom line is that, for most employees, the best incentive is they get to keep their jobs, and maybe get a pay raise once in a while. True, many companies dispense bonuses to employees based on the company's performance over a particular time period. This policy recognizes that each person in an organization, from management to the night janitor, has made some contribution to the success of the company and each should share somehow in the rewards from that success.

But salespeople are treated differently. Without a proper incentive system, some think, they won't do their jobs well enough, they might not make the extra call, not prepare their presentation properly, forget to close, take off a day and go to the beach.

Whether you use independent reps, your own direct sales force, or a combination of the two, you would like everyone who sells for your company to *want* to do the best job he or she can do for you. You want your salespeople to go at their jobs with enthusiasm as well as skill, and to perform superbly. To realize this requires putting together a team of people who are motivated for success. If they aren't motivated, they won't succeed. If they aren't motivated, you'd better see that they get that way—quick.

Since most people work for money, enhancing their motivation with the chance to make more money by selling more has become an ingrained part of our business culture. That wasn't always the case. When I started out in industry with my first job as a field sales engineer (a clever euphemism for salesman), our company's salespeople were all on straight salary. I would like to think that I possessed enough self-motivation to do the best job I knew how to do. As long as our performance reviews came on a regular basis and they resulted in decent pay raises we stayed happy. The best performers got the biggest raises. The lesser performers got smaller raises, or none at all. Which, of course, was an invitation to leave. We must have been doing something right because our company was far and away the market leader.

But times change. Most salespeople today are on some type of incentive compensation. The more they sell, the more they make.

The burden is on management to come up with an incentive package that makes the salespeople salivate while keeping the company solvent. No mean feat.

The Right Compensation Plan

Jim Carey heads up Carey Associates, Inc., a compensation consulting firm in Burlingame, California. I asked Jim to share with me his thoughts on compensating a typical sales force. The most common mistake managers make, he told me, was to consider the *financial* aspects of the plan before or instead of the *motivational* aspects. It's too bad that the same managers who have the marketing savvy to know that you focus on customer needs are the ones who install sales compensation plans that first take into account their *costs,* then (if ever) consider the *needs* of the sales force. Their primary consideration is how much the package is going to cost the company rather than how well it will motivate the sales force to greater performance. Sure, financial considerations are important; you have an obligation to your shareholders. But the most important consideration is what it will take to put together a team of stars.

Assuming you can get over that hurdle, you can get down to specifics. From Carey's perspective, most sales organizations will have some people who are strongly motivated to achieve, regardless of their compensation. They have so much pride in themselves and their abilities to achieve, they will set records regardless of the details of any compensation package. These are the type of people you look for and hope you get when building a sales team. Unfortunately, you can't find enough of them to staff the entire sales force. You round out your staff, whether you do it consciously or otherwise, with the middle-of-the-road people. These people are good, you hope, but they fall short of star status.

A good compensation package recognizes both classes of salespeople. When putting together the company's pay plan, you try to develop a package that not only satisfies your high achievers but also brings out, as Jim puts it, the strongest achievement-seeking traits in others, those for whom the drive to achieve is not a dominant part of their personality. You want to pay enough, but you want the pay package volatile enough to be interesting.

One of Jim's clients had acquired another company, which brought with it a sales force that had always been on straight salary, some of them for as long as 15 or 20 years. Jim worried that they would lose a good number of these people when they put them on the higher risk compensation program of the parent company. The company decided to build a "bridge" for the new people, offering them additional security by essentially guaranteeing at least as much income for the first six months as they had in the old company. That way they wouldn't get hurt financially until they could get used to the new scheme, which consisted of base salary plus incentives. Surprisingly, after a year on the new incentive program, some of the old straight-salary types came to the VP of Sales asking if the company would reduce the salary part of their income and get a greater percentage of their compensation from the incentives. The incentive part of the package was so attractive for them that they were willing to put more of their pay at risk to make more money.

Is That All It Takes?

Salespeople are a funny lot. In my experience it takes more than holding a carrot out in front of them to get them to pull the cart. Besides, we are talking about professionals here, real people, not mules. If you really want to ensure that the sales force is motivated to excel, look at some of the *nonfinancial* ways to get them moving and keep them moving.

First, salespeople will accept goals and quotas but they have to be *realistic* and *achievable*. Even if no money were involved, good salespeople will be demotivated if they are assigned quotas for their territory that they know they have scant chance of attaining. I could never understand how some companies can assign territory quotas without getting input and full, enthusiastic agreement from the reps themselves.

Second, salespeople need *support* from their managers and from the inside staff. Things like quick turnaround on quotations, competitive pricing, going out of one's way for a customer when the salesperson says it's the only way to get the business, management support in major sales projects, including participation on presentations and follow-up calls. Whatever it takes. When sales reps know they have the backup they need, they can be totally motivated. Without it, all the money incentive in the world isn't going to have much of an effect.

Third, salespeople are motivated when they know they're part of a company that is *committed* to going somewhere big. I never saw a successful salesperson who didn't believe in his or her product. You can't believe in your product unless your company is committed to making a product as good as can be.

88 DEMOTIVATION AND THE SALES FORCE

After all the effort you put into training your sales force and offering them what you and they both agree is a great pay package and a chance to make a lot of money, why would you turn around and do anything that would pop the bubble? Yet companies do that all the time, most of the time unwillingly. I say "most of the time" because I have heard of examples where management thinks that the sales force is a major expense and would like nothing better than to reduce the cost of operations by getting rid of it. That is the exception, but it does happen.

Most managements aren't so devious. Naive, perhaps, but rarely devious. Let's look at this example. Harry is hired to fill a sales representative position for a company selling mainframe software to major corporations like insurance companies, banks, defense contractors, food processors, and so forth. Harry gets the requisite product training, then gets out in the field calling on all his prospective customers. In a short period of time, it becomes obvious that Harry is a winner. Sales are way up, far exceeding expectations, not to mention Harry's quota, which he has left in the dust. In addition to his base salary, Harry receives a very substantial check regularly, reflecting his bonus for doing so well. Harry gets himself a new car and a fancy watch, remodels his house, and starts to put some money away for his children's education. Life is sweet.

One day Harry's regional manager invites him to lunch and introduces him to Fred, who will be taking over part of Harry's territory. It's a good deal for him, Harry is told. With a smaller territory, Harry can spend more time with his major customers and can get to some of the accounts he hasn't had time to call on. "Oh, by the way, Harry, we'll keep your sales quota the same for the time being, just to see how things go," says his boss. Harry turns over his notes and records for the customers Fred will now be handling. They all shake hands and get back to work.

As soon as Harry gets home that night, he starts to brush up his resume. Harry is down in the dumps. The word *screwed* keeps racing through his mind. Over the next few weeks he spends an increasing part of his time networking with his business contacts, checking out opportunities, going on an interview or two. Harry has done well enough that inertia keeps the territory producing even while his mind has been distracted from company business to personal business.

For the company, this was a no-brainer decision. Although Harry's managers are delighted with his work, they look at his results and figure that there must be a lot of business out there that even Harry can't get to. If the company can do so well with one person in this area, think how well it can do with two or even three.

Harry sees it differently. He has built up his territory for the company so that he is now making good money and living a good life. He's worked hard and he deserves what he gets. From his point of view, the company thinks he's making too much money. It's time to bring him down a peg.

Who is right? It doesn't matter. In this case, *perception is reality.* All that matters is that Harry has lost his motivation to succeed. The company, he believes, has let him down. So be it. It's time to move on. This is a classic case of a failure in sales management. No one ever explained to Harry what was going on or asked him his opinion on how to increase business in the territory. No wonder he's out looking for another job. When he leaves, the company will be no better off than before, perhaps even worse. Fred is still unproven. If he turns out to be a loser, not only will the company not increase its business, it will regress. Some management move.

Here's another scenario. Phil has been given a quota for the year of $2 million in sales. He makes his quota to spare and brings home a tidy sum of money for his efforts. During the planning cycle, he sits down with his manager and she tells him that he's done a fine job but she thinks he can still do better. Fair enough, thinks Phil. For the upcoming year his quota is boosted up to $2,500,000, a 25% increase. Foul, thinks Phil. The way he does his mental arithmetic, it looks like it will take a small miracle for him to hit that target and make as much money next year as he did this. Unfortunately, the mortgage and car payments won't go down proportionally. Phil thinks the company is playing games with his income. He turns off selling and turns on job hunting.

Who wins? Maybe Phil can win if he lands a better job. But the company *never* wins. Eventually, they substitute an unknown newcomer for a known high achiever. They lose months of productivity while they search for someone new and train her to a level where she can be trusted with the territory on her own. The company has shot itself in the foot.

Setting Quotas

When the going gets tough, some managers seem to think the best way to meet their sales targets is to put more pressure on the sales force. It's true, of course, that salespeople may get complacent, that maybe they get a little too fat and smug with generous commissions and bonuses. It doesn't hurt to once in a while take a good look at the commission structure or the incentive package or the sales targets and quotas. But chances are that declining sales are more a *marketing* problem than a *sales* issue. If you think you can improve sales performance by raising the bar, so to speak, look again. If your salespeople aren't performing up to your expectations, what makes you think higher quotas will make any difference?

Whether you raise quotas or reduce the size of the territory, it has the same effect. By micromanaging, you have disregarded the *motivational benefits* of an acceptable compensation plan and *demotivated* a good salesperson. And you call yourself a manager!

Money, or lack of it, isn't the only demotivator. Just as certain nonfinancial issues can give your salespeople a sense of belonging, purpose, and pride in the organization, their absence can be demoralizing. This is what I consider a short list of things that turn off a salesperson:

1. Lack of support from the inside staff. Inside sales and marketing people who respond slowly or not at all to field sales requests are embarrassing to a salesperson who is waiting for an answer to give a customer, for example.
2. Late delivery of customer orders. No salesperson likes to be an expediter. If shipments are late, that puts the company and him in a bad light with his customer. Dissatisfied customers consider competitive offers on the next buy.
3. Product quality problems. See above.
4. Overzealous control of expenses. No one should tolerate abuse of expense accounts. But sometimes you've got to give people a little slack. Salespeople are no different from other employees. They are uncomfortable when their judgment is questioned.
5. Ignoring the salesperson's recommendations. Joe Salesman may not know all there is to know about the total marketplace, but no one knows his territory or his customers better. When he recommends actions or new procedures that never get adopted, he's going to question whether anyone cares what he says or does.
6. Revolving door management. A salesperson I know complained to me that he had five different bosses in less than two years. If management takes so little care in selecting its leaders, what does that tell the salesperson about their commitment to excellence?

89 SELLING IS A TEAM SPORT

The salesperson going it alone, from prospecting to closing, is our traditional take on the selling process. After all, you've gone through great pains to hire people to work well on their own. If they have all the selling skills and all the needed product knowledge, the least you can expect is they go out on their own and bring in the orders. Unfortunately, this concept is more romantic than it is realistic.

In many cases, the "lone wolf" approach isn't in the best interests of the company or the customer. No matter how good they are, there are times when salespeople need support from others to get the big sale. Solution? T-E-A-M-W-O-R-K. Let's use it in a sentence. Effective selling calls for teamwork. The salesperson can't always do it alone. It is up to *sales management* to see that he doesn't have to.

Normal selling is a team effort. The salesperson leads the charge. Behind him is his immediate supervisor, his regional manager, perhaps. Behind them is the inside sales and marketing staff who get the best price and delivery, ensure that all the technical details have been worked out, that the product or service offered meets customer requirements and regulatory standards, and get the quote out on time.

Most day-to-day sales are handled smoothly as each member of the team does his or her job without any formal or conscious recognition that a team is involved. On the other hand, there not only are more complicated situations that require the team effort but also the teamwork is recognized and formalized. Three specific situations occur from time to time that you should be ready for.

Selling Across Territory Boundaries

The most common instance calling for a more structured team selling approach is when the buying decision or specification is in one territory and the actual purchase order is issued in another. In situations like this, salespeople have to work together to ensure that they present a common front to each customer facility, that there is no ambiguity in what they tell the customer with respect to pricing, terms and conditions, and the technical aspects of the sale. These cases often call for one of the salespeople involved to take the lead and to coordinate the process that, in some cases, can be international in scope.

Selling Across Product Lines

There are times when a major purchase calls for products and services from more than one division in the company. To further complicate the matter, the customer might be buying for more than one location, and some of the customer locations can be in overseas markets. Coordination in determining customer needs, prices for all or some of the products, compatible delivery schedules, and all the rest require a more structured team.

The Big Sale

"Team selling" to me has always implied the big project. "Big" is a subjective term and you can define it anyway you want, but to me any slice of business that could make or break the company is big. Any business that represents a significant percentage of your annual volume is big. In these cases you put together the team that leaves nothing to chance. Here is a typical breakdown of a team shooting for a major sale. The salesperson in charge of the account holds the customer's hand and acts as his advocate. The regional manager or the general sales manager lends backup support and interfaces more closely with senior management. The product manager coordinates the inside effort. If it is a technical product, engineering provides a representative to ensure that every one of the customer's technical questions or reservations are handled correctly. The CFO gets involved because there are financial terms and conditions that have to be worked out. The Director of Operations is involved because production scheduling is crucial to meeting the customer's delivery requirements. Finally, the CEO is part of the team because you can bet that the customer's CEO or senior management is also involved, by definition. You can see by now that this is no job for Willy Loman.

Team, Not Committee

One final thought. In cases like these, it's important to draw a distinction between team and committee. This isn't committee work. We are not looking for consensus. We are looking for *action with accountability*. Someone has to be in charge and responsible for the success or failure of the project.

90 "YOU MAY FIRE WHEN READY, GRIDLEY"

The flip side of successful hiring is successful firing. Letting people go is never easy. It is even more difficult when you have to tell people their performance doesn't measure up and they have to go. I am talking about letting someone go for cause, poor performance or otherwise, not about layoffs or downsizing or restructuring or any other euphemism for cutting costs or boosting profits. Apart from those sometimes necessary, albeit controversial actions, most of us agree that firing people should be a last resort. It is an action taken only because nothing else has worked to turn around a salesperson's performance.

From time to time I read in management-oriented magazines about some dynamic, hard-charging sales manager who puts intense pressure on his people to perform, then chops off the bottom 10% or so because they didn't meet his standards. It seems to work, I guess. Sales volume increases, but at what price? The sales manager gets to be a hero with the business press and the public, but the staff—or at least a significant part of it—bulks up on tranquilizers and ulcer treatments. The company then incurs the ongoing costs of replacing the removed salespeople and the cycle begins all over again. Meanwhile, those who survive the first cut begin the race all over again as a new crop of eager talent comes aboard nipping at their heels.

I don't have a lot of respect for managers who use the threat of firing to keep people on their toes, then carry through on their threats all too often. For one thing, it doesn't say much for a manager's leadership skills. Anyone can manage a star performer. Getting the most from average, even mediocre performers is the true test of sales management skills. For another, it's expensive to train people and put them in the field or on the retail floor, and it is more expensive to go through the process all over again when replacements are required. Finally, we are dealing with people, and I don't think it is appropriate to treat a person's livelihood casually. Most people work for the money. Interrupt the flow and the effect can be profound, even disastrous, on them and their families.

A Distasteful Task

And yet, what are you supposed to do if all the counseling and all the guidance and all the cajoling and all the threats don't change the fact that a certain person whose job is to sell does the job poorly? Take the case of Charlie. Charlie is a problem. Has been since he was hired two years ago. Although he's a likable guy, he's a long way from star performer or salesperson of the year. On the contrary. His almost never meets his quota. When you talk to him he'll tell you that his territory is too small, his quota is unrealistically high, the product line is wrong for his particular customers, or maybe that he's had some problems at home last month—but next month will be better. But if you look at the numbers month after month, study his call reports, make calls with him and watch how he relates to the customers, observe his presentation techniques and the way he manages his territory, you can't help coming to the conclusion that Charlie doesn't come up to standard—and never will. A change is necessary.

Of course, you agonize over it for a while. After all, you hired him. Firing an employee is probably the most distasteful task ever faced by a manager. If letting people go doesn't produce some agony for an executive, then that is not the kind of person I want to know.

Don't agonize for too long, however. It will waste too much time and won't do the misfit much good. The longer you retain ineffective salespeople, the worse off the company will be. Supervising their activities just to see that nothing slips through the cracks or cleaning up after them will take an inordinate amount of time, time that could be better spent backing up the rest of the sales force on the really big opportunities. Customers will feel better about your company when you make the change. Today's customer is sophisticated enough to recognize a poor sales performer. The rest of your sales force will feel better because they know old Charlie wasn't pulling his weight, and if he could get by without it, why should they work so hard?

Believe it or not, the longer you take to move on this, the worse off the employee will be. Our friend Charlie knows pretty much how he's doing. I have a theory that says no one knows better how poorly someone is performing than the poor performer himself. It may lessen your agony to know that he's so sure he's eventually going to get canned, he's already out looking for another job. If he isn't, he's not only incompetent, he's a fool. All the more reason to get rid of him. As a corollary to this theory, I believe that the poor performer is usually aware of his shortcomings and the growing doubts of his manager. He knows he's in trouble. The final fall of the ax comes as more of a relief than a surprise.

Want to avoid all this? Then take special pains to make sure you are hiring the right people to begin with.

91 MANAGE THE SALES FORCE EFFECTIVELY

During a discussion with a prospective client in the electronic component business, we got to talking about his field sales problems. The company used independent representatives throughout the country, directed by marketing management in the home office. In this company, sales management was the responsibility of the marketing director.

When I asked the company president how he felt about the current field organization, he offered that, like most such forces, some reps were very good, some not so good, and some were horrible.

Then he said a few things that really piqued my interest. First, he told me about a phone conversation with one rep whom he had not heard from for some time. The rep, it turns out, didn't know the name of the company's director of marketing nor had he ever spoken with him, even though the firm had been under contract for several years. Not once in those years had he ever been contacted by the company's marketing management. All his contact was with the application engineers and sales correspondents in the home office, and those discussions were few and far between. You can guess for yourself how much business was coming out of that territory.

The president's next horror story was about how two members of a second rep firm dropped into the plant one day unannounced. They said they were in the area for other purposes and came by the plant to say hello. They hadn't heard from anyone in the organization for so long they wanted to make sure the company was still in business. What does that say about how well this sales operation has been managed? What does it say about how much business these guys were producing?

The final story shared with me by one of the company's inside marketers was the saga of the rep who thought it was perfectly all right to handle competing lines. He swore that the lines weren't competitive, but a comparison of product data sheets and sales literature left no doubt that they clearly were. It doesn't take a high-priced management consultant to know what to do in a case like this, but the simple fact that this story was being told in the present tense was enough to tell me that this company had a real problem in sales management.

Whose fault was it? There's plenty of blame to go around. First, the reps in question have to take some of the responsibility. They were obviously not putting in much effort to sell the line. Although applications vary from territory to territory, the very nature of this product category dictated that there had to be some business out there. Some supplier was getting the business in those territories. Unfortunately it wasn't this company.

The lion's share of the blame, however, goes with the principal. There wasn't an acre of real estate in the country not covered by an independent rep organization. On paper, at least, every one of the reps was qualified, handled complementary lines, and was highly regarded. The principal, however, never "managed" the reps. They did joint calls, of course, but never on a systematic basis, and without a program to make the reps bend over backward working for them.

How to deal with reps? It is a well-known but unwritten rule when dealing with reps that you respect their independence. Truth be known, they tolerate joint calls but they would rather you weren't there in the first place. So you don't want to take up too much of their time. After all, yours is not the only company they are working with. When you are out on sales calls together, it is only common courtesy to let them sell their other lines while you are there, just good form to let them make a call or two that have nothing to do with you. Sure.

Just in case you didn't pick up on the irony in the above paragraph, what I really mean is this: If you allow the reps to control how you spend *your* time with *your* customers, you are conforming to conventional thinking. And when you conform to conventional thinking you are just that—conventional. You are not any better or worse than your competition, and that means you have no competitive edge. You should not be looking for a fair share of their time. You should be looking for an *unfair* share, more time than conventional thinking would have you deserve.

Don't get me wrong. Dealing with reps is not about being adversarial. If the reps don't want you around, it's probably because you haven't earned your way into their hearts. And the best way to do that is to *help them make money*. The more the better. If they know you are there to help them make money, they'll give you more time than even you are willing to spend with them.

Consider a company like Powers Process Controls of Skokie, Illinois. H. L. Singer, president of this unit of The Crane Company, spent five years as Vice President for Sales and Marketing before taking over the top job, so he brought with him lots of marketing expertise and sales management skills. The company's business is split approximately 50-50 between two major markets, industrial instrumentation, and commercial and industrial plumbing products. Both markets are handled through reps and stocking distributors under the overall supervision of the company's regional managers.

When I asked H. L. (he goes by his initials, "H. L.") what he was especially proud of and what he considered the major reason for his company's success, he said one of the most important factors in helping the company achieve its goals was effective sales management.

Interestingly, he said his biggest competition was not so much other suppliers—he competes with some very big companies—but from the reps' other lines. If the rep is working for another principal during any given time frame, you effectively have no sales representation during that period. Typically, each rep allocates the time spent for each principal essentially in proportion to the amount of revenue realized. Thus, if PPC is in the top three of any reps' line card, it would normally get about eight hours or 20% of the time. H. L. maintains that if he can get *two more hours a week* of the rep's time, that will increase the available time for PPC by 25%. If you put those extra hours to good use, you are talking about a major increase in sales productivity. What PPC concentrates on, then, is getting a bigger share of the rep's time. To do that they leave very little to chance.

For example, it is usual practice in industry for the rep to set up appointments for joint calls. The regional manager arrives on the scene, makes the presentation, presents the offer, answers questions, handles objections, and closes the sale. The manager departs. The company gets the order and the rep gets the commission. Generally, the rep is content to see it happen this way. It's less work for the same amount of money. All he has to do is make the appointment and let the principal do the work.

Not so with PPC. As early as a month to six weeks before a proposed visit, the regional manager determines in discussions with the rep what the territory needs, the type of calls he or she wants to make (i.e., engineering calls, calls to purchasing, calls on distributors, and so forth), then asks the rep to set up appointments and confirm them at least two weeks in advance. None of this picking the manager up at the airport and telling him "I tried to get in touch with the buyer at XYZ but he'll be tied up all day. We'll stop by Amalgamated and see if Charlie is in." That's a sure way to waste everyone's time.

Prior to each call the regional manager will go through a series of questions with the rep, something like this:

"What is the objective of this call?"

"Who will we be talking to?"

"What stage of the selling cycle are we in?"

"What is their interest level?"

"What customer objections do you anticipate?"

"How will we overcome them?"

"What role should the manager play? Observer? Backup? Take an active part?"

After the call, the manager and rep sit down together and review how it went. At PPC, the managers make conscious efforts not to jump on the sales reps' mistakes. The first thing the manager asks is, "What did you do right? What did you do to feel good about that call?" Then he might shift to a question like "What would you do differently?" This gives the rep an opportunity to assess his own performance. Most reps, or anyone else, for that matter, know in their hearts what they've done right or wrong. It's PPC's experience that when the atmosphere is positive and open, reps can be much harder on themselves than when someone else critiques them, and much more open to change.

And so it goes throughout the day. After each call, there is an assessment and an agreement on what to do next for that particular prospect or customer.

What is so unusual is that we are talking here about *independent* representatives, not company-employed salespeople. I commented to H. L. that one would not expect reps, as independent businesses, to be so cooperative, particularly when it came to reviewing selling techniques. After all, they might tell you that you engaged their firms for their selling skills. He agreed that that could be a problem. PPC's approach, however, is to be very positive, to do everything it can to help the rep sell more and *make more money* doing it. PPC sells a technical product. Most reps aren't so familiar with the product that they can immediately present it well. What the managers do is help them through the process so that they can, after a reasonable time, present the product themselves. Not only can they do it, but the PPC attitude is so positive, they *want* to do it.

92 WHEN ALL ELSE FAILS, COLD CALL

The selling technique that has always been the device of last resort is the cold call. Cold calling, for those lucky enough to have never needed to resort to this method, refers to picking up the phone and calling someone who doesn't know you and asking for an appointment. It also refers to dropping in on that same someone unannounced and asking for an audience either at that moment or at some future time. "Smokestacking," another term for the same thing, apparently originated in former days with a salesperson driving through an area looking for smoke coming out of chimneys, a sign that if the company was doing well enough to fire up its furnaces, it was worth dropping by to make a presentation.

Actually, I don't recommend dropping in cold. It may work, but if it doesn't, the salesperson has wasted a lot of time, time that could probably have been put to better use. You can make many more phone calls in the same time it takes to drive to a cold prospect, sit in the reception room, and wait and hope that someone will see you. On the other hand, if the salesperson is driving by late in the afternoon with no more appointments for the day, what has he or she got to lose by walking in and presenting a business card?

Cold calling, either by phone or in person, is a tough way to make a living. Ask yourself how many calls you get from telemarketers offering long-distance services, newspaper subscriptions, health insurance, time-share vacations, and countless other products and services. Then ask yourself how many times in the last year you actually bought something from an unsolicited phone call. I rest my case. If you like to make cold calls, then you might also enjoy pushing sharp sticks into your ear. Unless you thrive on rejection, cold calling is a tough way to get business. Not for the faint of heart.

Yes, there are exceptions. I once spent an hour or so with a prospective client who said he actually enjoyed making cold calls. He told me he worked his way through college selling gravestones on the telephone and the job prepared him well for a career in sales and marketing. He could call anyone, anywhere, anytime. He loved it. But he is definitely the exception. Rejection is not something that we enjoy.

But there comes a time every so often when the phone doesn't ring or the good leads stop coming in. I hope it never happens to you but it's happened to me. The reasons this could happen are what this book is about, but if it happens it happens. Rationalizing doesn't do any good. You've got to get the selling machine going again.

Cold calling has its definite place in the hierarchy of selling techniques. When you throw new salespeople out in the field and tell them to get out there and hustle, they may be lucky to have a list of contacts. But if they don't, they better get on the phone and start dialing for dollars.

What Have You Got to Lose?

The thing about cold calling is you have everything to gain and very little to lose, except some time that you could have spent on the golf course. I once purchased and listened to a set of audiotapes based on the book *Successful Cold Call Selling* by Lee Boyan. I would like to say that I bought the program as part of my ongoing research into sales and marketing skills and techniques. In fact, I was looking for some help in getting my own consulting practice going. (The secret is out. Marketing consultants can have trouble marketing their own businesses just like anyone else.)

Probably the greatest cause of aversion to cold calling is the fear of rejection. That fear, at least for me, doesn't go away. But the potential benefits to me and my business by cold calling were so great that I tried to overcome that fear. From Lee I learned to ask myself, "What is the worst thing that could happen to me as a result of this call?" It is highly unlikely that the other party is going to curse at me for calling. It is extremely unlikely that, as a result of my call, someone will search me out and smash my kneecaps. So, really, what is so terrible? I have never done business with these people. If they won't see me, I won't be doing business with them in the near future. Thus, the worst possible thing that could happen to me is that I will be no better off than I am now. Life will go on. The sun will rise and set. I will continue to look for more business.

Another way of looking at cold calls is risk versus benefit. Sooner or later someone will agree to see the salesperson. When that happens, and he or she closes the sale, the revenue from that transaction may far outweigh the time it took to go through a long list of negative responses. In my case, even after 15 years in this business, the single biggest client I ever got in terms of billing came from a cold call.

Get your people to make cold calls to fill in time or turn stagnant territories around. The rewards far outweigh the negatives.

12

GOD IS IN THE DETAILS

It is very difficult to distinguish what characteristics make one company successful and another an also-ran. We all strive for excellence. No one deliberately sets out to fail. We look for ways to better ourselves and our companies and to gain that elusive competitive edge. My vote for what is *most* important in achieving that competitive edge is a conscientious attention to detail. In this world, details count. Strategies don't work if they aren't implemented properly, and implementation eventually involves specifics and details.

Brian Heimbigner is Vice President for Business Development at Resources Conservation Company in Bellevue, Washington. RCC is one of the leading designers and builders of large evaporators used typically in wastewater treatment for power plants, pulp paper mills, and chemical plants all over the world. These installations run anywhere from $2 million to $40 million, so there is a lot at stake with each job, especially when there aren't that many of them around at those prices. RCC makes a special point about attention to detail. Brian calls it "differentiation at the level of human service," and he listed for me several things RCC focuses on before, during, and after these important projects:

- *Good communications skills*—For most of their customers, English isn't the native tongue. You have to be able to get your message across without risk of misunderstanding.
- *Timely responses*—Time is money, and we are talking about big money. Delays hold up subcontractors and that adds to the cost of the project.
- *Accuracy of information*—Engineering information has to be correct. Misinformation can cause a disaster.
- *Honesty*—Mistakes are inevitable in large projects. How the company admits to them and handles them is important in maintaining customer confidence.
- *Meeting deadlines and commitments*—Do what you say you are going to do, when you say you are going to do it.
- *Adherence to standards*—There are internationally accepted technical standards and there are local standards. The company has to be aware of and comply with all of them.

What is so interesting about this list is how *ordinary* and *down to earth* all this is. But imagine if you will the consequences of ignoring any part of it. In RCC's case, not only is the company on the line for millions of dollars but also the environment is at risk. I won't say that following this list is a guarantee for success, but I can say with confidence that ignoring any part will make success that much less certain.

Speaking of details . . .

93 BE CAREFUL HOW YOU ANSWER THE PHONE

Sometimes egos get in the way of common sense. In few places are egos more a factor than with regard to the telephone. Answering your own phone isn't fashionable. I would like to see its return to acceptability. If you disagree, perhaps you should listen in once in a while on how your people answer the phone.

I once phoned a business prospect, the president of a small electronics company, following up on a conversation we had had at an industry meeting the previous week. The telephone receptionist advised me that he wasn't in and offered to leave a message for him to return the call. So far so good. When she asked me what the call was about, I said that he knew me and was expecting my call. Her voice suddenly chilled. "I doubt it," she said. When I asked her why she would say that, she told me she had never heard of me. At this company, apparently, being known by the telephone operator is the only valid proof of credibility. I left the message but I didn't expect a call back, nor did I get one.

For today's executive, time is a scarce commodity. No one likes to be interrupted by unwanted phone calls. If you don't have a specific need at a specific time, you would just as soon have the telemarketer or the cold caller intercepted by your trusty gatekeeper. But since this receptionist didn't know me, I could just as easily have been a prospective customer. Is your time worth missing a call like "Mr. Executive, I've heard some good things about your product and we may be interested in placing a large order with you?" Or perhaps I was the important banking contact your survival depended on, calling "about that million dollar credit line we discussed the other day. . . ." Those are calls you may never know about because an untrained operator overzealously guards your privacy.

It scares me to think how much business is lost because of poor telephone etiquette. From that point of view, telephone answering is every bit as much a marketing issue as pricing and sales presentations are. It's a business risk that doesn't have to be.

On a particularly tough day in my office, I was trying to crank out a final report on a consulting project. As usual, the stockbrokers, long-distance telephone companies, health-care providers, and newspaper subscription salespeople were ganging up on me over the phone. Finally, I was interrupted by what I thought was one call too many. A woman started out with what seemed to be one of those canned sales pitches where they ask "how are you today?" as if they really cared. I interrupted her and said a few words about getting to the point. Maybe I wasn't too polite (I wasn't), because the next thing she said was that I didn't sound very nice and she would prefer not to do business with me, then she hung up.

After a brief moment of shock that she would hang up on *me,* the "abused" party, I started going over in my mind just what she said in the beginning of the call. The truth is, I never really knew whether she was the zillionth telemarketer of the day, or someone who actually was calling me to engage my services. To this day, and it happened several years ago, I wonder whether unintended rudeness cost me the consulting assignment of my life.

How It's Supposed to Be

A. J. Weller Corporation is a small industrial products company based in Shreveport, Louisiana. After making a few calls to Tom Edwards, the CEO, I began to notice a pattern. First, every time I called, the phone rang no more than once before it was picked up. Always. Second, when I asked for Tom, the call was put through immediately and Tom picked up his own phone. This is pretty refreshing stuff in a voice-mail world of recorded messages and endless menu choices.

I asked Tom whether all this was just coincidence or was it a matter of policy. When it comes to customer service and putting the company in the best light, he commented, "Our policy is 'why not do the obvious?'"

Why not, indeed. No voice-mail menu of options here. Just a pleasant voice offering to connect you to the party of choice, no further questions.

But what of the risk of someone calling that he didn't want to talk to? No problem. The greater risk was for someone he really wanted to talk with to get turned away.

94 STAY OUT OF "VOICE-MAIL JAIL"

Tom may have the right idea for his company, but he is definitely bucking the trend. In bygone days, when you wanted to talk to someone, you picked up the phone and dialed the main number and an operator would connect you to the right extension. If the person wasn't in, the operator would take your name and number and your party just might call you back. If the person you were calling was important enough, a secretary would take the message. Chances are your party was tied up in a meeting because important people are always at meetings. When the person called you back, you were at a meeting yourself and someone left a message for you. Over time great stretches of forest were stripped clean to produce the countless pink "While You Were Out" message slips that piled up on the desks of busy people.

Voice mail, the breakthrough technology for the nineties, has changed the way we do business. Now, instead of leaving a message with a secretary, you can leave a voice message directly on someone's line. You still may not get a return call, but at least you can hope that your party got your message. Say what you will about the technology, once the program is set up and running, it will always get the message right. Since messages aren't on little slips of paper, they can't be misplaced or overlooked. Most systems I've seen allow you to save messages for as long as you want.

I am not suggesting a conspiracy here, but it looks suspiciously like marketers of voice-messaging systems have taken advantage of the downsizing mania to sell systems that replace people to reach people who are scrambling around to make up for the people who voice mail did away with in the first place.

Or so it seems.

Any Negatives?

There are all sorts of voice-messaging systems, beginning with the tape-driven answering machines that started this revolution back in the seventies. The ones that seem to get the most criticism are the multimenu systems used mostly by large corporations. My bank has so many options, suboptions, and sub-suboptions that you can get yourself off in a never-never land of "press one for . . ." alternatives that can kill an hour or so without ever getting to talk to a real live person. Whatever happened to user-friendly?

Speaking of user-friendly, the myth is that these systems are designed to make it easier for callers to have their questions answered and their needs satisfied. In truth, the benefits seem to accrue to the receiving party, rather than to the caller. There is a serious concern here. Companies that install these elaborate "menu-upon-menu" systems are saying to their customers that the burden of finding a solution to your problem or an answer to your question is on you. Get through the maze on your own. You'll get no help from us until you've solved the riddle. What does that say about where companies put their priorities?

But in the normal course of a business day, you run into the more typical voice-mail system, which is in effect an elaborate telephone answering machine using digital techniques instead of analog tape. It's use is so common today that I am truly surprised when a live person answers the phone. The paradox with voice mail is that by eliminating the written word, you depersonalize normal human intercourse. You leave a message on my machine and I leave a reply on yours, then you leave another and I leave another. We can conduct our entire business without ever having an actual conversation. I am not sure that is such a good thing. What does that do for the relationship idea we talked about in Chapter 5?

But Voice Mail Is Here to Stay, You Say

In spite of my reservations, let's face it, the technology is going to be here for a while. We better learn how to live with it and use it properly. There even appears to be a certain etiquette associated with its proper use. The first rule I ran into said it was gauche to leave bad news on a message. "I'm sorry that your order has run into manufacturing problems and it will be shipped six months late" is not something one wants to hear when checking messages. Or how about the one a consultant friend of mine got recently that said, in effect, "We've decided not to use your services. Have a nice day." Definitely gauche.

The challenges for marketers brought on by voice-messaging technology are twofold. First, getting to potential customers and, second, letting customers get to *you*. If you suspect, like I do, that many people use these systems more to screen calls than to take messages when they are away, then *persistence* is your most important tool. You have to call as many times as necessary until someone gets tired of hearing from you. You have to leave a clear message that states why you are calling and what's in it for the called party. Clear. Precise. Short. Often.

If you want to make it easy for customers to get to you, the most obvious solution is to answer your own phone or have a message taken by a real live person. If that isn't possible, return the customer's call as soon as possible. If the original message included enough information, then the call back should include all the answers to the customers. If the customer isn't in when you call back, enjoy the endless game of cybertag.

95 REVIEW AND IMPROVE PROCESSES

There has been so much said about Total Quality Management and business process reengineering that I was apprehensive about including this Section. But in the combined context of attention to detail and No-Nonsense Marketing, I will go ahead with it. Processes are the way we do things, and there are lots of things we do that cry out for being done differently and better.

Changing Processes

One of the reasons I have been so skeptical about the benefits of "flavor-of-the-month" techniques is that they have always seemed to me as other ways of saying what management should be doing in the first place. In the course of gathering material for this book, I talked to dozens of managers, mostly of successful but small companies. At no time during the course of these discussions did I ever hear one of them attribute their success to instituting TQM or reengineering their processes. Yet that's exactly what happened. Whatever name you give it, good managers are out there doing whatever it takes to satisfy customers and succeed. If what it takes is *change,* change is what good managers implement.

From a marketing perspective, processes aren't as clearly defined as in other disciplines. Yet they are critical to customer support and customer satisfaction. This constitutes, I suppose, a wish list of things I'd like to see improve over things I've seen.

- I would like to see *faster handling of internal paperwork* so that information can be put in the customer's hands before competition gets there. After all these years working with industrial and technology-based companies, I have grown weary of the excuse, "it's somewhere in engineering," when a marketer asks about an overdue proposal. It seems it's always in engineering, except when it's in accounting for a credit check or numbers check or any other kind of check.

- I would like to see *more attention paid to how customer complaints are handled.* How many times have I heard someone say she was so mad at the company she got on the phone and called the president? "Of course, I didn't talk to him but his secretary was very nice and promised someone would get right back to me." That isn't customer service, that's gatekeeping. It's protecting the president from getting involved with things beneath the dignity of the office. If the president or some other member of the executive suite can't take a few moments to listen to a customer, it says a lot about dedication to customer service.

- I would like to see a concerted effort to *speed up the handling of customer orders* and radically cut down on shipping time. I can't see any justification for companies to take seven days or more to ship stock items. I buy software and computer hardware from a catalog, and phone in the order through a toll-free number. As long as they get my order by 9:00 P.M. Eastern Time, I will get delivery the *very next day.* Total shipping charges for this premium service? Three dollars. Three dollars! That is the essence of No-Nonsense Marketing.

Nor can I understand why a company trying to sell to an OEM market would take eight weeks to deliver samples or test units when they are essentially modifications of stock units. If you aren't in a hurry for the *sample* order, what is the customer to expect from *production* deliveries?

- I would like to see *telemarketers drop their canned spiels* and talk to me like they knew what they were talking about. I expect them to sound like they were sincerely interested in me as a customer. I understand that their managers do not want them to deviate from a script that works, but when they sound like they are reading from that script, I look to hang up immediately.
- I would like to see *technology applied to the selling process,* but only when it makes a difference. Cellular phones and pagers have become vital communications tools for the salesperson in the field. Notebook computers can serve a useful purpose such as checking inventory or price. But they are very heavy address books to lug around. There was a time when a formal sales presentation meant overhead transparencies or, to get really fancy, 35mm slides. You dropped your overheads on a projector and ran through your presentation without the necessity to even lower the room lights. Today, good presentation software allows everyone to have quality visuals. That's fine, but not enough, because today's technology allows us to do things we never dreamed of. Like lugging along a laptop computer connected to a special projector that puts images on the screen directly from the computer. The laptop, typical cost of about $2,000, weighs 6 pounds, not including spare batteries, power cords, and so forth. The projector, $6,000 or so, weighs about 20 pounds, maybe more. That's $8,000 worth of hardware weighing 26 pounds or more. Compare that with a quality overhead projector costing about $300 and transparencies, even color transparencies, running about a dollar apiece. Oh, and one other thing. The overhead projector is usually resident in the conference room so you don't even have to bring your own. So much for the benefits of technology.

Summary: There's got to be a better way. Find it and put it to use.

96 MOVE FAST

"Speed kills."

"Haste makes waste."

"Slow and steady wins the race."

"Look before you leap."

We are culturally biased toward the careful and cautious. As much as we would like to think of ourselves as hard-charging, dynamic executives, most of us take pride in our careful and reasoned approach to our business problems. Not thinking through the effects of our actions leads to mistakes, sometimes costly mistakes.

But it is a competitive world, after all. I have another maxim that I would recommend following rather than the ones at the top of this section. It may be somewhat inelegant but it will serve the purpose. *The early bird catches the worm.*

Why Wait?

I was sitting in a client's office recently as he took a call from what turned out to be a prospective customer. When the call ended, the CEO passed the message and contents of the call to his newly hired VP for Sales and Marketing who had started with the company that very day. Later that afternoon, the new VP joined in our discussions and casually remarked about the results of *his* conversation with the same prospect, what information he was passing on, and how he sized up the opportunity. I was impressed. This was obviously a take-charge guy. Sure, he was hardly burdened down with a workload after only half a day on the job and the opportunity might eventually prove to be nothing of any consequence. The important point, however, is that there was *no delay, no procrastinating, no rationalizing.* It would have been easy for him to think that he was too new to risk talking to a prospect about subjects he was barely familiar with. On the other hand, there is *no time like the present* to receive a baptism of fire. As it turned out, the inquiry was real and it suggested some market opportunities that the company hadn't previously considered.

What might have happened if he didn't call when he did? Well, the customer might have asked someone else, which would be the most likely consequence. If the competitor was as eager as he should have been, the customer would have gone that route. Which is the whole point.

Speed of action is one of the most important guidelines I can think of.

It means getting new products out the door *fast.* I can think of numerous examples where the first company on the market did not end up the ultimate market leader. Sony's Betamax was the first videocassette recorder. VHS technology swept away the market. The British-built Comet was the first commercial jet transport. The first *successful* commercial jet aircraft was the Boeing 707 and Boeing continues to dominate that market. Yet I would have to say that far more first-to-market products maintain their leadership. Xerox copiers, Sony Walkman, Du Pont's nylon, and so on.

It means responding to customer requests *immediately.* The surest way to get a customer down on you is to ignore or delay a response.

It means *cutting the lead time* required to ship production items. Leach Relays in Buena Park, California, cut their delivery time from six weeks to three days. Any way you want to measure the size of the market they serve, it will show that they have a better than 50% share.

It means picking up on a new technology and converting it to products *before your competitor does.* The buggy whip is the usual metaphor for obsolete products. Staying with an obsolete technology can only hurt.

It means reacting to market changes *without hesitation.* Market changes mean changing customer requirements, shifting social trends, new legislation that changes the way you have to do business.

It means reacting to competitive moves *without hesitation.* Strategists have elegant words for this, usually based on the military analogy. Defensive strategy, flanking defenses, and preemptive strikes. I just call it getting off your butt and doing something about your competitors before they do you in.

97 DON'T LEAVE THE CUSTOMER WAITING FOR AN ANSWER

Responding to customer inquiries is such a fundamental part of doing business one wonders why this should ever be a problem. But it often is. Watch my lips. Fast responses are *good*. Late responses are *bad*. Customers and prospects like answers to their questions as quickly as possible. Getting back with an answer long after you should is inexcusable.

Picture this. A salesperson gets a voice-mail message from a customer asking for a call back. Although it's someone she has never done business with or knows much about, the salesperson returns the call promptly. When she gets the customer on the phone, she gets a question about price and delivery in certain quantities. The salesperson, although unimpressed with the quantities involved, writes the query down in her notebook, places a call to the product manager, leaves a voice-mail message, of course, then trots off to her next call.

A week later, going through her notes, the salesperson realizes that she still owes a return call, makes a quick call to the product manager, who says she needs more information before she can give an answer. After a rather heated discussion about whose responsibility it is for follow-up and so forth, the salesperson has her information and calls back the customer. The customer, sly devil that he is, thanks her very much for the information and promises to get back with his decision as soon as he can. He never will.

As it turns out, the customer conveyed the same message to four prospective suppliers. Three of the four responded within 24 hours. The best offer among the three was chosen, an order was placed, and delivery had already begun. While our heroes were busy ignoring each other, the customer was busy putting the products to use. What do you think the chances are for getting an inquiry from this customer next time around? There is no amount of sales training that will compensate for stupidity or indifference.

When a customer poses a question, you have to treat it as a request for clarification on the long road to making a purchase. It is not humanly possible for each of us to know all the answers to all the questions a customer or prospect might ask. For the salesperson, the question may be too technical in nature to respond without checking with the technical staff. For the technician, the question may involve price or delivery information that he or she isn't qualified to discuss without further input. Whatever, the reason, there are plenty of cases where you just don't have the answers readily available.

The fact that you don't know the answer doesn't make the customer's question less valid. If a satisfactory answer is holding up the sale, you had better get the answer, or your competitor will get the order.

Put yourself in the customer's place for a moment. There is an information gap and you need that information before you can make an informed decision. It may be about price or delivery or it may be a technical question. You call the supplier for the information. You call several suppliers for the same information. You talk to all of them, and they all promise to get right back. Meanwhile you are on a deadline. You've got to place an order immediately or miss your own commitment to *your* customer. The next morning you get three answers back, one of which is something you can live with: Zap. There goes the order.

He who hesitates is lost.

One path to wisdom, of course, is training. The more knowledge you can impart to your sales force, the more likely they can speak with confidence and certainty when customers ask. But training will never substitute for common sense. Common sense says you get back to your customer as soon as you can. The faster the better. No one wants to lose an order. Sloppy performance not only loses the immediate order, it pretty much assures that you will not even know about the next requirement.

Summary: Respond to customer requests as quickly as is humanly possible. Your business depends on it.

98 NEVER GIVE UP—IT AIN'T OVER TILL IT'S OVER

I once talked with a sales manager who went on and on about how much he demanded of his sales staff. I took something away from that discussion that has stayed with me for these many years. In telling me how good he was, he described an incident when he was a field salesman. The way he told it, a buyer broke the bad news that a major order was going to the competition. As the salesman left the customer's plant, all he could think about was the lost order and what he might have done better to have won it. Suddenly, he made a U-turn and sped back to the customer plant, where he asked the buyer that very question, "What could I have done better to have got the business?" The buyer, flattered that anyone would even ask and impressed that this fellow was still interested in the details of this order, told him what the competitor offered. To make a long story short, the salesman had one more chance to match or beat the competitive offer, and he took full advantage of the opportunity. Then, when all the details were out on the table, he delivered the coup de grâce by asking for the order again. This time, he got it. A happy ending, a story our sales hero could tell prospective employees for the rest of his career.

The moral of this tale is that when you think the order is lost, it may not yet be. It never hurts to ask for the order one more time. And again, if you are still not sure it's over. And again. In the immortal words of Yogi Berra, "It ain't over till it's over."

Can You Ever Get a Second Chance?

Speaking of getting a second chance, I have always been of the opinion that you only get one chance to hurt a customer. Miss a critical delivery or deliver an inferior product and your relationship is history. During a discussion with the CEO of a midsized manufacturing company, I casually dropped that thought on him in the context of customer satisfaction. "I disagree," he came back. "Under certain conditions you *can* get a second chance." We talked about it further and I've since come up with a modest list of those times where you may, just may, get back on the good side of the customer, even though you probably don't deserve it. For instance:

- You may be the customer's only choice because your product or service is unique.
- Your price is so good, the customer can't afford *not* to give you another try.
- You and the customer have had such a fine relationship over the years that they are willing to bend over backward for you.
- You make up for it in other ways, like outstanding customer service and responsiveness.
- You cry and plead and say you're sorry. (Don't laugh. It works sometimes.)

99 MAKE DECISIONS AT THE LOWEST POSSIBLE LEVEL

I am not fond of the word *empowerment*. It is a fancy word that is supposed to mean management has delegated decision making to the worker bees. It rarely works out that way.

I probably learned about delegation during leadership training as a young naval officer, or perhaps I got it from some management training program I went through decades ago. Wherever it came from, I know deep in my heart that people are better workers if they are trusted to make decisions without referring everything to their managers. Good leadership is expecting your people to take care of things without coming to you for each and every decision. You do a better job of serving customers when you allow your employees to make decisions on the spot.

The best-run organizations empower their people to make decisions at the lowest possible level. When Nordstrom welcomes its new employees, each is given the Nordstrom Employee Handbook, actually a five-by-eight-inch card on which the Nordstrom Rules are printed. It says, in part:

> "Rule #1: Use your good judgment in all situations. There will be no additional rules."

That sends a strong signal to employees that they have the confidence and support of management to do the right thing. The right thing for the customer.

Colleen Barrett is executive vice president at Southwest Airlines. Actually, her title is Executive Vice President-Customers, which tells you where the second-ranking executive in the company puts the emphasis. Ms. Barrett makes a special point about people acting on their own to do what's right. They call it P.O.S., Positively Outrageous Service. That comes from people doing what they have to do to make the organization work, independent of any company rules and regulations. They must be doing something right. Southwest's performance and service have always been at or near the top in the airline industry.

As for sales and marketing people, when your people are out on the front line talking to customers and dodging competitors, you want them to know what to do *instinctively*. If the sales manager thinks the only way to get a particular order is to make a major concession, then he or she should be able to make that decision on the spot. Management should backup its managers by honoring the commitment. If the customer says she needs a certain price, the salesperson on the scene should be able, within obvious limits, to make the concession and come home with the order. Margins only count in penmanship lessons. For the rest of us, it's better to get the order.

I know it's the way the game is played, but I have always found it curious—and when I'm personally involved, infuriating—the way car salespeople will agree on a price with the customer, then run it past the sales manager, who kicks it back for a higher price. These people have devised a process that formalizes the concept of the nonempowered employee.

What Does Empowerment Mean for You?

Picture this. You are busy at your desk working through the final details of a strategy to finally win over a major account. They have been doing business with the competition for ten years, ever since your company's late delivery shut down their production line for lack of parts. It's an old story, but all the players are new at your company and theirs, and the prospect is encouraging you to give it your best shot. As you begin to reach for the phone to make an appointment for one final meeting and closing the deal, you look up to see your product manager in front of you.

"What's up, Charlie," you cheerfully ask. "Sorry to bother you," he says, "but I need your approval on some changes I think we should make to the new widget brochure." Before you can get the right expletive past your lips, you remember that you had had a lot to say about the brochure during its design stage and it was very clear to your people that "ownership" of the brochure was yours. In a moment or two, you are fully immersed in the details. When you complete your ad hoc meeting, you realize that you've missed the chance to call your prospect that day because of the three-hour time difference. Oh well, we'll do that tomorrow.

Picture this: Same scene. Same customer. Same possibilities. Same Charlie. This time he hands you a form for your signature indicating your approval of his upcoming travel itinerary. In your company, department heads or above must approve travel plans for the hoi polloi. This is the corporate equivalent of asking teacher for permission to go to the bathroom. Charlie's a big boy. He gets a decent salary. He has a lot of responsibilities that he handles very well. If you don't trust him to use his travel budget wisely, what *do* you trust him to do?

Just think of all the extra time you'll have if you didn't spend half the day listening to stories and making decisions that someone else could have made just as effectively without involving you. This is a book about marketing, especially down-to-earth marketing, so I am trying to avoid even a hint of touchy feely lessons on motivation or human relations. But I must say this. As part of marketing management, you would be far better off if you surround yourself with people who not only know their jobs well but also can *act independently.* If you already have those people and don't loosen up on the tether, you are mismanaging.

100 STAND BEHIND WHAT YOU SAY

You are only as good as your word. The reputation of your company—and you, for that matter—depends on the truthfulness of what you say and claim. There are one or two practical reasons why honesty and ethical behavior are always the best policies. First, customers will tear you to pieces if you are caught lying to them. Figuratively, of course. Of course. The best you could hope for is a big hole in your sales volume for a long time. On the other hand, the market will respect you for the truth, no matter how distasteful. In the automobile industry, there have been so many manufacturers' recalls to correct defects in certain models that customers are conditioned to hearing about them. Car manufacturers today voluntarily announce recalls rather than wait for government mandates. Good policy. Tell the truth. Fix the problem. Get on with life.

The second reason is that misrepresentation will land you in court, defending yourself and your company in a lawsuit. This is a litigious age we live in. The chances of being sued are much better when you get caught in a lie or a half-truth.

If you claim certain performance characteristics for your product, you had better make sure you can back that up with test data or third-party testimonials. If your people make promises, you have to back them up. You may not like it, but the world will not end if you give in to a particular commitment to a particular customer. It's called empowerment. See the previous section.

Standing Behind Your Product

Is the warranty you provide a statement of your intent to support your product, or is it a legal document that you hide behind to limit your liability? Of course it's both, I know. But a warranty to me is the way you put your money where your mouth is. Although I fully understand the need to put some boundaries around the time you will be expected to support a product at no charge, a rigid adherence to the terms of the warranty is self-defeating. Each customer sees his or her own situation as unique. All customers want their product to last forever, but most are realistic enough to expect it to break down eventually. It's when it breaks down uncomfortably close to the warranty limits, on the wrong side, of course, that the customer becomes testy. That's when you can either shine or withdraw into the legal shell.

I have an Olympus handheld microcassette recorder that I use for dictating notes to myself. I rarely leave my office without it. What is important to me in such a device is the size. The smaller the better. I am willing to pay a premium to get something small and lightweight. The one I bought was at the high end of the price for similar products but it was the one I had to have.

Wouldn't you know it, it stopped working one day and left me digging for the original sales receipt and the warranty statement. It turned out that I had exceeded the original 90-day warranty by about a week. To me, a 90-day warranty is like no warranty at all. Companies that limit their warranties to 90 days are telling their customers they have no confidence in their product. In any case, at least I had one thing going for me. I bought it at a reputable retail store. When I took it into the nearby Circuit City, they noted it was no longer in warranty, but *they replaced it anyway.* They talked me into buying a service contract for the new one for about 20 dollars, which was a fair exchange for getting a new recorder without any hassle.

I recently purchased an Apple PowerBook notebook computer. I had heard about some Apple technical problems with their notebooks, but I was caught with an immediate need and no desire to give up on the Apple Macintosh after nine years of use.

One day I sorted through my mail and found a letter from Apple Computer. They confirmed that there might be problems with certain PowerBooks and my model was one of them. Not to worry, they said. They will repair those problems if I have them at no cost to me. Call them and they will schedule the repair. Once the repair is on the schedule they will send a freight-paid shipping container, pick up the package, repair the computer, and send it all back via overnight air. If I don't have a problem now, not to worry, either. They will repair those problems if they ever show up for as long as they service those models, which in the United States, they said, is seven years after they end production of the particular model. Seven years. Now that to me is putting your money where your mouth is. What more could you ask for in a manufacturer taking responsibility for its products?

101 EVERYONE HAS TO BE A CUSTOMER ADVOCATE

Advocate *n.* One who argues for a cause; a supporter or defender.

—American Heritage Dictionary

The customer is king. Or queen. Whatever, titles aren't important. Service is. I am very much impressed with manufacturers who empower (there's that word again) any worker on an assembly line to stop the line should there be a problem with the unit coming along. Companies who do this are telling their workers that each of them is an advocate for the customer, each of them has the right and obligation to act on the customer's behalf, regardless of the short-term cost to the company. I like it.

From the worker on the assembly line to the Chief Executive Officer, *everyone* in an organization has to keep the best interests of the customer at heart. Everyone has to be an advocate for the customer. Salespeople and marketers have traditionally been the organization's customer advocates. In the businesses I grew up in, I always felt like we sales and marketers were the only ones in the company who really cared about the needs of the customer. Today it isn't enough.

The engineer must develop products that meet the precise needs of the customer. In the balance between company profit guidelines and customer-friendly products, both are important, but there are no profits if customers don't buy.

The operations manager must ensure that internal systems are focused entirely on getting quality products through the process in time to meet customer delivery needs. What else would count? When management sends down cost and labor guidelines, the operations manager has to stand up and be counted. "We can't satisfy customer needs, boss, if this restriction is enforced" has to be said forcefully enough to get the point across.

The chief financial officer has a stake in customer satisfaction. Credit policies have to be realistic and workable. Credit checks have to be timely. Nobody wants to see the company get itself involved with poor credit risks, but the decision-making process should be weighted in favor of accepting a customer rather than against it.

And so it goes. Each department in the organization has a stake in seeing that the customer's needs are met. Within each department, every person has to take it upon himself or herself to stand up and be counted.

But what about the company's interests? Where is the obligation to the one who pays the employees' salaries? Here's a radical, albeit unoriginal thought: The best interests of the company are served by taking care of the best interests of the customer. Good companies have always been customer-oriented. What I am saying, and I can't stress this too much, is that marketers are not the only ones who should be thinking about the customer. On the contrary. I would like to see everyone in the organization, regardless of department assigned, to take the part of the customer in everything they do. The question each person should ask is, "What does this action mean to the customer?"

That's the only attitude that matters.

13

SOME CONCLUDING THOUGHTS

One hopes to conclude a work like this with some profound observation, something that will be the author's legacy. It's hard to be profound when you've spent all your time telling your clients and readers to get back to basics. But there is something I have to share with you.

I was once interviewed for an audiotape series that included some questions and answers on marketing. The interviewer wanted my comments on customer service, particularly how I felt about too much service. Can you reach a point of diminishing returns trying to please everyone? I answered that I could never define what too much service was. I didn't know then and I still don't know a practical way to set limits.

I have read articles that claim striving for 100% customer satisfaction is wasteful. You can never please everyone. Intellectually I agree. Practically, however, I can't think of a good way to put boundaries on customer service. Though I can't please everyone, I can't stop trying. Customers may not expect all that you do. That is why you should give them *more* than they expect.

102 ALWAYS GIVE THE CUSTOMER MORE THAN WAS EXPECTED

This is point number 102 in a book that only promises 101. As I said in the introduction, 101 isn't a definitive number. Perhaps over time the number will grow to ten times 101. As a matter of fact, I can add one additional comment that both illustrates the point and gives what I think is as sound advice as you could get. Not only should we strive to meet customer expectations, but we should strive to *exceed* them.

By now you've all probably read the heroic customer service stories associated with a particular department store or hotel chain or warehouse hardware store or major electronics manufacturer. Whether half of those stories are true or not, they illustrate that people go to extraordinary lengths to please their customers.

There are things you can do that can exceed your customers' expectations that may fall short of "extraordinary" or "heroic" but still give that extra measure that is both appreciated and ultimately rewarded with more business from them. Things like special packaging, delivery arrangements, unquestioned response to unusual customer requests. They may not be the stuff of legends but they can very well be the stuff that keeps the customer happy and, important for you, coming back.

Here is something I experienced firsthand. Upon returning from a business trip I discovered that I had left my personal organizer in the seat pocket of the last plane I was on, a United Airlines 737 into Burbank, California. This was a pretty traumatic thing for me since it contained my address and telephone list as well as all my notes for the previous few days. With little hope of ever finding it again, I called the airline's lost and found number and described what I had mislaid, my flight, and seat number as best I could remember any of them. I had all but given it up for lost when, the next day, I got a call from the United station manager in Burbank telling me they had found the book and would send it to me. You can imagine how surprised I was and how good I felt about United when the doorbell rang at my home late that afternoon and a gentleman from the United ground staff at Burbank stood there with my organizer in his hand. He told me he lived in the same town I did and, instead of mailing it, he thought he would just drop it off on the way home, figuring I needed it pretty bad. That is what I call giving the customer more than is expected.

You can do that, too. When customers have a problem, stay with the problem until it is solved. Nights and weekends if necessary. When they need your presence, even if they don't ask for it, get on an airplane and go there.

Good luck.

INDEX